AF522695

NATURAL RESOURCES, CONSERVATION MANAGEMENT AND HEALTH CARE

NATURAL RESOURCES CONSERVATION, MANAGEMENT AND HEALTH CARE

By

Prof. Madireddi V. Subba Rao

Ph.D. (SVU), D.Sc. (IOU, Colombo)

DISCOVERY PUBLISHING HOUSE PVT. LTD.

NEW DELHI-110 002

Published by:
Tilak Wasan
DISCOVERY.PUBLISHING HOUSE PVT. LTD.
4831/24, Ansari Road, Prahlad Street
Darya Ganj, New Delhi-110002 (India)
Phone: +91-11-23279245, 43764432
Fax: +91-11-23253475
E-mail: parul.wasan@gmail.com
info@discoverypublishinggroup.com
web: www.discoverypublishinggroup.com

***First Edition:* 2011**
ISBN: 978-81-8356-802-9

Natural Resources, Conservation, Management and Health Care

Printed at:
Shree Balaji Art Press
Delhi

DEDICATED TO

కీ॥శే॥ మాదిరెడ్డి రామరావుగారు కీ॥శే॥ ఆదిలక్ష్మమ్మగారు

My Beloved Parents
Late Sri Madireddi Rama Rao and
Late Smt. Adilakshmamma

and

TO MY RESPECTED TEACHERS
Prof. Ratan Singh, Agra University
Prof. K. Pampapati Rao, S.V. University, Tirupati
Prof. K.G. Rajabai Naidu, S.V. University, Tirupati

Prof. Madireddi V. Subba Rao, Ph.D.
Editor
E-mail: mvsubbarao_enra@yahoo.co.in

Preface

In recent years, our glorious Mother Earth has seen exponential population growth, rapid urbanization and industrialization, indiscriminate disposal of industrial wastes and emissions, degradation of forest cover, depletion of non-renewable energy resources, hazards of industrial chemicals, extinction of rare and endangered species, etc.

To sustain life on the earth, the planet's natural resources must be carefully preserved. Preservation requires prodent use of our limited land, air and water resources. Inhabitants must consider how their current life styles are going to affect the quality of life during future generations.

In the past 30 years, scientists have made great strides in the study of the environment. After defining environmental problems, scientists now suggest various means for saving our planet Earth.

Humanity must accept responsibility for the present fate of our planet. Industrialists and environmentalists alike must unite as trail blazers in the environmental revolution.

They need to identify and study calamities such as tsunami, earthquakes, cyclones, and floods, to develop social services and control measures during such mishaps.

Now-a-days health care is essential for the control of diseases such as malaria, filaria, jaundice, meningitis, cancer, tuberculosis, and AIDS. It is the responsibility of scientists and physicians to respond to these challenges by providing authoritative assessment of the possible effect of these changes and to develop systems that provide early warning and analysis of impending environmental problems for the protection of humanity and conservation of natural resources.

I thank to M/s Discovery Publishing House Pvt. Ltd., New Delhi for their neat execution of printing and bringing out this book in time.

Finally, I am thankful to all the contributors for their excellent contribution to this book on "Natural Resources, Conservation, Management and Health Care", which is a source of valuable asset. I heartily welcome any criticisms or suggestions regarding the contents of this book that would help to revise and to make this more applicable.

PROF. MADIREDDI V. SUBBA RAO, Ph.D.

Editor

Contents

Contributors

1. Dr. M.V. Subba Rao (Dr. Madireddi V. Subba Rao) Editor, Senior Professor, Head & Coordinator (Retired) Dept. of Environmental Sciences. Andhra University, President, Environmental Research Academy, Intl., 50-120-8/1, Seetammadhara North Extn., Visakhapatnam 530013, Email: mvsubbarao_enra@yahoo.co.in
2. Dr. Barry Walden Walsh, President, Selbyana, Selby Botanical Gardens, Sarasota, Forida, USA, 34236
3. Dr. B.N. Rao, Reader in Zoology (Retired), Mrs. A.V.N. College, Visakhapatnam-530 002, A.P.
4. Dr. P.S. Rajasekhar, Dept. of Environmental Sciences, Andhra University, Visakhapatnam-530003, A.P., E.Mail: psrsekhar@hotmail.com
5. Dr. M. Rama Murthy & G. Pruthiv Raj, Dept. of Zoology, B.V.K. College, Visakhapatnam-530 016, A.P.
6. Dr. Y. AVASN, Maruthi, Dept. of Environmental Studies, GITAM University, Visakhapatnam-530 035. E-mail: a_yellamraju@yahoo.com
7. A. Radhika (Ankala Radhika), Dept. of Computers Science Engineering, SRK Institute of Technology, Enikepadu, Vizaiwada-520 008, A.P. E.Mail: radhisunil@yahoo.com
8. Dr. M. Aruna Kumari, Dept. Environmental Sciences, Andhra University, Visakhapatnam-530013, A.P.
9. Dr. B.P. Das, Orissa University of Agriculture & Technology, Bhubaneswar-641 012, Orissa State.
10. Pusp Kumar, IFS (Retd.), Ex PCCF, Govt. of AP, Aranya Bhavan, Hyderabad-500004
11. Dr. V. Venkateswarulu, Professor (Retired), Dept. of Botany, Osmania University, Hyderabd-500007
12. Dr. V.V. Sarma, Scientist, National Isntitue of Oceanography, LB Colony, Visakhapatnam-530017
13. Dr. P.J. Rao, Dept. of Chemical Engineering, Andhra University, Visakhapatnam-530 003, A.P.
14. Mantri Shyam Prasad, Secretary, AP State Human Rights, Lawsons Bay Colony, Visakhaptnam-530 017
15. Dr. S. Ramakrishna Rao, Professor, Dept. of Civil Engineering, Andhra University, Visakhapatnam-530003, A.P.

16. Dr. Madhavi Madireddy, MS, (Wisconsin, USA), FEnRA, Manager, PRO Health Care Hospital, #2707, River Ridge Drive, Waukesha, Wisconsin, USA 53189. E.Mail: mvsmadhavi@hotmail.com
17. Dr. AVR. Brahmanandam, MS, Consultant, Paediatric Surgeon, Nankem Hospital, Coonoor, Nilgiris, Tamil Nadu, 643 191, Email: nanadseniorl@yahoo.co.in
18. Dr. A.V. Subba Rao, MD, Cardiologist, SV. Heart Care Center, Rajahmundry, EG. Distt., A.P.-533 013, E-Mail: avsubbarao2000@yahoo.com
19. Dr. N.K. Chandrasekhar, MS, Chief Executive & Ophthalmic Surgeon, Nankem Hospital, Coonoor, Nilgiris, Tamil Nadu. E-Mail: Nankem_nk@yahoo.co.in

CHAPTER

1

BIODIVERSITY CONSERVATION OF EASTERN GHATS FORESTS OF ANDHRA PRADESH WITH SPECIAL REFERENCE TO SPECIES RICHNESS : AN OVERVIEW

MADIREDDI V. SUBBA RAO

Keywords: Biodiversity, Conservation, Eastern Ghats, Andhra Pradesh, Species Richness

ABSTRACT

The variety of physiographic and climatic conditions of the Eastern Ghats support a wide range of biodiversity both rich in flora and fauna and a wide variety of habitat conditions. Apart from mangrove forests, the Eastern Ghats have largely dry and moist deciduous forests alternately occupying scrub jungles. Our dense forests are now limited to a few pockets. The main reasons are the deforestation and swidden or shifting type of cultivation by tribal. In fact, the survival problem is common to all wildlife, which has led to the extinction of cheetah and has pushed the tiger to the brink. This has led to drastic reduction in biodiversity for both plants and animals. The present status of species richness of faunal groups is presented.

INTRODUCTION

The Eastern Ghats are a long chain of broken hills and crystalline metamorphic rocks and have a line of mountain ranges running from North-East to South-West with parallel ridges with an elevation ranging from a few metres to 1750 metres. High at Biligirirangan Hills forming their southern tip in Tamil Nadu.

These Eastern Ghats are spread over three States in India namely Orissa (3 districts), Andhra Pradesh (14 districts) and Tamil Nadu (7 districts). In Andhra Pradesh, the Eastern Ghats run through 14 districts (Figure 1.1) as a continuous chain with interruption between Godavari and Krishna deltas and in parallel ridges in the remaining districts. Perennial rivers like Godavari, Krishna and Pennar have their origins in Western Ghats while the ephemeral ones like Nagavali, Vamsadhara and Sarada have their origin in Eastern Ghats.

The Eastern Ghats are not a range of mountains or escarpments like the Western Ghats but an assemblage of series of much broken isolated hills representing weathered relics of peninsular India, including hills of various altitudes, plateau, escarpments, mesa and the butts, intermountain basins, valleys and gorges.

Considering the ecological conditions, the Ghats in Andhra Pradesh have been classified into three major regions, namely: (1) Northern Ghats; (2) Central Ghats (3) Sourthern Ghats (Fig. 1.1).

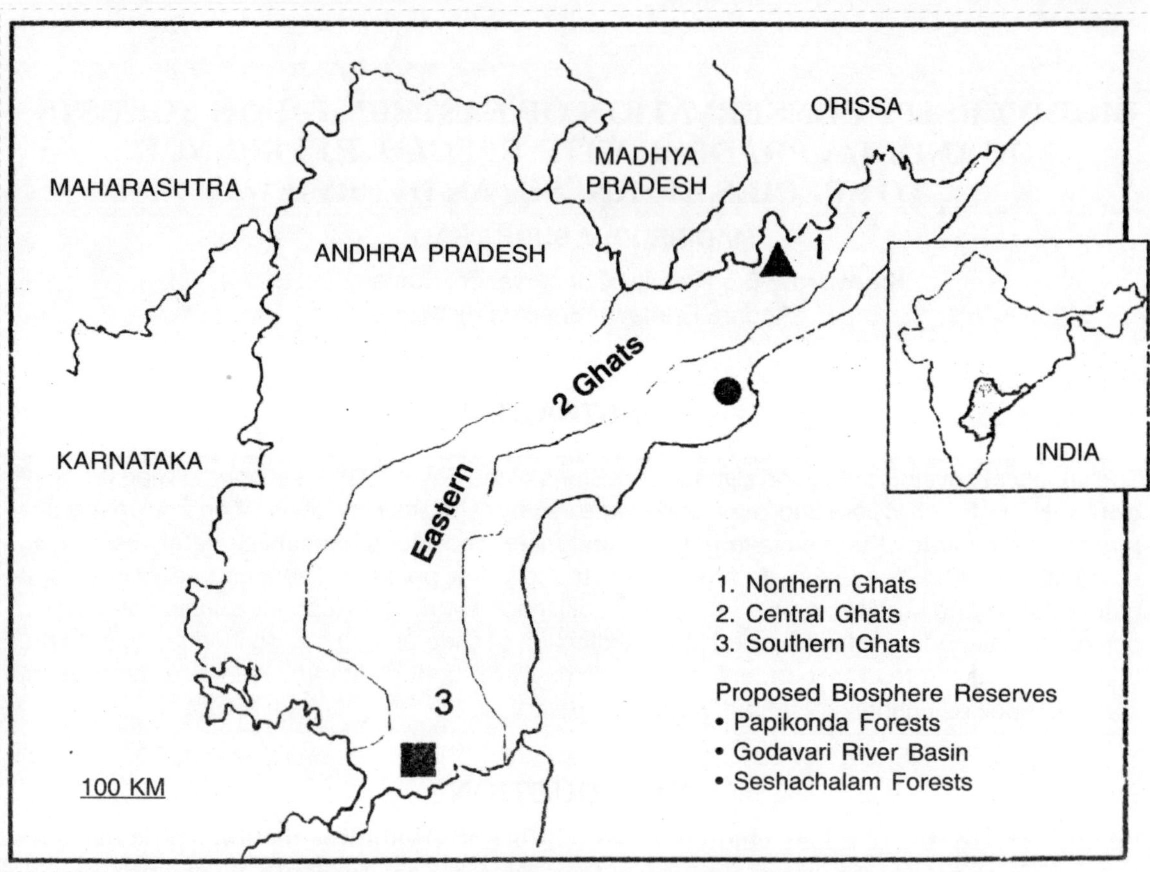

Fig. 1.1. The Eastern Ghats region is classified as having three zones : (1) Northern Ghats, (2) Central Ghats, and (3) Southern Ghats. Also shown are the locations of proposed Biosphere Reserves (Subba Rao 2000).

The Northern Ghats

The Northern Ghats consists of the foothills, plateaus and the coastal plains. The forests of Northern Ghats are located in Sileru, Machkund basin and the basin of the major river Godavari covering the districts of Srikakulam and Khammam. The coastal areas with foothills and hillocks of Eastern Ghats run parallel to the Bay of Bengal. The Northern Ghats have an average elevation ranging from 1100 to 1200 m with Mahendragiri near Orissa State boarder having the highest elevation point of 1501 m.

Vegetation : The semi-evergreen forest of vegetation constitutes moist vegetation while moist to dry deciduous vegetation riverines and streams. The foothills and the plateaus are covered by dry deciduous and occasionally scrub type of vegetation. The vegetation cover is classified into three strata as described by Legris and Meher-Homji (1982). They are the upper canopy, intermediate stories and ground covered with scrubs. The vegetation is mostly characterized by the presence and prominence of the sal, (*Shorea Kobusta*), whereas the general floristic composition of the deciduous type is constitutes teak, (*Tectona grandis*). The density varies from 0.3 per cent to 0.8 per cent.

The Central Ghats

The Nallamalai are mostly the formations in the central region of Eastern Ghats in the districts of Guntur, Prakasam and Kurnool. These are continuous ranges with an elevation ranging from 750 to 1000 metres. The river Krishna flows through the Nallamalai, and the perennial streams support the forests with tropical, semi-evergreen, moist and dry deciduous types of vegetation.

The three broad types of Nallamalai forests are upper canopy, dry and moist deciduous isolated patches and evergreen vegetation along perennial streams. After the rainy season, the grass cover is often continuous and gradually disappears during summer (Table 1.1).

Table 1.1. Distribution of Forest Types and Important Plant Species in the Eastern Ghats of Andhra Pradesh, India

Group	Forest type	Plant species	Distribution area
A	Semi-evergreen	*Michelia champka* *Mangifera indica* *Artocarpus lakoocha* *Dellina pentagyna* *Bridelia tomentosa* *Xylla xylocarpa* *Polyalthia cerasoides* *Macaranga peltata* *Pittosporum napaulense*	Northern Eastern Ghats
B	Moist deciduous	*Terminalia tomentosa* *Xylla xylocarpa* *Anogeissus latifolia* *Adina cordifolia* *Pterocarpus marsupium* *Schleichera trijuga* *Bridelia retusa* *Careya arborea* *Polyalthia cerasoides* *Kydia calychina* *Dendrocalamus strictus*	Northern Central Ghats

Group	Forest type	Plant species	Distribution area
C	Dry deciduous	*Terminalia alata* *Terminalia chebula* *Pterocarpus marsupium* *Madhuca longifolia* *Cassia fistula* *Sterculia urens*	Central and Southern Ghats
D	Scrub type	*Lantena camera* *Albizia amera* *Acacia chundra* *Anogeissus latifolia* *Xerophis spinesa* *Euphorbia tiricallia* *Hugonia mystex* *Dodonaea viscosa* *Cassia auriculate* *Carissia apinarum* *Eupatorium* spp.	Southern Ghats
E	Mangroves	Acanthus ilicifolius Avicennia officinalis Bruguiera cylindrica Bruguiera gymnorrhiza Excoecaria agallocha Lumnit/era racemosa Rhizophora candellana Sesuvium portulcastrum Sonneratia apetala	Coastal Plains

The Southern Ghats

The Seshachalam and Erramalais are formations of the southern ghats in Andhra Pradesh State through the districts of Chittoor, Nellore, and Anantapur. They are comparatively smaller ranges with dry conditions. These Ghats annually receive lower rainfall under higher temperature and less humid conditions. The main vegetation is dry evergreen, deciduous to scrub type of vegetation mostly of the thorny type (Table 1.1).

Ecological Significance : Fifty per cent of the Andhra Pradesh State forest area lies in the Eastern Ghats of which 1.0 million hectares lies in the Northern Ghats and 2.2 million hectares in Central and Southern ghats. When compared to the forests of Central and Southern Ghats, the forests of Northern Ghats are inferior although they are extensive in density and quality. The Central and Southern Ghats receive low rainfall with higher temperature when compared to Northern Ghats. The hills of Eastern Ghats are steep in nature and are studded with a number of peaks.

Physiography : In general, the Eastern Ghats are made up of variety of rocks such as khondalites, charnockites, gneises and schits of igneous and sedimentary origin (Krishnan, 1958). Though the ancient metamorphic rocks are of diverse material of highly complex substances of different ages (2400 million years old or Jurassic age). The sedimentary rocks formed in Eastern Ghats are highly metamorphosed. They include quartz, mica schists, manganiferous sediments and crystalline lime stones. A conspicious member is khondalite which consists of quartz garnets and sillimanite-graphic schists. It has also phosphorous-rich granites, alumina, iron and bauxite.

Climate : The climate of the Eastern Ghats is typically tropical and has a good thermal potential, sufficient enough to support the most luxuriant development of forest types of vegetation. The climate of the Eastern Ghats can be divided into three seasons: 1. Summer (March-May); 2. Rainy (June-October); 3. Winter (November-February).

The northern Eastern Ghats are characterised by low temperature, high humidity and medium to heavy rainfall. The Southern ghats have high temperature and relatively low humidity and rainfall. The temperature ranges from 41°C during summer to low of 6°C during winter. The annual rainfall from 1200 to 1500 mm.

Forests : In 1900, forests covered 40 per cent in India's goegraphic areas. In 1964, the forest cover was 34 per cent. Today it is reduced to 10 to 11 per cent only.

The forests of the Eastern Ghats apart from mangrove forests (Table 1.1) in Andhra Pradesh State are largely dry with moist deciduous alternately occupying scrub jungles. Now our dense forests are limited to a few pockets. The main reasons are the deforestation and the swidden or shifting cultivation by tribals from Adilabad district along with river Godavari in Karimnagar district from Srisailam to Nallamalai ranges.

Tribals : Of the 33 recognised (Scheduled) tribal groups of Andhra Pradesh, 27 live in the Eastern ghats. The Chenchus and Yanadis are the dominant groups in the Southern ranges. The Government of India has recognized the Chenchus and Kondareddi as primitive tribal groups.

The main problem in the Eastern Ghats are swidden or shifting type of cultivation, monoculture practice, timber exploitation and industrial activity. Now the efforts are on to increase forest cover through afforestation and Joint Forest Management (JFM) programmes which are in progress.

FLORAL COMPOSITIONS

The vegetation of the Eastern Ghats is mainly of two types, *i.e.* : (1) Dry deciduous and (2) Moist deciduous. However, there are a few patches of semi-evergreen sprinkled at random in association with highly elevated areas of the moist deciduous type. On the other hand, a vast spread of the dry deciduous forests degraded into thorny scrub alone exists.

The North Eastern Ghats consist of mixed deciduous types, both moist and dry, as well as semi-evergreen patches. The Southern Ghats to a great extent support dry deviduous and thorny scrub (Table 1.1). The interesting medicinal plants of Eastern Ghats of Andhra Pradesh are shown in Table 1.2.

Table 1.2. Interesting Medicinal Plants of Eastern ghats of Andhra Pradresh, India

Acacia nilotica (Linn.) Wild. sp. Indica (Benth.) Brenan	*Cleome viscosa* Linn.
Achyranthes aspera Linn.	*Clerodendrum serratum* (Linn.) Moon
Adenia wightiana (Wall. Ex Wt. & Arn.) Engl.	*Cocculus hirsutus* (Linn.) Diels
Adhatoda zeylanica Medic.	*Coldcnia procumbens* Linn.
Acrva lanata (Linn.) Juss.	*Colebrookea oppositifolia* Smith
Ailanthus excelsa Roxb.	*Cordia dichotoma* Forst.
Alangium salvifolium (Linn f.) Nees	*Costus speciosus* (Kocnig) Smith
Albizia lebbeck (Linn.) Benth	*Cryptolepis buchananii* Roem. & Schult.
Andrographis echioides (linn.) Nees	*Datura metel* Linn.
Andrographis panichulata (Burm. F.) Nees	*Digera muricata* (Linn.) Mart.
Annona squamosa Linn.	*Ecbolium viride* (Forsk.) Alston
Argemone mexicana Linn.	*Eclipta prostata* (Linn.) Linn.
Aristolochia bracleata Lamk.	*Euphorbia hirta* Linn
Aristolochia indica Lamk.	*Eurphorbia tirucalh* Linn.
Asparagus racemoss Wild.	*Evolvulus alsinoides* (linn.) Linn.
Asystasia gangetica (Linn.) Aanders.	*Ficus heterophylla* Linn.
Azadirachta indica A. Juss	*Oloriosa superba* Linn.
Balanitis aegyptiaca (Linn.) Del.	*Gmelina arborea* Roxb.
Boswellia serrata Roxb. Ex. Coleb.	*Grangea maderaspatana* (Linn.) Poir..
Bndelia ratusa (Linn.) Spreng.	*Guizotia abyssinicia* (Linn.) Cass.
Bunchanania axillaris (Dres.) ramamurthy	*Gymnema sylyestre* (Retz.) R. Br.
Caesalinia bonduc (Linn.) Roxb	*Helicteres isora* Linn.
Calotropis gigantica (Retz.) R. Br.	*Hemidesmus indicus* (Linn.) Schult.
Carica papaya (Lour) Cogn.	*Holarrhena pubescens* (Buch.-Ham.) Wall, ex Don
Cassia occidentails Linn.	*Ichnocarpus frutescens* (Linn.) R. Br.
Catharanthus roseus (Linn.) G. Don	*Ipomea aquatica* Forsk.
Celosia argentea Linn.	*Jatropha gossypifolia* Linn.
Ceropegia candelabrum Linn.	*Kalanchoe pinnata* (Lamk.) Pers.
Cleistanthus collinus (Roxb.) Diels	*Kirganelia reticulata* (Poir.) Baill.
Cleome gynandra Linn.	*Lepidagathis cristata* (Retz.) Wt. & Arn.
	Leucas cephalotes (Roth) Spreng.

Limonia elephantum (Correa) Panigrahi	*Ricnus communis* Linn.
Litsea monopetala Pers.	*Rubia cordifolia* Linn.
Macaranga peltata (Roxb.) Muell.	*Rungia pectinata* (Linn.) Nees.
Madhuca longifolia (Keon.) Macb.	*Salacia chinensis* Linn.
Mallotus phillippensis (Lamk.) Muell.	*Schrebera switinioides* Roxb.
Martynia annua Linn.	*Semecarpus anacardium* Linn. f.
Mollugo cerviana (Linn) Ser.	*Solanum indicum* Linn.
Ocimum americabum Linn.	*Solanum sarrattense* Burm. f.
Ocimum gratissunum Linn.	*Solena heterophylla* Lour.
Ocimum sanctum Linn.	*Soyniida febrifuge* (Roxb.) A. Juss.
Passiflora foetida Linn.	*Stemodia viscosa* Roxb.
Pergularia daemia (Forsk.) Chiov.	*Strynchnos nux-vomica* Linn.
Phyla nodiflora (Linn.) Green	*Terminalia cordifolia* (Willd.) Hook. f.
Phyllanthus embilca Linn.	*Trianthema poortulacastrum* Linn.
Phyllanthus amarus Schum. & Thonn.	*Tridax procumbens* Linn.
Piper triocum Roxb	*Vitex altissima* Linn. f.
Rauvoltia serpentina (Linn.) Benth.	*Vitex negundo* Linn.

FAUNAL COMPOSITION

Eight species of amphibians and 41 species of reptiles have been recorded in Eastern Ghats of Andhra Pradesh State (Subba Rao,1992) (Table 1.3). Important species include a golden gecko, (*Calodactylus aureus*), which has been reported from this part for the first time and four other reptiles with new destributional records. Nineteen species of rare and endangerd species of birds (Table 1.4) and 46 species of mammals have been recorded in Eastern Ghats of Andhra Pradesh State (Table 1.5).

Besides faunal diversity, the status of the individual species with their distribution, habitat and abundance in herpetiles and mammals were studied.

Andhra Pradesh has a rich variety of wild animals: over 1000 species of mammals, 500 varieties of birds and nearly 100 species of herpetiles besides several terrestrial and aquatic forms of life. In the Indian sub-continent, 35 per cent of the Vertebrates are distributed in the Eastern Ghats forest of Andhra Pradesh. Some of the endangered animals are, the tiger, leopard, fishing cat, Asian elephant, black buck, chinkara, four-hourned antelope, mouse, deer, slender loris and smooth Indian otter. The threatened birds are the Indian Bustard and Jerdon's courser. Among reptiles, salt water crocodiles, once found throughout the coastal marshy plains, have disappeared from their original habitat (Subba Rao and Bustaid,1992). The golden gecko (*Glodactylus aureus*) is one of the rarest species found only in the Eastern ghats of Andhra Pradesh, at Seshachalam hills in Chittoor district (Daniel, 1985) and Ananthagiri hills of Visakhapatnam district (Subba Rao, 1989). After

100 years, it was rediscovered in these two places. Another important reptile species, the limles lizard (*Barkudia insularis*) is also endemic to Visakhapatnam (Subba Rao,1992).

Table 1.3. Distribution of Herpetilian Fauna in the Eastern Ghats of Andhra Pradesh, India

Class	Order	Family	Species
Amphibia	Anura	Ranidae	*Rana hexadactyla*
			Rana cyanophlyctus
			Rana *tigrinr*
			Rana cressa
		Bufonidae	Bufo melanostictus
			Bufo fergusonil
		Rhacophoridae	Rhacophorus leucmystax
Reptilia	Testudinata	Chelonidae	Lepidochelys olivacca
			Eretmochelys imbricata
			Chelonia mydas
		Emydadae	Lissemys punctata granosea
			Kachuga tectus tentenca
		Testudinae	Geochelone elegans
	Loricata	Crocodylidae	Crocodylus porosus
			Crocodylus palustris
	Squamata		
	Sub-order: Sauria		
		Gekkonidae	Hemidactylus prashadii
			Hemidactylus brooki
			Hemidactylus gigonteus
			Hemidactylus reticulatus
			Calodactylodes aureus
		Agimidae	Calotes versicolor
			Calotes nemoricola
			Calotes calotes
			Psammophilus blanfordenus
			Citana ponticeriana
		Chamaeleonidae	Chamaeleon zeylenicus
		Scincidae	Mabuya beddomii
			Mabuya carinata
			Lygosoma dussumieri
			Riopa punctata

Class	Order	Family	Species
			Barkudia insularis
		Varanidae	Varanus bengalensis
	Ophidia	Typhlopidae	Typhlops beddomii
		Biodie	Python molurus
			Eryx johni johni
		Colubridae	Oligodon arnensis
			Amphiesma stolata
			Atretium schistesum
			Dryophis pulverulentus
			Enhydris enhydris
			Lycodon striatus
			Lycodon trevancoricus
			Lycodon auricus
			Natrix piscator
		Elapidae	Bungarus molurus
			Naja naja naja
			Naja hannah hannah
		Viperidae	Vipera russelli

Table 1.4. List of Rare and Endangered Avian Fauna Present in the Eastern Ghats and Surronding Areas of Andhra Pradesh, India

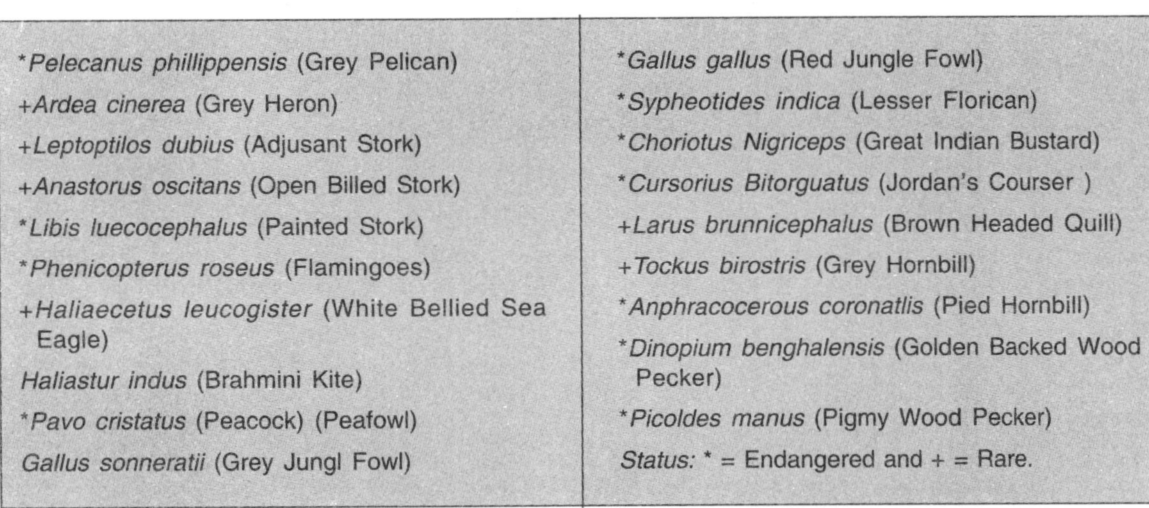

**Pelecanus phillippensis* (Grey Pelican)	**Gallus gallus* (Red Jungle Fowl)
+*Ardea cinerea* (Grey Heron)	**Sypheotides indica* (Lesser Florican)
+*Leptoptilos dubius* (Adjusant Stork)	**Choriotus Nigriceps* (Great Indian Bustard)
+*Anastorus oscitans* (Open Billed Stork)	**Cursorius Bitorguatus* (Jordan's Courser)
**Libis luecocephalus* (Painted Stork)	+*Larus brunnicephalus* (Brown Headed Quill)
**Phenicopterus roseus* (Flamingoes)	+*Tockus birostris* (Grey Hornbill)
+*Haliaecetus leucogister* (White Bellied Sea Eagle)	**Anphracocerous coronatlis* (Pied Hornbill)
Haliastur indus (Brahmini Kite)	**Dinopium benghalensis* (Golden Backed Wood Pecker)
**Pavo cristatus* (Peacock) (Peafowl)	**Picoldes manus* (Pigmy Wood Pecker)
Gallus sonneratii (Grey Jungl Fowl)	*Status:* * = Endangered and + = Rare.

Table 1.5. Distribution of Mammals in the Eastern Ghats of Andhra Pradesh, India

Parenchinus nudiventris (Hedgehog)	*Lutra vulgaris* (Water otter)
Suncus caeruleus (Musk Shrew)	*Sus cristatus* (Indian Wild Boar)
Tupia ellioti (Tree Shrew)	*Tragulus meminna* (Mouse Deer)
Pteropus giganteus (Indian flying Fox)	*Axis axis* (Chital or Spotted Deer)
Rousettus leschenaults (Fulvous fruit Bat)	*Muntiacus muntjac* (Barking Deer)
Taphozous melanopogon (Bearded sheath tailed Bat)	*Cerus unicolor* (Sambar)
Pipistrellus coromandra (Indian pipistrelle)	**Bos gaurus gaurus* (Indian Bison)
**Loris tardigradus* (Slender Loris)	**Bubalus bubalis* (Wild Buffalo)
Macaca muletta (Rhesus Monkey)	*Antelope cervicapra* (Black Buck)
Macaca radiata (Bonnet Monkey)	*Gazella benneti* (Indian Bison)
Presbytis entellis (Common Langur)	*Boselaphus tragocamelus* (Nilgai or Blue Bull)
**Penthera tigris* (Tiger)	*Tetracerus guadricornis* (Four Horned Antelope)
Panthera pardus (Indian Panther)	**Elephas maximus* (Indian Elephant)
Felis vierrina (Fishing Cat)	*Funamnbulus palmarum* (Stripped Palm Squirrel)
Felis chaus (Jungle Cat)	*Ratufa indica* (Indian Giant Squirrel)
Viverricula Indica (Indian Civet Cat)	*Mus booduga* (Indian Field Mouse)
Herpestes mungoose (Common Mungoose)	*Mus rattus rattus* (Common House Rat)
Hyaena Hyaena striata (Hyaena)	*Bandicoota bengalensis* (Bandicoot Rat)
Canis pallipes (Indian Wolf)	*Gerbillus indica* (Indian Gerbelle)
Canis aureus (Indian Jackal)	*Hystrix indica* (Porcupine)
Vulpes bengalensis (Indian fox)	*Lepus nigricollis* (Common Hare)
Cyon alpinus (Wild Dog)	*Manis crassicaudata* (Scaly Ant-liater)
Melursus ursinus (Sloth Bear)	

Status : * = Endangered

ACHIEVEMENT

For the first time in India, a comprehensive study on the Herpetofaunal and Mammalian resources of the Eastern Ghats of Andhra Pradesh State was made based on a systematic survey and intensive investigation including species richness. During the study, 8 species in 4 families belonging to class Amphibia and 4 species in 13 Families and 4 Orders of class Reptilia have been recorded. A very important species of reptile is the golden gecko, *Calodactylus aureus,* which has been reported from Ananthagiri hills of Visakhapatnam district of eastern Ghats (Subba Rao, 1989) along with four other reptiles with new distributional records. Another important reptile species, the limbless lizard, *Barkudia insularis,* is also endemic to Visakhapatnam (Subba Rao,1992). Nineten speies of rare and endangered birds and 46 species of Mammals in nine orders have been recorded in Eastern Ghats of Andhra Pradesh State (Subba Rao, 1993). Of these Insectivora are represented by 3 species; Chiroptera 4; Primates 4; Carnivora 14; Artiodactyla 11; Rodenta 7; and Proboscidae, Lagomorphamad Pholidota, one species each respectively (Table 1.5).

Besides faunal discovery, status of the individual species, with their distibution habitat, abundance in Herpetiles and Mammals was studied.

Comprehensive management programmes for the conservation of threatened and endangered species of reptiles such as Olive Redley sea turtle, *Lepidechelys olivacea*; colour changing lizard, *Chamealeon zeylanicus*; and monitor lizard, *Varanus begalensis* have been developed.

CONSERVATION AND MANAGEMENT

Since more than half of the faunal composition is already endangered/threatened, it is essential that a balanced environment should be established forthwith to ensure continuing diversity. Faunal resources in three regions are mainly depleted through (1) Economic exploitation, (2) Habitat destruction and (3) Casual ignorance. Most of the herpetilian habitats are being lost, degraded or decimated due to human activity. Woody habitats are the most affected areas but scrub jungles and fallow lands are also rapidly deteriorating. In the Eastern Ghats of Andhra Pradesh, there are number of organism facing severe habitat loss; among the reptiles: the Indian chamaeleon, golden gecko, and limbless lizard; among birds; Jerdan's Course Indian Bustard, and Lesser Florican, and among Mammals; slender loris, musk deer and black buck. As for aquatic ecosystems; the fresh water and estuarine habitats are actually threatened. Many of the water bodies are deteriorating either due to erosion or siltation.

Human activity in the Eastern Ghats region falls into two categories: The first includes approved forest operation by the Government, rural agricultural and tribal development programmes and many other developmental activities undertaken by individuals or local bodies of the Government. The second category comprises all activities of man that lack prior approval and violate the existing acts, (for example, swidden or shifting cultivation, collection of forest produce and game, etc., no work has been done on the sanctuaries of Biosphere Reserves in Andhra Pradesh, except for a few working plans prepared by the Andhra Pradesh Forest Department. These plans are mainly directed toward social forestry programmes of plantation and deal very little with the development of wildlife and their habitats.

Survey data on "Habitat trends" indicate that all seven recognized habitats of Herpetiles in the Eastern Ghats of this region are being fragmented at an alarming rate. Hence, habitat development is the most vital component of management programmes. The management programmes suggested below will not only help to improve the habitat of these Herpetiles, but also help (1) to ensure a balanced ecosystem, (2) to conserve native flora and fauna and (3) to serve as a model to extend the same to other regions. As a first step in this direction, it is essential to protect certain areas from human activities. Based on the quality of Eastern Ghat's environment and species diversity, it is proposed to create six Biosphere reserve areas. Creation of these Biosphere Reserve Zones will have manifold uses besides developing a continuous stretch in the region that will enable native flora and fauna to survive in their natural conditions. These biosphere reserves have to be monitored by an independent body appointed for the purpose by the State Wildlife Wing, and necessary legislations have to be made so that all the departmental activities in the area by the Governments, Quasi-governments are carried out as per the instructions of the Biosphere Executive Body. The executive body will be equipped with personnel of proven capabilities in the concerned field, and the necessary infrastructural financial and administrative facilities must be provided to them.

The following conservation measures should be taken immediately for the protection of wildlife and its management:

(1) protection of natural habitat,

(2) maintenance of the viable number of species in protected areas (Santcuaries, National Parks and Biosphere reserves),

(3) establishment of Biosphere Reserves for plants and animal species,

(4) protection through Legislation and

(5) education of the environmental protection.

PRESENT STATUS OF EASTERN GHATS

In India, National Forest Policy is prescribed for 33 per cent forest cover. The forest departments control 23 per cent (about 75 million hectares) of total land area. The satellite imagenary shows 9 per cent (28 million hectares). In India, the Eastern Ghats from the chief mountain ranges along with the Himalayas, the Vidhya and Western Ghats. However, information regarding the ecological aspects of these Ghats is meagre. Human activity by way of various development schemes and other practices is observed to be the chief threat to the ecology of this region.

Swidden of shifting type of cultivation is a major agricultural practice of the local tribals in the region. This practice results in the loss of valuable plant cover and removal of invaluable top soil affecting fertility. Complete disappearance of certain plant species at Aruku and Ananthagiri is noticed.

The devolopment of monoculture results in altered microclimatic conditions and mineral cycles and poor underground vegetation. Construction works like roads, buildings, laying down of railway tracks and electrical cables made the area easily accessible, causing increased threat to the ecological balance. As a result, sensitive species like many Bryophytes are increasingly becoming sparse in areas where they are very luxuriantly griming a decade ago. Mining activity is a basic reason of degradation of forests. Ever-growing demand for timber and firewood is resulting in increased rates of deforestation in the areas leading to many adverse changes in the environment.

In brief, industrialization is at the root of ecological disruption of the region as the ecosystem simultaneously acts as source (*e.g.* in supplying of wood for paper industry) and sink (*e.g.* water bodies receiving industrial discharge) of industries development. The reason for wildlife resources depletion is mainly due to destruction of natural habitat, expansion of agriculture, urbanization and industrialization, overgrazing by domestic animals, poaching for meat, skin, fur, ivory, eggs and export of some species.

ACKNOWLEDGEMENTS

Accomplishment of a task of this nature in a short time is impossible without the co-operation of many individuals, institutions and departments. I express my grateful thanks to various organizations, namely (1) Ministry of Environment, Forests and Wildlife, Government of India that sponsored the Herpetiles and Mammalian resources projects of the Eastern Ghats of Andhra Pradesh and granted complete financial assistance and support; (2) the authorities of the Andhra University and Andhra Pradesh State Forest Department; and (3) Integrated Tribal Development Authority of various regions of Eastern Ghats of their full co-operation and encouragement.

REFERENCES

Daniel J.C. 1985. The golden gecko in Seshachalm hills, *Hornbill* 3; 17-19.

Ellis J. L.. 1982. Wild plant resources of Nallamalais on the Eastern Ghats. *Proc Nat. Sem. Eastern Ghats*, Andhra University, Visakhapatnam, pp. 65-68.

Krishnan M. S. 1958. *Introduction to the Geology of India.* Higginbothams Pvt Ltd., Madras.

Legris P. and V. M. Meher-Homji 1982. The Eastern Ghats: Vegetation and Bioclimatic aspects. *Proc. Nat. Sem. Eastern Ghats*, Andhra University, Visakhapatnam, pp. 1-18.

Subba Rao M. V. 1989. *Management on Conservation of Herpetofaunal Resources of the Eastern Ghats, Andhra Pradesh. Final Technical Report*, Ministry of Environment and Forests, Government of India, New Delhi.

Subba Rao M. V. 1992. *Herportofaunal survey in and around Visakhapatnam. Final Technical report*, University Grants Commission, New Delhi.

Subba Rao M. V. and H. R. Bustard 1992. Studies on the conservation and management of the Indian Crocodiles, *J. Environ. Biol.*, 3(2); 83-93.

Subba Rao M. V. 1993. *Ecology and Management of the Mammalian Resources of Eastern Ghats, Andhra Pradesh. Final Technical Report*, Ministry of Environment and Forests, Government of India, New Delhi.

CHAPTER

2

SHOERELINE RESTORATION AT THE MARIE SELBY BOTANICAL GARDENS : A CASE STUDY+

BARRY WALDEN WALSH

ABSTRACT

Global interest in restoring natural shorelines has increased in the aftermath of the December 2004 tsunami that wreaked havoc on open beaches bordering the Indian Ocean. In contrast, areas with coastal mangrove forests reported less catastrophic damage. Shorelines with native vegetation also are best able to withstand the wave action of tropical storms. A case study of the Shoreline Restoration Project undertaken in 1997 at the Marie Selby Botanical Gardens in Sarasota, Florida, USA, provides data that may be useful to those designing such projects today.

INTRODUCTION

The Marie Selby Botanical Gardens, a 14-acre peninsula bordered by Sarasota Bay and Hudson Bayou in downtown Sarasota, Florida, U.S.A., has a thriving mangrove forest lining its shores; but this has not always been the case. In the early 1900s, mangroves and associated coastal plants native to the shoreline were removed by developers. In their place, cypress seawalls, popular at the time, were installed (Fig. 2.1), and boat channels were dredged for navigation. This clearing of the waterfront to "improve the view" was part of a trend that greatly reduced mangrove ecosystems worldwide.

Prior to the settlement of Sarasota in the 1890s, the shoreline of Sarasota Bay and connecting bayous were lined by red, black, and white mangroves and their upland neighbor, the buttonwood tree (see Hoist 2000 and Table 2.1 for scientific names). Florida mangroves are among those species forming the forest tidal wetlands that once protected much of the world's tropical and subtropical coasts.

In 1921, William and Marie Selby constructed a winter residence in Sarasota on bayfront property that would become part of Selby Gardens. William and his father had sold Selby

+Reproduced from EnRA *Souvenir*, 2005, organised by Prof. M.V. Subba Rao at Andhra University.

Oil and Gas to the firm that became Texaco. Marie, a founding member of the Sarasota Garden Club, set out to create a seashore garden, introducing exotic species such as bamboos and banyans. She did preserve the native live oak hammocks on the site; and over the years, as the wooden seawalls deteriorated, the Selbys allowed the bulkheaded shoreline to revert to a sandy beach, upon which native mangroves recolonized naturally.

Fig. 2.1.Shoreline Restoration of Mangroves at the Maire Selby Botanical Gardens, Sarasota, Fl, USA.

Marie Selby bequeathed her home and gardens "for the enjoyment of the general public"; and in 1973, the Marie Selby Botanical Gardens was established as a non-profit organization, specializing in research and display of epiphytic plants such as Orchids and Bromeliads. Selby Gardens opened to the public in 1975 and that same year published the first issue of the research journal *Selbyana*.

By the 1980s, recolonizing mangroves had reached shrub height. To showcase the return of these natives, the Gardens added an elevated wood-plank Baywalk to provide visitors the experience of walking through a mangrove forest without disturbing the plants [Fig. 2.1(2)]. Interpretive signage was installed along the Baywalk explaining the ecological value of mangroves (Desmon 2002).

Selby Gardens gradually acquired adjoining properties, including a parcel with a cypress seawall still intact and, next to that, a property with the Christy Payne mansion built in 1934. Only a few scattered mangroves remained on these sections of shoreline, and behind the Payne mansion, a natural-seepage wetlands had been filled to create a grass lawn sloping from the house down to water's edge.

The 1997 effort to restore native coastal vegetation included a number of endangered plant species. In 1998, the Selby Gardens Shoreline Restoration Project won First Place in the Institutional/Educational category of the Design with Natives Landscape Awards. In presenting the award, the Florida Native Plant Society recognized Selby Gardens for use of native species in restoring coastal vegetation along 600 feet of its shoreline on Sarasota Bay. Criteria included wildlife habitat value, visual amenities, and low maintenance features, such as independence from routine irrigation or fertilization. The Awards Committee also considered public information efforts to showcase the landscape, such as plant identification, interactive paths, guided tours, interpretive signage, and community lectures.

This Chapter considers how Selby Gardens went about the project planning, design, permitting, funding, acquisition of native plant stock, planting, installation of paths and signage, and finally monitoring.

PLANNING AND DESIGN

Cooperating with Selby Gardens on the Shoreline Restoration Project were the William G. Selby and Marie Selby Foundation (a separate philanthropic group founded by the Selbys), the Sarasota Bay National Estuary Program (then a division of the U.S. Environmental Protection Agency), the Department of Environmental Protection (DEP, a State agency), the Southwest Florida Water Management District (a regional agency), and the City of Sarasota.

Annemarie Post, Director of Horticulture at Selby Gardens, coordinated the project and was one of three designers who worked on the restoration. Alien Burdett, DEP Environmental Restoration Coordinator, handled project engineering, including the various government permits required by coastal management laws and regulations. Alien Shuey assisted with plant selection. Post worked with Burdett, Shuey, and Sarasota landscape designer Chris Fusca on design and plant selection.

The restoration addressed the need to protect coastal zone natural habitats, wildlife habitats, shoreline species, and freshwater resources. As part of the project, Selby Gardens discontinued use of well water for irrigation and connected to the City of Sarasota wastewater reclamation plant. The project also addressed the need to educate schoolchildren and adults on the impact of these environmental issues. The Selby Foundation was the major funder of the project, underwriting the recreation of the natural seepage lagoon on the lawn of the Christy Payne Mansion. The shoreline restoration linked to the lagoon by a marsh flat serves the community as a Florida Yards and Neighborhoods demonstration site. The plantings of native vegetation provide a model landscape for residents, especially those just moving to the area from northern States. The DEP funded the purchase of lagoon grasses, and the Sarasota Bay National Estuary Program funded interpretive signage, brochures, and an educational exhibit on the restoration in the Learning Center at the Gardens.

Restoration planning, design, and permitting (federal, state, and local) began in 1995, and the preparatory stage took nearly 2 years. Installation of the project began in January 1997, with the removal of exotic plant species from the shoreline and excavation of the lagoon and marsh flat that extends toward the bay. Adjacent to the marsh, a shell mound was constructed of sand and shell.

Volunteers from local businesses and the Serenoa Chapter of the Florida Native Plant Society assisted Selby Gardens grounds staff and volunteers with the planting of salt- and wind-tolerant species. During a Community Planting Day in February 1997 more than 4000 plants were planted in less than four hours (Post 1997a). On the shell mound and shoreline in front of the Selby Gardens Activities Center and greenhouses, 80 volunteers from local businesses and organizations helped with the planting of coastal species.

MANGROVES

Although mangroves had recolonized the southern portion of the Selby Gardens peninsula, the shoreline in front of the Payne Mansion and the nearby Activities Center had only a few existing mangroves in 1997. These native trees were competing with invasive exotic species. The restoration began with the removal of the competing invasive trees from the shoreline. This was accomplished without disturbing the established mangroves, which included a mature black mangrove, several white mangroves, and a number of red mangroves and buttonwoods. One hundred potted red mangroves [Fig. 2.1(3)] were planted in among the existing trees, and 1000 bare-root plants of smooth cordgrass were planted to help stabilize the beach and encourage natural seeding by mangroves (Lewis & Durstan 1975, Odum & Mclver 1990). Potted sand cordgrass and saltmeadow cordgrass also were planted.

LAGOON AND MARSH

One-third of an acre was excavated on the lawn of the Christie Payne Mansion to recreate a freshwater/brackish lagoon. Functioning as a stormwater retention pond, the lagoon also provides wildlife habitat and supports a marsh flat containing native grasses [Fig. 2.1(4)]. The excavation, conducted by bulldozers, uncovered an extensive deposit of peat, documenting that the area was originally a freshwater wetlands. The lagoon and native marsh vegetation restored the ability of the area to intercept runoff, allowing it to percolate through vegetation and sediment instead of flowing directly into the bay. The lagoon and marsh help protect Sarasota Bay by filtering out pollutants such as fertilizers, pesticides, and oils carried from urban landscapes to roads in stormwater runoff.

Plants were selected according to the several habitats involved in the restoration. Species that grow naturally in freshwater/brackish marshes were planted around the lagoon and in the marsh flat, including black rush and leather fern. Species adapted to freshwater wetlands were planted beyond the lagoon along the northern boundary wall of the Gardens forming a windbreak of native Florida trees. These species include salt-tolerant trees such as buttonwoods, Florida royal palm, southern red cedar, oaks, and stoppers (Post 1997b).

SHELL MOUND

As part of the shoreline restoration, a cactus scrub mound, composed of sand and shell, was constructed adjacent to the marsh flat. Native trees, such as south Florida banyan and gumbo limbo, were planted on the mound, along with native cacti species (see Table 2.1).

Table 2.1. Native Florida plants used in the Shoreline Restoration Project at the Marie Selby Botanical Gardens (MSBG), 1997-1998.

Scientific name	Common name	Family	Distribution	Plants		Status*	Plot
				No.	Size		
Acer barbatum Michx.	Southern sugar maple	Aceraceae	Florida, SE USA	1	3-gal.	—	D31
Acer rubrum L.	Red maple	Aceraceae	Fla., E. USA	2	15-gal.	—	D31
Accelorrhaphe wrightii (Griseb. & Wendl.) Wendl.	Paurotis palm, Everglades palm	Arecaceae	Fla., W. Indies	1	12-ft. mature MSBG transplant	FDA: T	D31
Acrostichum danaeifolium Langsd. & Fisch	Leather ferm	Adiantaceae	Fla., Trop. America	100	3-gal	FDA: T	D29 D31
Agarista populifolia (Lam.) Judd.	Pipestem	Ericaceae	Fla.	6	1-gal.	—	I32
Amorpha fruticosa L.**	Bastard indigo	Fabaceae	Fla., SE	2	3-gal.	—	D29
Annona glabral L.	Pond apple	Annonaceae	Fla., W. Indies, Trop. America	3	3-gal.	—	D31
Ardisia escallonioides Schlecht. & Cham.	Mariberry	Myrsinaceae	Fla., W. Indies, Mexico	9	3-gal.	—	D23 D27

(Contd.)

Table 2.1 (Contd.)

Scientific name	Common name	Family	Distribution	Plants		Status*	Plot
				No.	Size		
Argusia gnaphlodes (L) Heine	Sea lavender	Boraginaceae	Fla., W. Indies	3	3-gal.	—	D23 D27
Asimina tetramera Small**	Pawpaw	Annonaceae	Fla.	3	1-gal.	—	D31
Avicennia germinans (L) L.	Black mangrove	Avicenniaceae	Fla., Trop. America	Existing tree	Mature, native to site	—	D31
Bacopa monnieri (L) Pannell	Water hyssop	Scrophulari-aceae	Fla., SE USA., Trop America	Colonies on lagoon & marsh flat edges	Colonized after excavation	—	D27 D29 D31
Blechnum serrulatum L.C. Rich.	Blechnum	Blechnaceae	Fla., SE USA	20	1-gal.	—	D31
Borrechia frutescens DL.	Sea-oxeye daisy	Asteraceae	Fla., W. Indies Mexico	Existing plants	Native to site	—	D27 D29 D31
Bumelia tenax (L.) Wild.	Tough bumelia	Sapotaceae	Fla, SE USA	1	3-gal.	—	I32
Bursera simaruba (L.) Sarg.	Gumbo limbo	Burseraceae	Fla., Trop. America	2	3-gal.	—	D23 D27
Callicarpa americana L.	Beautyberry	Verbenaceae	Fla., SE USA, W. Indies	15	3-gal.	—	D31
Canella winterana (L.) Geartner	Cinnamon bark	Canellaceae	Fla., W. Indies	1	2-gal.	FDA: E	D31
Canna flaccida Small	Yellow canna	Cannaceae	Fla., SE USA	20	1-gal.	—	D31
Capparis cynophallophora L.	Jamaica caper	Capparaceae	Fla., W. Indies	3	3-gal.	—	D23 D27
Capparis flexuosa (L.) L.**	Limber caper	Capparaceae	Fla., W. Indies	1	3-gal.	—	D23 D27
Capraria biflora L.	Goat weed	Scrophulari-aceae	Fla., Trop. America	1	1-gal.	—	D31

(Contd.)

Table 2.1 (Contd.)

Scientific name	Common name	Family	Distribution	Plants		Status*	Plot
				No.	Size		
Carya glabra (Mill.) Sweet	Pignut hickory	Juglandaceae	Fla., E.	1	30-gal.	—	I32
Celtis laevigata Wild.	Hackberry, sugarberry	Ulmaceae	Fla., Mexico, W. Indies	1	30-gal.	—	I32
Celtis pallida Torr.**	Thorny hackberry	Ulmaceae	Fla.	1	3-gal.	FDA: E	D23 D27
Cephalanthus occidentalis L.	Buttonbush	Rubiaceae	Fla., N. America	4	1-gal.	—	D31
Cereus eriophorus L. Pfeiffer var. *fragrans* (Small) L. Bens.**	Fragrant prickly apple	Cactaceae	Fla.	4	3-gal.	FDA: E CITES: 2 USFWS :E	D23 D27
Cereus gracilis Mill. var. *aborginum* (Small) L. Bens.**	Prickly apple cactus	Cactaceae	Fla.	3	1-gal.	FDA: E CITES: 2 USFWS: C2	D23 D27
Cereus robini (Lem.) L. Benson**	Tree cactus	Cactaceae	Fla., Cuba	1	3-gal.	FDA: E CITES: 2 USFWS: E	D23 D27
Chamaecyparis thyoides (L.) BSP. **	Atlantic white cedar	Cupressaceae	Fla., E. USA	1	3-gal.	—	I32
Chiococca alba (L.) Hitchc.	Snowberry	Rubiaceae	Fla., W. Indies	1	3-gal.	—	D31 I32
Chrysobalanus icacao L.	Horizontal cocoplum	Chrysobalan-aceae	Fla., Central America	7	1-gal.	—	D27
Chrysobalanus icacao L.	Red-tipped cocoplum	Chrysobalan-aceae	Fla., Central America	10	3-gal.	—	D31
Conocarpus erectus L.	Buttonwood	Combretaceae	Fla., Trop. America	10 Existing tress	10-gal. Native to site	—	D27 D29 D31
Conocarpus erectus L. var. *sericeus* Fors. ex DC.	Buttonwood silver	Combretaceae	Fla., Trop. America	4	10-gal.	—	D31
Comus foemina Mill.	Swamp dogwood	Comaceae	Fla., SE USA	6	3-gal.	—	D31
Crataegus crus-galli L.**	Cockspur hawthorne	Rosaceae	Fla., E. USA	1	1-gal.	—	I32

(Contd.)

Table 2.1 (Contd.)

Scientific name	Common name	Family	Distribution	Plants		Status*	Plot
				No.	Size		
Crataegus flava Ait.**	Summer haw	Rosaceae	Fla., E USA	1	1-gal.	—	D31
Crinum americana L.	Swamp lily, string lily	Amaryllid-aceae	Fla., SE USA	15	1-gal.	—	D31
Cyperus planifolius L.C. Rich	Beach sedge	Cyperaceae	Fla., W. Indies	Existing plants	Native to site	—	D29
Dalbergia ecastophyllum (L.) Taub.	Coin-vine	Fabaceae	Flat., Trop. America	Existing plant	Native to site	—	D31
Dennstaedtia bipinnata (Cav.) Maxon	Cuplet fern	Pteridaceae	Fla., Trop. America	2	1-gal.	FDA: E USFWS :E	D31
Diospyros virginiana L.	Wild persimmon	Ebenaceae	Fla., SE USA	2	3-gal.	—	I32
Dodonaea viscosa (L.) Jacq. **	Varnish leaf	Sapindaceae	Fla., Pantropics	3	1-gal.	—	D23 D27
Eleocharis geniculata Torr.	Spike rush	Cyperaceae	Fla., E. USA, America	Colonize diagoon margins	After excavation	—	D27 D29 D31
Encyclia tampensis (Lindl.) Small	Butterfly	Orchidaceae	Fla., W. Indies	2 clumps	Aprox. 10 pseudo-bulbs	—	D31
Emodea littoralis Sw.	Golde creeper	Rubiaceae	Fla., W. Indies	12	4-in.	FDA: T	D23 D27
Erythrina herbacea L.	Coral bean	Fabaceae	Fla., SE USA, W. Indies	3	3-gal.	—	D31
Eugenia axillaris (Swartz) Willd.	White stopper	Myrtaceae Myrtaceae	Fla., W. Indies, Centr. America	10	3-gal.	—	D23 D27 D31
Eugenia foetida Pers.	Spanish stopper	Myrtaceae	Fla. W. Idies	10	3-gal.	—	D23 D27
Forestiera segregata (Jacq.) Krug & Urban	Florida privet	Oleaceae	Fla., W. Indies	1	3-gal.	—	D31
Halesia diptera Ellis	Silverbell	Styracaceae	Fla., SE USA	1	3-gal.	—	I32

(Contd.)

Table 2.1 (Contd.)

Scientific name	Common name	Family	Distribution	Plants		Status*	Plot
				No.	Size		
Hamamelis virginiana L.**	Witch hazel	Hamameli-daceae	Fla, E. USA	1	3-gal.	—	I32
Helianthus debilis Nutt.	Beach sunflower	Asteraceae	Fla.	12	4-in.	—	D23
Heliotropium polyphyllum Lehm.**	Heliotrope	Boraginaceae	Fla., S. USA, Centr. Amerca, W. Indies	3	1-gal.	—	D31
Hibiscus coccineus Walt.	Swamp hibiscus	Malvaceae	Fla., SE USA	6	1-gal.	—	D29
Hibiscus moscheutos L.	Swamp rose mallow	Malvaceae	Fla., E USA	1	3-gal.	—	D29
Hydrangea quercifolia Bartram**	Oak-leaf hydrangea	Saxifragaceae	Fla., SE USA	1	3-gal.	—	I32
Hymenocallis palmeri S. Wats.	Alligator lily	Amaryllidaceae	Fla., SE USA	1	7-gal.	—	D31
Ilex Cassine L. L.	Dahoon holly	Aquifoliaceae	Fla., SE USA	1	7-gal.	—	D31
Ilex glabra (L.) A. Gray	Gallberry	Aquifoliaceae	Fla., SE USA	2	3-gal.	—	D31
Ilex myrtifolia	Myrtle-leaf holly	Aquifoliaceae	Fla., SE USA	1	10-gal.	—	D31
Ilex vomitoria Ait.	Yaupon holly	Aquifoliaceae	Fla., SE USA	7	7-gal.	—	D31
Illicium parviflorum Michx. ex Vent.	Yellow star anise	Illiciaceae	Fla.	7	7-gal.	FDA : E USFWS: C2	D31 I32
Ipomoea pescaprae (L.) R. Br.	Railroad vine	Covolvulaceae	Fla., Pantropics	Existing plants	Native to site	—	D27
Iris hexagona Walt.	Blue flag iris	iridaceae	Fla. SE USA	24	1-gal.	—	D29 D31
Itea virginica L.	Virginia willow	Saxifraga-ceae	Fla, E USA	3	3-gal.	—	D31
Iva frutescens L.	Marsh elder	Asteraceae	Fla., SE USA W. Indies	Existing plants	Native to site	—	D29 D31
Jacquemontia pentantha (Jacq.) G. Don	Jacquem-ontia	Convolvula ceae	Fla., W. Indies	1	3-gal.	—	D31

(Contd.)

Table 2.1 (Contd.)

Scientific name	Common name	Family	Distribution	Plants		Status*	Plot
				No.	Size		
Jacquemontia reclinata House**	Jacquem-ntia	Convolvulaceae	Fla., W. Indies	2	1-gal.	FDA: E USFWS: CA	D29
Jacquinia keyensis Mez.	Joewood	Theophrast-aceae	Fla. W. Indies	1	1-gal.	—	D31
Juncus roemerianus Scheele	Black rush	Juncaceae	Fla., SE USA	3400	4-in.	—	D29 D31
Juniperus silicicola (Sm.) L.H. Bailey	Southern red cedar	Cupressaceae	Fla., SE USA	2 Plus existing trees	12-ft. B & B Native to site	—	D31 D31 I32
Laguncularia racemosa Gaerth. F.	White mangrove	Combretaceae	Fla., Trop. America, Africa	Existing trees	Native to site	—	D31
Lantana involucrate L.**	Lantana	Verbenaceae	Fla., W. Indies	3	1-gal.	—	D23 D27
Licania michauxii Prance	Gopher apple	Chrysobal-anceae	Fla., SE USA	7	1-gal.	—	D23 D27
Lycium carolinianum Watt.	Christma-*sberry*	Solanaceae	Fla., W. Indies	1 Existing plants	2-gal. Native to site	—	D31
Lyonia lucida (Lam.) K. Koch**	Fetterbush	Ericaceae	Fla., SE USA	1	3-gal.	—	D31
Magnolia ashei Weatherby**	Ash Magnolia	Magnoliaceae	Fla., Texes	1	3-gal.	FDA: E	I32
Magnolia grandiflora L.	Southern magnolia	Magnoliaceae	Fla., SE USA	1	30-gal.	—	I32
Magnolia grandiflora L. cv. Little Gem	Little gem	Magnoliaceae	—	1	10-gal.	—	I32
Magnolia grandiflora L cv. St. Mary	St. Mary	Magnoliaceae	—	1	10-gal.	—	I32
Magnolia virginiana L.	Sweet bay	Magnoliaceae	Fla., E USA	1 1	30-gal. 10-gal.	—	D31
Mastichodendron foetidissimum (Jacq.) H.J. Lam**	Mastic tree	Sapotaceae	Fla., W. Indies	1	3-gal.	—	D23 D27

(Contd.)

Table 2.1 (Contd.)

Scientific name	Common name	Family	Distribution	Plants		Status*	Plot
				No.	Size		
Morus rubra L.**	Black mulberry	Moraceae	Fla., E. USA	1	1-gal.	—	I32
Myrcianthes fragrans (Sw.) McVaugh	Simpson's stopper, twinberry	Myrtaceae	Fla., Trop. America	11	7-gal.	USFWS: C2	D23 D27
Nephrolepis cordifolia (L.) Presl.	Sword fern	Davalliaceae	Fla., Pantropics	40	1-gal.	—	D31
Ocotea coriaceae (Sw.) Britt.	Lancewood	Lauraceae	Fla., W. Indies	1	3-gal.	—	D31
Opuntia humifusa (Raf.) Raf.**	Prickly pear cactus	Cactaceae	Fla., SE USA	1	3-gal.	FDA: T CITES: 2	D23 D27
Peperomia humilis (L.) A. Dietr.	Peperomia	Piperaceae	Fla., W. Indies	Several plants	Mounted on tree stump	FDA: E	D31
Persea borbonia (L.) K. Spreng.	Red bay	Lauraceae	Fla., SE USA	1	15-ft. B & B	—	D31
Pinus elliottii var. *densa* Engelm	South Florida slash pine	Pinaceae	Fla.	Existing tree	Native to site	—	D29
Piscidia piscipula (L.) Sarg.**	Jamaican dogwood	Fabaceae	Fla., W. Indies Trop. America	1	3-gal.	—	D31
Pithecellobium unguis-cati (L.) Benth.	Cat's claw	Fabaceae	Fla., W. Indies Centr. America	1	3-gal.	—	D23
Plumbago scandens L.	Wild plumbago	Plumbagi-naceae	Fla. Trop. America	6	4-in.	—	D31
Polypodium polypodioides (L.) Watt	Resurrection ferm	Polypodiaceae	Fla., E. USA, Trop. America	Several clumps	Native to site	—	D31
Pontedaria cordata L.	Pickerelweed	Pontederaceae	Fla., E. USA,	Colony at edge of lagoon	Seed in acquired plant material?	—	D31
Prunus angustifolia Marsh.	Chicksaw plum	Rosaceae	Fla., SE USA	1	1-gal.	—	I32

(Contd.)

Table 2.1 (Contd.)

Scientific name	Common name	Family	Distribution	Plants		Status*	Plot
				No.	Size		
Psychotria nervosa Benth.	Wild coffee	Rubiaceae	Fla., Trop. America	30	1-gal.	—	D31
Psychotria sulzneri Small	Wild coffee, dull	Rubiaceae	Fla., W. Indies	12	1-gal.	—	D31
Quercus austrina Small**	Bluff oak	Fagaceae	Fla., SE USA	1	3-gal.	—	I32
Quercus laurifolia Michx.	Laurel oak	Fagaceae	Fla., SE USA	Existing trees	Native to site	—	D31 I32
Quercus michauxii Nutt.**	Basket oak	Fagaceae	Fla., SE USA	1	3-gal.	—	I32
Quercus virginiana Mill.	Live oak	Fagaceae	Fla., SE USA	Eixsting trees	Native to site	—	D23 D27 D29 D31
Randia aculeata L.	White indigo berry	Rubiaceae	Fla., Trop. America	5	3-gal.	—	D23 D27
Rapanea Punctata (Lam.) Lundell = *Myrsine guianensis*	Myrsine	Myrsinaceae	Fla., W. Indies	9	7-gal.	—	D23 27
Rhapido-phyllum hystrix (Pursh) Wendl. & Drude	Needle palm	Arecaceae	Fla., E. USA	11	7-gal.	FDA: CE	D31 I32
Rhizophora mangle L.	Red mangrove	Rhizopho-raceae	Fla., Trop. America	10 90 Plus existing trees	10-gal. 3-gal. Native to site	—	D23 to D31
Roystonea elata (Bartram) Harper	Florida royal palm	Arecaceae	Fla.	3	3-gal. Planted 1998	FDA: E	D31
Ruellia caroliniensis subsp. *ciliosa* (Pursh) R.W. Long	Wild petunia	Acanthaceae	Fla., SE USA	40	1-gal.	—	D31

(Contd.)

Table 2.1 (Contd.)

Scientific name	Common name	Family	Distribution	Plants		Status*	Plot
				No.	Size		
Sabal minor (Jacq.) Pers.	Dwarf palmetto, bluestem	Arecaceae	Fla., SE USA	5	7-gal.	FDA: T	D31
Sabal palmetto (Walt.) Lodd.	Cabbage palm	Arecaceae	Fla.	6 1 Existing trees	20-ft. B & B Transplant from D29 Native to site	State tree of Florida	D31
Sagittaria latifolia Willd.	Arrowhead	Alismataceae	Fla., E. USA, Calif., Mexico	Colony at edge of lagoon	Seed in acquired plant material?	—	D31
Scaevola plumieri (L.) Vahi**	Inkberry	Goodeniaceae	Fla.,	7	1-gal.	FDA: T	D23 D27
Sesuvium portulacastrum L.	Sea purslane	Aizoacee	Fla., SE USA, W. Indies	Existing plants	Native to site	—	D27
Sophora tomentosa L.	Necklace pod	Fabaceae	Fla., W. Indies	3	1-gal.	—	D23 D27
Spartina alterniflora Loisel	Smooth cordgrass	Poaceae	Fla., SE USA	1000	Bare-root plants	—	D23 to D31
Spartina bakeri Merrill	Sand cordgrass	Poaceae	Fla., SE USA	100	1-gal.	—	D29 31
Spartina patens (Ait.) Muhl.	Saltmeadow cordgrass	Poaceae	Fla., SE USA	100	1-gal.	—	D23 to 31
Styrax americana Lam.	Snowbell	Styracaceae	Fla., SE USA	2	3-gal.	—	D31
Suriana maritima L.	Bay cedar	Surianaceae	Fla., Trop. America	6	3-gal.	FDA: E	D23 27
Taxodium distichum (L.) L. Rich.	Bald cypress	Taxodiaceae	Fla., SE USA	Existing mature tree	Planted in 1980s?	—	D31
Taxus floridana Chapman	Florida yew	Taxaceae	Fla.	1	3-gal.	FDA: E USFWS: C2	I32
Thelypteris kunthii (Desv.) Morton	Wood fern	Thelypteridaceae	Fla., E. USA	40	1-gal.	—	D31

(Contd.)

Table 2.1 (Contd.)

Scientific name	Common name	Family	Distribution	Plants		Status*	Plot
				No.	Size		
Tradescantia ohiensis Raf.	Spiderwort	Commeli-naceae	Fla., E. USA	24	1-gal.	—	D29 D31
Tripsacum dactyloides (L.) L.	Eastern gamma-grass	Poaceae	Fla., SE USA, Trop. America	12	1-gal.	—	D31
Ulmus alata Michx.	Winged elm	Ulmaceae	Fla., SE USA	1	3-gal.	—	D31
Ulmus americana L.	Florida elm, American elm	Ulmaceae	Fla., SE USA	1	7-gal.	—	D31
Ulmus crassifolia Nutt.	Cedar elm	Ulmaceae	Fla., SE USA, Mexico	1	1-gal.	—	D31
Urechites Lutea lutea (L.) Britt.	Wild	Apocynaceae	Fla., W. Indies	1	3-gal.	—	D31
Vibumum obovatum Walt.	Walter's viburnum	Caprifo-liaceae	Fla, SE USA	5	3-gal.	—	D31
Viola affinis Le Conte**	Florida violet	Voilaceae	Fla., SE USA	12	1-gal.	—	I32
Viola primulifolia L.**	Primrose-leaved violet	Violaceae	Fla., SE USA	12	1-gal.	—	I32
Woodwardia areolata (L.) Moore	Netted chain ferm	Blechnaceae	Fla., SE USA	40	1-gal.	—	D31
Yucca aloifolia L**	Spanish bayonet	Agavaceae	Fla., SE USA, W. Indies, Mexico	Eixsting plants	Native to site	—	D27
Zamia integrifolia L.f.	Coontie	Zamiaceae	Fla., W. Indies	10 5	3-gal. 1-gal.	FDA: CE CITES: 2	D23 D27 D31
Zanthoxylum fagara (L.) Sarg.	Wild lime	Rutaceae	Fla., Tex., W. Indies	2	3-gal.	—	D23 D27 D31

Source : Horticulture Department, Marie Selby Botanical Gardens, 1997-1998.

Key to designated status

*(1997): Endangered (E), Threatened (T), Candidate for Federal Listing with substantial evidence for vulnerability (C1), Candidate for Federal Listing with some evidence for vulnerability (C2), Commercially exploited (CE), Convention on International Trade in Endangered Species of Wild Fauna and Flora (CITES) Appendix I (1), CITES Appendix II (2), Florida Department of Agriculture and Consumer Services (FDA), U.S. Department of the Interior/Fish and Wildlife Service (USFWS).

Note: B&B (balled and burlap). Low site survival rate (2005).

MONITORING

An endowed monitoring programme was part of the project design to track the return of native flora and fauna to the shoreline. Soon after the excavation and planting, Post (1997a) reported that two mallard ducks had taken up winter residency in the lagoon and increased numbers of wading birds were observed along the restored shoreline.

Monitoring revealed that the sand-to-shell ratio of the cactus scrub mound favoured trees over cacti. Another finding has been that native plant stock raised in the area has a better survival rate than nursery stock raised further north in the state. Shoreline restoration projects benefit from locally raised plant nursery stock. A bald cypress planted prior to the Restoration Project is well established in the freshwater natural seepage area, where it is sending up characteristic knees visible along the path. Over the years, storm damage has impacted the shoreline at Selby Gardens, most recently the four major hurricanes and Christmas Day storm of 2004. Where the land previously sloped down to the water, there is now a low escarpment, but mangroves continue to grow and propagate seaward of the escarpment helping to stabilize the shoreline.

CONCLUSION

Cooperation and funding by the sponsoring agencies were key components of the project, as was community support provided by volunteers who helped Selby Gardens staff plant thousands of native plants.

Harry Luther, curator of living collections at Selby Gardens, during a tour of the shoreline restoration, observed that progress is good at the 8-year mark, but it will take 50 years to truly evaluate the success of the project. It is not just what we plant, but what recolonizes the shoreline naturally.

The lagoon, marsh, and shoreline continue to be monitored for signs of feral flora and fauna. Positive indicators include native plant colonizers such as the red mangrove seedlings taking root on their own in among the cordgrass [Fig. 2.1(5)]. Elsewhere a yucca plant that may have floated in has taken root among the branches of a mature mangrove.

Another recent colonizer is a healthy looking screw-pine (Pandanus sp.), which is not a pine but a monocot tree with prop roots, some species of which form mangrove-like forests along the shorelines of the Old-World tropics. Selby Gardens has a screw-pine growing some distance from the water; however, this species, popular with Sarasota landscapers, has seeds that float, which may explain its unannounced arrival on the beach at Selby Gardens. Although invasive species can pose a threat to native vegetation, for the time being, Selby's volunteer screw-pine is doing its part to stabilize the shoreline.

REFERENCES

1. Desmon, Lee. 2002. Native plants at Selby Gardens. *The Palmetto* 21(3): 6-7.
2. Hoist, Bruce. 2000. *Field Guide to the Mangroves of Florida*. Selby Botanical Gardens Press, Sarasota, Florida, USA.

3. Lewis, III, Roy R. and Frank M. Dunstan. 1975. The possible role of Spartina alterniflora Loisel. in establishment of mangroves in Florida. pp. 82-100. In: Lewis, R.R., (ed.) Proceedings of the Second Annual Conference on Restoration of Coastal Vegetation in Florida. Hillsborough Community College, Tampa, Florida, USA.

4. Odum, W.E. and C.C. McIvor. 1990. Mangroves. pp. 517-548 in Myers, R.L. and J.J. Ewel, eds. *Ecosystems of Florida*. University of Central Florida Press, Orlando, Fla.

5. Post, Annemarie. 1997a. Horiticulture: New Garden, Familiar Sites. Marie *Selby Botanical Gardens Bulletin* 23(4): 3.

6. Post Annemarie. 1997b. Horticulture: Surrounded by Beauty. *Marie Selby Botanical Gardens Bulletin* 24(2): 4.

CHAPTER

3

PRESENT DAY PROBLEMS AND PERSPECTIVES OF ORCHIDS IN EASTERN GHATS OF ANDHRA PRADESH , INDIA

MADIREDDI V. SUBBA RAO

Keywords: Orchids, Eastern Ghats, Andhra Pradesh India, Problems, Perspectives

INTRODUCTION

The Eastern Ghats are a long chain of broken hills and crystalline metamorphic rocks and have a line of mountain ranges running from Northeast to Southwest with parallel ridges with an elevation ranging from a few meters to 1750 m high at Biligirirangan hills forming their southern tip in Tamil Nadu.

The Eastern Ghats spread mainly through three States in India, namely Orissa (3 districts), Andhra Pradesh (14 districts) and Tamil Nadu (7 districts). In Andhra Pradesh, the Eastern Ghats run as a continuous chain with interruption between Godavari and Krishna Deltas and in parallel ridges in the remaining districts (Fig. 3.1). Perennial rivers like Godavari, Krishna and Pennar have their origins in Western Ghats while the ephemeral ones like Nagavali, Vamsadhara and Sarada have their origin in Eastern Ghats.

The Eastern Ghats are not a range of mountains of escarpments like the Western Ghats but an assemblage of series of much broken isolated hills representing weathered relics of peninsular India, including hills of various altitudes, plateaus, escarpments and intermountain basins, valleys and gorges.

The Eastern Ghats region in Andhra Pradesh (Subba Rao, 1997) have been classified into three major regions considering the ecological conditions namely (1) Northern Ghats (2) Central Ghats and (3) Southern Ghats (Fig. 3.1).

The Northern Ghats

The Northern Ghats consist of the foot hills, plateaus and coastal plains. The forests of Northern Ghats are located in Sileru, Machkund basin and the basin of the major river Godavari covering the districts of Srikakulam and Khammam. The coastal areas of foothills and hillocks of Eastern Ghats run parallel to the Bay of Bengal. The Northern Ghats have an average elevation ranging from 1100 to 1200m with Mahendragiri near Orissa state border having the highest elevation point of 1501 m.

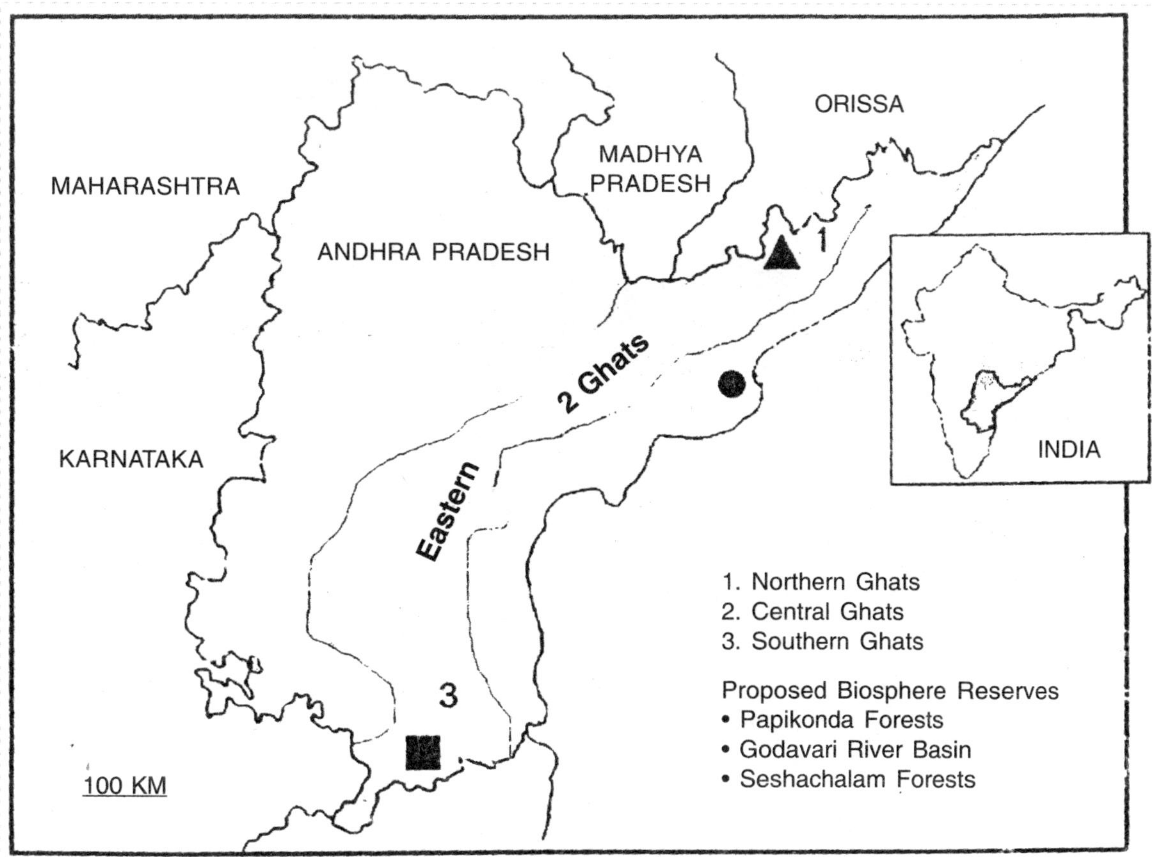

Fig. 3.1. The Eastern Ghats region is classified as having three zones : (1) Northern Ghats, (2) Central Ghats, and (3) Southern Ghats. Also shown are the Locations of Proposed Biosphere Reserves (Subba Rao 2000).

Vegetation : The semi-evergreen forest of vegetation types are prevalent in moist vegetation while moist to dry deciduous vegetation constitutes the river and stream borders. The foot hills and the plateaus are covered by dry deciduous and sporadically scrub type of vegetation. The vegetation cover is classified into three strata as described by Logris and Meher-Homji (1982). They are upper canopy, intermediate stories and ground covered with scrubs (Fig. 3.2). The vegetation is mostly by the presence and prominence of the sal, *Shorea robusta,* whereas the general floristic composition of the deciduous type is teak, *Tectona grandi.* (Subba Rao, 1997).

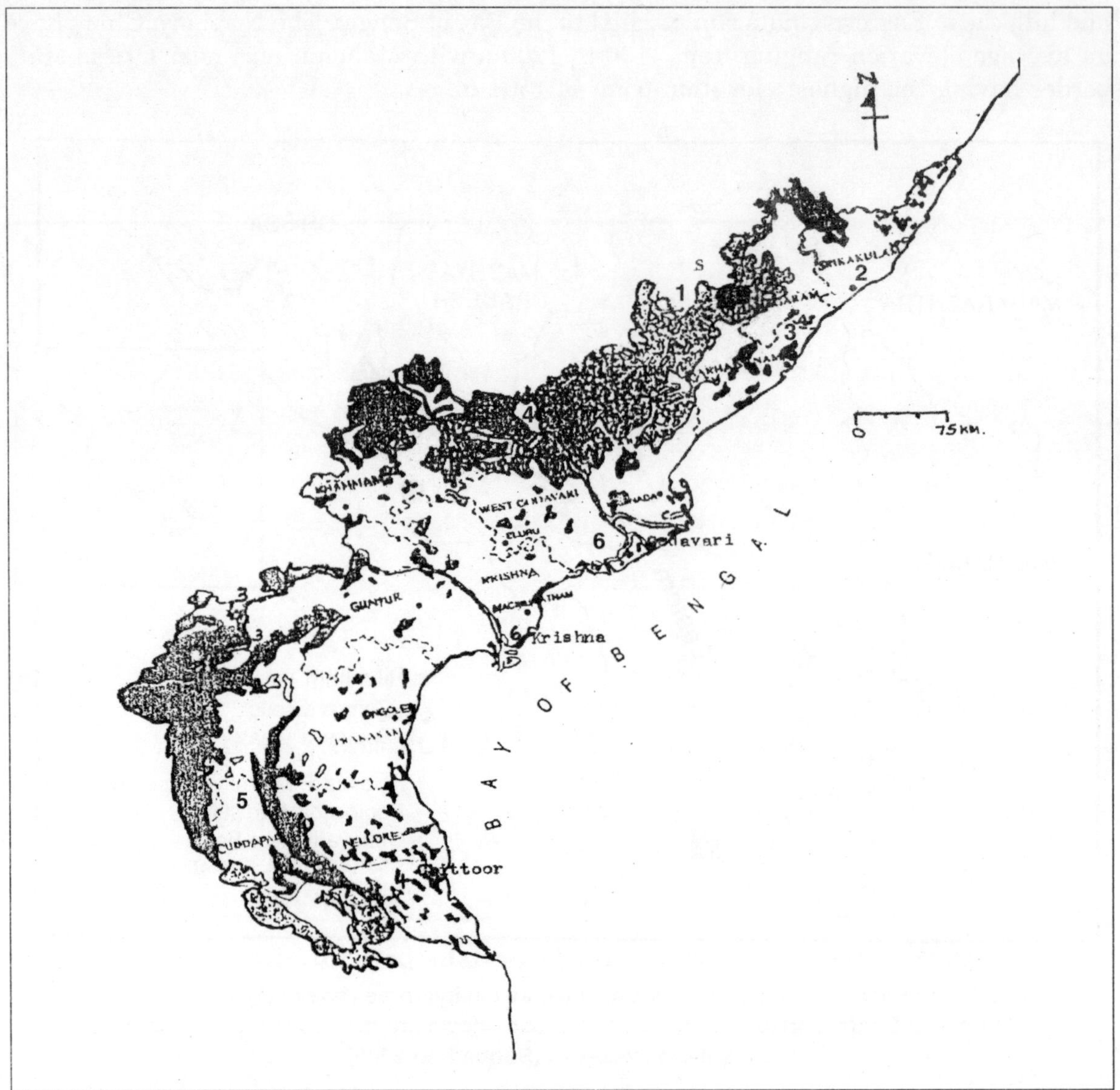

Fig. 3.2. Forest Types in Eastern Ghats of Andhra Pradesh

1. Southern Tropical moist mixed deciduous forests.
2. Sal (*Shorea robusta*) forest, peculiar kind of forest formed in the Vizianagaram district of Andhra Pradesh.
3. Southern Tropical dry deciduous forest.
4. Red Sandars (Chittoor district) of Southern Ghats.
5. Scrub Forest.
6. Littoral and Mangrooves at Krishna and Godavari rivers basins.

The Central Ghats

The Nallamalais are mostly the formations in the central region of Eastern Ghats in the districts of Guntur, Prakasam and Kurnool. These are continuous ranges with an elevation ranging from 750 to 1000 metres. The river Krishna flows through the Nallamalai and the perennial streams support the forests with tropical, semi-evergreen, moist and dry deciduous types of vegetation. The three broad types of Nallamalai forests are upper canopy dry and moist deciduous isolated patches and evergreen vegetation along perennial streams. After the rainy season, the grass cover is often continuous and gradually disappears during summer (Table 3.1).

Table 3.1. Distribution of forest types and important plant species in the Eastern Ghats of Andhra Pradesh, India

Group	Forest types	Plant species	Distribution area
A	Semi-evergreen	*Michelia champaka* *Mangifera indica* *Artocarpus lakoocha* *Delleniapentagyna* *Bridelia tomentosa* *Xylia xylocarpa* *Polyalthia cerasoides* *Macaranga peltata* *Pittosporum napaulense*	Northern Eastern Ghats
B	Moist deciduous	*Terminalia tomentosa* *Xylia xylocarpa* *Anogeissus latifolia* *Adina cordifolia* *Pterocarpus marsupium* *Schleichera trijuga* *Bridelia retusa* *Careya arborea* *Polyalthia cerasoides* *Kydia calycina* *Dendrocalamus strictus*	Northern and Southern Ghats
C	Dry deciduous	*Terminalia alata* *Terminalia chebula* *Pterocarpus marsupium* *Madhuca longifolia* *Cassia fistula* *Sterculia urens*	Central and Southern Ghats

Group	Forest types	Plant species	Distribution area
D	Scrub Type	*Lantana camera* *Albizia amara* *Acacia chundra* *Anogeissus latifolia* *Xerophis spinesa* *Euphorbia tirucalli* *Euphorbia antoguonum* *Hugonia mystex* *Dodonaea viscosa* *Cassia auriculata* *Carissa apinarum* *Eupatorium species*	Souther Ghats
E	Mangroves	*Acanthus ilicifolius* *Avicennia alba* *Avicennia officinalis* *Bruguiera cylindrica* *Bruguiera gymnorrhiza* *Excoecaria agallocha* *Lumnitzera racemosa* *Rhizophora candellaria* *Sesuvium portulacastrum* *Sonneratia apetala*	Coastal plains

The Southern Ghats

The Seshachalam and Erramalais are formations of the Southern Ghats in Andhra Pradesh state through the districts of Chittoor, Nellore and Anantapur. They are comparatively smaller ranges with dry conditions. These Ghats annually receive lower rainfall under higher temperature and less humid conditions. The main vegetation is dry deciduous and thorny type (Table 3.1).

Tribals : The State of Andhra Pradesh consists of 33 tribal groups. The Government of India has identified 12 scheduled tribes as primitive tribal groups (PTG). There are two types of tribes based on the ecological and geographical distribution, known as (1). Plain and (2). Hill tribes. A total of 30 tribes inhabit in the hill tracts of forests in the Eastern Ghats. Their population is 31,71,000 (Government of India census, 2001).

Ecological Significance : Fifty percent of the Andhra Pradesh state forest areas lies in the Eastern Ghats of which 1.0 million hectares lie in the Northern Ghats and 2.2 million hectares in Central and Southern Ghats. When compared to the forest of Central and Southern Ghats, the forests of Northern Ghats are inferior even though they are extensive in density and quality. The Central and Southern Ghats receive low rainfall with higher temperature when compared to Northern Ghats. The hills of Eastern Ghats are steep slope in nature and are studded with a number of peaks.

Physiography : In general, the Eastern Ghats are made up of a variety of rocks such as khondalites, charnockites, gneisses and schist of igneous and sedimentary origin (Krishnan, 1958). The sedimentary rocks formed in Eastern Ghats are highly metamorphosed. They include quartz, mica schists, manganiferous sediments and crystalline lime stones. A conspicuous number is khondalite which consists of quartz, iron and bauxite.

Climate : The climate of the Eastern Ghats is typically tropical and has a good thermal potential, sufficient enough to support the most luxuriant development of forest types of vegetation. The climate of the Eastern Ghats can be divided into three seasons: (1) Summer (March-May); (2) Rainy Season (June-October) and (3) Winter (November-February).

The Northern Eastern Ghats are characterized by low temperature, high humidity and medium to heavy rainfall. The Southern Ghats have high temperatures and relatively low humidity and rainfall. The temperature ranges from 6°C in winter to 41°C in summer. The annual rainfall varies from 1200 to 1500mm.

Forests : In 1964, the forest cover was 34 Percent. Today, it is reduced to 13 Percent only. The forests of the Eastern Ghats apart from mangrove forests (Table 3.1) in Andhra Pradesh state are largely dry with moist deciduous alternately occupying scrub jungles. Now our dense forests are limited to a few pockets. The main reasons are the deforestation and the swidden or shifting cultivation by tribals.

OBSERVATIONS

India has 1400 species of Orchids belonging into 184 genera whereas Eastern Ghats have 128 species and 43 genera. Sikkim is the natural habitat of 475 species and 100 genera and Arunachal Pradesh State consist of 515 species and 110 genera of Orchids. The Orchid plants, their uses and status in Eastern Ghats of Andhra Pradesh have shown in Table 3.2 and Fig. 3.3. The endemic species of Orchids are *Bulbophyllum panigrahianum, Eria meghasaniensis, Habenaria panigrahiana, H.p.varparviloba* and *Liparis vestita.* The rare orchids in Eastern Ghats are *Bulbophyllum macraei, Diploprora championi* and *Goody era fumata.* The ornamental Orchids which are introduced into the gardens are: *Aerides adonata, Dendrobium species, Papilionanthe teres, Pecteilis gigantea.*

PROBLEMS

The present status of Eastern Ghats is over exploitation of natural resources, beyond carrying capacity. There is a heavy human and live stock pressures. Due to deforestation, the loss of biodiversity including Orchids is common. Another problem is swidden or shifting cultivation. In Eastern Ghats the literacy is 10 Percent and the economic conditions of the tribals are poor. There is no safe drinking water in many parts of Eastern Ghats. The soil erosion is due to the shifting cultivation. The large scale deforestation, destruction of native germplasm plants and erosion of biodiversity are common. The grazing lands are due to large scale exploitation, Lack of improved water management system, Incidence of fire is due to phases of burning during process of shifting cultivation, Encroachment of forest area, Population pressure on land, Loss of productivity, Habitat and genetic diversity, Wide spread of poverty and loss of indigenous knowledge, depleting ground water resources, sedimentation and water quality problems are some of them, which are constraints of Orchids conservation in Eastern Ghats of Andhra Pradesh.

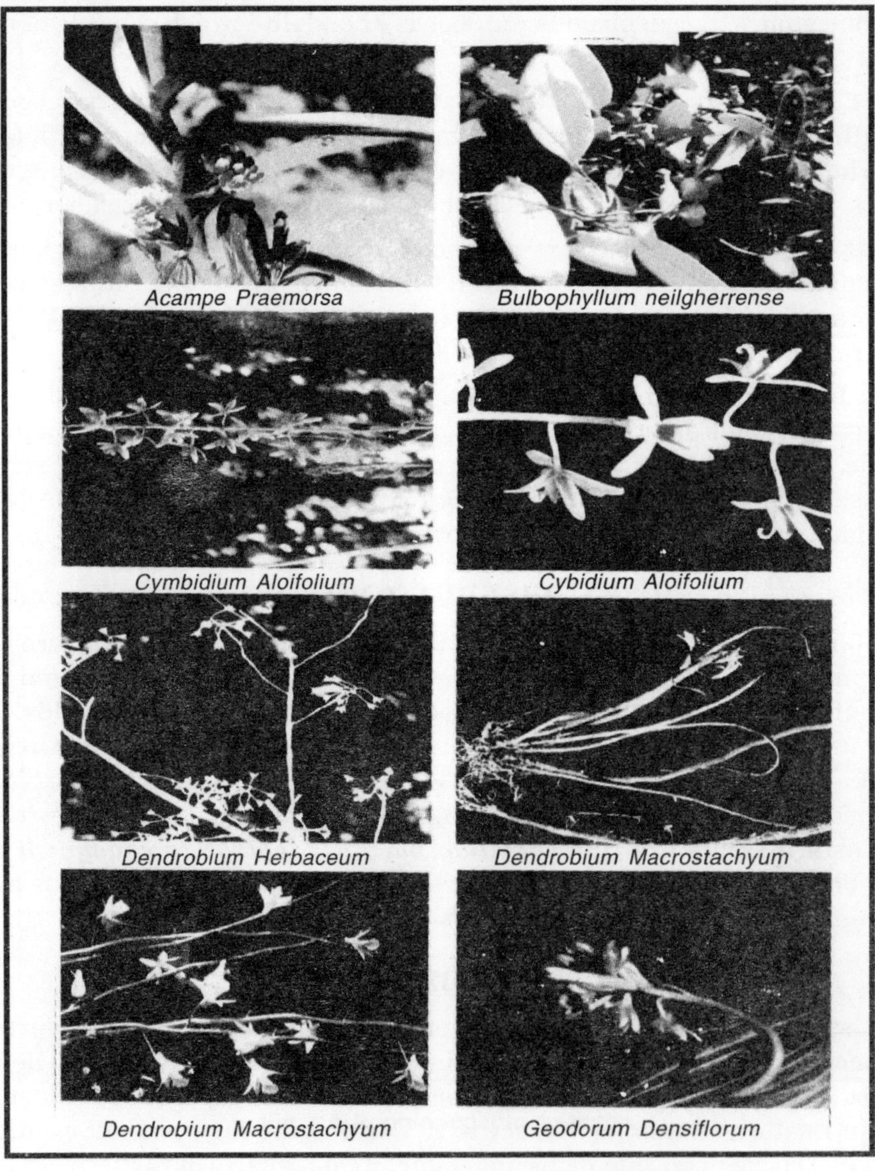

Acampe Praemorsa — *Bulbophyllum neilgherrense*

Cymbidium Aloifolium — *Cybidium Aloifolium*

Dendrobium Herbaceum — *Dendrobium Macrostachyum*

Dendrobium Macrostachyum — *Geodorum Densiflorum*

Fig. 3.3 Orchids in Eastern Ghats of Andhra Pradesh

Fig. 3.3. Orchids in Eastern Ghats of Andhra Pradesh, India.

Table 3.2. List of Orchids and Uses in Eastern Ghats of Andhra Pradesh, India

Sl. No.	Name of the Orchid Species	Uses
1.	*Acampe Praemorsa* (Roxb)	Setting of Fractures
2.	*Bulbophyllum neligherrense*, Neil	Good Health
3.	*Cymbidium* aloifolium (L)	Fractured bones & Foot cracks
4.	*Dendrobium herbaceum*, Lindl	Ear ache
5.	*D.macrostachyum*, Lindl	Ear ache and Ear drops
6.	*Eulophia epidendraea* (Koen)	Anorexia
7.	*Geodorum fensiflorum* (Lam)	Insect bite and wounds
8.	*Habenaria guecifera*, Lindl	Poisonous bite, cuts & wounds
9.	*H. Longicormiculata*, Graham	Leucoderma
10.	*H. Plantaginea*, Lindl	Scorpion bite, cuts & wounds
11.	*H. Roxburghii*, Nicolson	Snake bite
12.	*Luisia zeylanica*, Lindl	Setting of fractures & pus forming wounds
13.	*Malaxis acuminata*, D. Don	Tonic medicine
14.	*M. rheedei*, Sw	Insect bite & Rheumatism
15.	*Nervilia aragoana*, Gaud	Ointment for wounds
16.	*N. plicata* (Andr)	Insect bites
17.	*Oberonia wightiana*, Lindl	External tubers on body
18.	*Peristylus lawi*, Wt	Insect bites
19.	*Pholidota imbricata* (Roxb)	Rheumatic swellings
20.	*Vanda tessellata* (Roxb)	Rheumatism and Dysentrey
21.	*V. testacea*, Lindl	Bone fractures in cattle

Factors Responsible for Degradation of the Forests in Eastern Ghats are

1. Population explosion in Eastern Ghats hills
2. Increased cattle population
3. Abject poverty
4. Poor social economic conditions
5. Pressure on the forest for food, small timber beyond its carrying capacity
6. Illegal encroachment for cultivation (shifting cultivation)
7. Influence of antisocial elements such as smugglers, poachers etc.
8. Fires, soil erosion, land degradation, moisture losses.

PERSPECTIVES

Conservation : The Eastern Ghats have some "Ecological Islands" that harbour endemic Orchids. It is prudent to consider these areas of narrow endemics as Biosphere reserves for preservation of the interesting Orchids. Hence, the need for an integrated rapid forest management for "Sustainable forest productivity and harvest, and resource monitoring on a continuing bases with public participation. Holistic planning with long term monitoring of resources, identifying commercially harvestable species and quantities in time frames. The management practices probably cover silvicultural practices, Orchid species selection, fire and fertilizer, grazing, litter and moisture effect. The practices should improve the forest litter, organic matter content and decrease soil erosion, and thus control the loss fertility. Polyculture or mixed forest development matching the topography will help proper rapid conservation and environment of Orchids in Eastern Ghats. Introduction of exotic species should be carefully done based on the economic needs, overall land and forest productivity, and ensuring that it dose not become a weed or host for many diseases and pests. Hence, action plan should be implemented.

Joint forest management (JFM) and demanded for formation of Vana Samrakshna Samathis (VSS) are necessary to discard the swidden or shifting cultivation by the tribals. Moreover, there is necessary for improvement of the land, soil, water quality through watershed management or rain water harvesting. For this purpose construction of water ponds are required. Tissue culture techniques of Orchids should be encouraged for propogation of the plants. Development of Orchid societies in each state of India is recommended. The self help groups for improving the environment and education and achieving the real sustainable development of natural resources including Orchid plants.

Finally declare all the present orchid flora in Eastern Ghats as Sanctuaries / National parks and conserve Orchids systematically.

ACKNOWLEDGEMENTS

The author acknowledge his sincere thanks to Prof. Y.C. Simhadri, Vice-Chancellor, Andhra University, Visakhapatanam for the encouragement. Thanks are also due to Prof. S.M. Mukherjee, Rector, Gitam College of Engineering for his suggestions and encouragement. Finally, thank the organizers of IOCC planning committee especially Dr. Wesley Higgins and Dr. Bruce Rinker for the invitation to Prof. Rao and partial financial support to participate in the International Orchid Conservation at Marie Selby Botanical Gardens, Sarasota, Florida, USA.

REFERENCES

Government of India Census, 2001. Government of India Press and Publication Division, New Delhi.

Legris P. and V.M. Meher-homji 1982. The Eastern Ghats: Vegetation and Bioclimatic aspects. *Proc. Nat. Sem. Eastern Ghats.* Andhra University Press,Visakhapatnam, pp. 1-18.

Krishnan.M.S.1958. *Introduction to Geology of India.* Higginbothams Pvt. Ltd., Madras.

Subba Rao, M.V. 1997. Development and management of ecohamlets for the consevation of Eastern *Ghat forests in the V izianagaram District. Final Technical Report,* Ministry of Environment and Forests, Government of India, New Delhi, pp. 1-60.

CHAPTER

ECONOMICALLY SIGNIFICANCE OF THE ORCHIDS IN INDIA

M V SUBBA RAO

In ancient India, Orchids were described as medicinal and ornamental plants. The pharmaceutical values of alkaloids, flavonoids, terpenes and glycosides are present in Orchids which have been used for therapeutic purposes. The eye ailments can cure through the flowers from *Vanda coerules* and *Dendrobium nobile.* The amoebic dysentery is controlled by the use of *Paphiopedilum insigne.* The treatment of nervous disorders is checked through *Cymbidium elegans, Cypripedium pubescans* and *Epinectis latofoia.* The tubers of *Eulophia. dilectal* are believed to cure scabies and other skin diseases. The roots of *Planthera bifolla* are used to treat dysentery. Decoction of *Vanda tessalata is* used for bronchitis and woofing cough. The paste of roots, *Dactylorhiza hatagirea* is used as health tonic for bone fracture patients. As tonic and for treatment of rheumatism, pimples, boils and asthma, the orchids of Orchids *latifolia, Eulophia latifolia, Dendrobium alpestre* and *Liparis restrala* are uaed. *Malaxis wallichii* is used for the increase of life span. Vanilla, the favourite flavour is extracted from green pods of *Vanilla plantfolia.* The leaves of *Goodyera, Ceretostylis, Liparis* and *Renanthera* are used for food. The tribals eat the tubers of Eulophia, Habinaria and Cynorchis raw as food. Many Orchid flowers have a pleasant smell. *Phalenepsis* produces a Lilly like scent during daytime and rose like scent at night. Hence extracted from this Orchid for medicinal value. Therefore, the Orchids are economically important for various medicinal uses.

Orchids: Medicinal Uses

At present, natural products represent over 50 per cent of all drugs in clinical use, in which natural products derived from higher plants represent 25 per cent of the total. WHO estimated that over 80 per cent of the people in developing countries rely on traditional remedies such as herbs for their daily needs and about 855 traditional medicines include used the extracts of crude plants. This means that about four billion of the world population depends upon the resources of plants for drugs/medicinal purposes.

Many infectious diseases are known to be treated with herbal remedies throughout the history of mankind. At present plant materials continue to play a major role in primary health care as therapeutic remedies in many developing countries.

Demand for Medicinal Plants in Market

About 95 per cent of plants are used in traditional medicines, which are collected from the forests and other natural resources. The plants collected from different sources show wide disparity in therapeutic values and also much variation in market rates. According to latest estimate, there are about 8000 licensed pharmacies of ISM in the country. The annual demand of the global market is $32 million medicinal plants from developing countries. The herbal drug production in our country has been estimated to be Rs. 4,000 crores in the year 2000. Out of 20,000 medicinal plants of Indian origin are used throughout the world.

A number of higher plant species on Earth is estimated around 2,50,000. Of these, only about six per cent have been screened for biological activity and only 15 per cent have been pharmacologically screened.

Medicinal Use of Orchids

India has 1400 spp. of Orchids with 180 Genera. North Eastern Ghats of India are rich in Orchids. Eastern Ghats have 128 spp. of Orchids with 43 Genera. The tuber of terrestrial species of "Eulophia" and "Habenaris" is used in both '*ridhi*' and '*virdhi*' drugs of *Astavarga* group. These drugs in the form of tonic are used for blood purification, unconsciousness,

Fig. 4.1. Red Ginger

Fig. 4.2. Odontoglossum grande

Fig. 4.3. Cymbidium cultum

Fig. 4.4. Pophiopedilum cultium

Fig. 4.5. Phragmopedilum hybridum

Fig. 4.6. Brassocattleya

Fig. 4.7. Pendrobium noble

leprosy, retaining youthfulness. Additionally several other species are used to cure wounds and fractures. Whereas the Orchids of *Habinaria edgeworthii, H. intermedia, Malaxis muscifera* and *Ephemerantha macraei* are important ingredients of rejuvenating tonic and most commonly used in ayurvedic formulation of "*Chyawan Prash*" Fig. 4.1 to 4.7.

Endemic Species of Orchids in Eastern Ghats are:

(*a*) *Bulbophyllum panigrahianum*

(*b*) *Era meghasanierrsis*

(*c*) *Habinaria panigrahiana*

(*d*) *H. P. varparviloba*

(*e*) *Liparis vestita*

Rare Orchids in Eastern Ghats are:

(*a*) *Bulbophyllum macraei*

(*b*) *Diplopora champloni*

(*c*) *Goodyera*

Problems : Over exploitation of wild species for medicinal, ornamental and scientific purposes.

Habitat destruction,

Macroclimatic changes,

Podu or shifting cultivation.

Solutions : Afforestation, JFMGT, Tissue Culture technique of propagation, Protection of Habitat, Development of Orchid societies, Declare Biosphere reserves /Sanctuaries.

Table 4.1. Ethnomedicinal Use of some Orchid Species

Species	Plant Parts	Treatment for
Aerides multiforum Raxb	Juice of stem & Leaf	External Deworming
Eria tomentosa Hook, F	Juice of whole plant	Medicinal bath for ague
Euophia nuda Lindl.	Tuber & Flower	Bronchitis,Vemifuge & Tumor
Dendrobium ariaeflorum Giff.	Whole Plant	Narcotic
Dendroblium denudans D.Don	Extract	Narcotic
Dactylorhizo hatagirea D.Don	Root &Tuber	Astringent Healing Bone fracture Expectorant, tonic & Wound healer
Habenaria plantaginea Lindl.	Root	Piles & wound Healer
Saccolabium papillosum Lindl.	Whole plant	Healing cracked bone

Table 4.2. Medicinal Uses of some Orchids

Species	Medicinal use
Acampe papillosa	Root is employed under the name Rasna, used for rheumatism, sciat-ica, neuralgia, syphilis and uterine diseases.
Aerides odorata	The ground fruit used for healing wounds. Juice of leaves to heal boils in ears and nose.
Anoectochilus regalis	Stem and leaves as ingredients in certain medicinal oils
Calanthe sylvatica	Flowers used to stop nose bleeding
Calanthe triplicata	Roots as ingredient of local medicine to treat swollen hands; with other ingredients roots chewed for diarrhoea, Flowers as a painkiller in caries, Pseudobulbs as a masticatory, gastrointestinal disorders.
Cephalanthera longifolia	Roots and Rhizome as tonic
Corymborkis veratrifolia	Fresh leaf juice as an emetic to cure fever in children
Crepidium acuminatum	Bulbbous stem used in drug *Rishabhak* of *Ashtavarga* for strength, enchances sperm formation, and prevents diseases born by *vaata pitta* and *kapha*
Cremastra appendiculata	Paste of roots used for toothache and as emollient. Tuber used for abscesses, scrofula, and freckles and as an antidote to snakebite.
Cymbidium aloifolium	Pounding the plant with ginger and extracting the mixture with water is used to induce vomiting and diarrhoea, to cure chronic illness, weakness of the eyes, vertigo and paralysis. Used as an ingredient of oil to cure benign and malignant tumours.
Dendrobium no bile	Fresh and dried stems used in preparation of Chinese drug *Shih-hu* for longevity and as an aphrodisiac, stomachic, analgesic.
Dendrobium jenkinsi	Fresh and dried sterns used in preparation of Chinese drug *Shih-hu*
Dienia muscifera	Decoction of tuber used as tonic to strengthen kidneys
Echioglossum williumsoni	Terete Leaf juice applied by Monpa tribe to cure swellings of hands and legs and bone fractures.
Eria pannea	Decoction of roots and leaves used in bathing in cases of ague

Table 4.3. Medicinal Uses of some Orchid Species

Orchid Species	Medicinal use
Arundina graminifolia	Scrapped bulbous stem applied on heels to treat cracks.
Aerides crispum	Its plants are powdered, boiled in neem oil, filtered, 2-3 drops of oil are put into the ear once at night to cure earache.
Acampe praemorsa	Roots used for treating rheumatism
Coelogyne ovalis	Aptly called as *Jeevanti*, and the whole plant is used in Western and Southern parts of India for cough, urinary infections and eye disorders.
Cymbidium hookerianum	Seeds applied on cuts and injuries as hemostatic
Dendrobium ovatum	Juice obtained by hand crushing the stems is used on patients suffering from constipation and stomachache.

Orchid Species	Medicinal use
Dendrobium densiflorum	Leaves crushed to paste with salt and applied on fractured area to bone
Eulophia nuda	*Amarkana* in Sanskrit), is a ground orchid and used as an appetiser and for treating tumours and bronchitis.
Flickngeria nodosa	'*Purusharatna*' in Kannada, and '*Jiwanti*' in Ayurveda. This orchid is used to treat asthma, bronchitis, throat infections, etc.
Goodyera repens	Roots and leaves for female disorders, stomach and bladder diseases, chewed leaves applied to reptile bites. Mashed leaves prevent rash in infants.
Goodyera schlectandaliana	Tincture of the plant in rice wine is used as a tonic for internal injuries and to improve circulation.
Limodorum sapthulatum	Flowers commonly called *Swarnapushpa*, and flowers of *Habenaria diphylla*, commonly called *Jeevahi Purusharatna* are used to cure asthma.
Malaxis rheedei	It is used as a tonic. It also forms one of the ingredients of the important Ayurvedic drug known as '*Ashtavarga*', which has immense therapeutic value.
Nervilia oragoana	To cure eye infection
Pyamnadenia orchidis	Salep made from digitate tubers used as aphrodisiac, tonic
Phaius tancarvilleae	Paste of Pseudobulbs is used to heal swellings in hands and legs, poultice to soothe pain of abscess.
Pholidota chinensis	Aqueous extract of pseudobulbs is taken for scrofula, feverish stomach-ache, and toothache. Tincture is used for internal bleeding, hemorrhaege, asthmatic cough, tuberculosis, and dysentery.
Pholidota imbricate	Pseudobulbs finely macerated in mustard oil and applied on joints for rheumatic pains.
Pleione maculate	Pseudobulbs used in liver complaints and stomachache
Ponerorchis chusua	Tubers used for diarrhoea, dysentery and chronic fever
Rhynchostylis retusa	Roots (Rasna) for rheumatism. Plant used against Asthma, Tuberculosis, nervous twitchings, cramps, infantile epilepsy, vertigo, palpitation, kidney stone, and menstrual disorders.
Salyrium nepalense	Tubers eaten by Monpa tribe for Malaria, dysentery, also aphrodisiac
Spathoglottisplicata	Decoction of the boiled plant used for rheumatism and used in hot as a foment.
Tropidia curculioides	Decoction of plant given for cold stage of malaria, decoction of boiled roots given for diarrhoea
Vanda corulea	Leaf juice for diarrhoea, dysentery, external application for skin diseases
Zeuxine strateaumatica	The tubers are used as a tonic in combination with the roots of *Cymbidium aloifolium* in Uttara Kannada district

CHAPTER

5

ECOLOGY AND THE DISTRIBUTION OF LIMBLESS LIZARD, BARKUDIA INSULARIS, ANNANDALE (REPTILIA, SAURIA, SCINCIDAE)

M.V. SUBBA RAO AND B.N. RAO

ABSTRACT

Barkudia insularis, Annandale (Reptilia, Sauria, Scincidae) is a limbless lizard and was first reported in 1916 by Cravely from a remote island of the Indian lagoon, Chilka lake, Orissa. After four decades, the species was recorded from the red loamy soils of the Andhra University Campus, Visakhapatnam (17°42' N and 82°18' E). Seven decades have passed since the discovery of this species, but information on it is scanty and limited to mere description only.

The present study is aimed to provide baseline information on this species to understand its ecology, which would help in protecting this rare limbless lizards, *B. insularis* for conservation, status and the distribution.

B. insularis is an elongate limbless lizard which leads a secretive subterranean in the gardens and densely vegetated areas on the Andhra University Campus. The ecology, habit, habitat, conservation and the distribution of *B. insularis* were studied.

INTRODUCTION

Studies on rare Scincid limbless lizard, *Barkudia insularis,* Annandale was made during 1989-99 at the Andhra University Campus, Visakhapatnam (17°42' N and 82°18' E), a coastal city of the State of Andhra Pradesh, India.(Fig. 5.1).

The limbless lizard, *Barkudia insularis*, is the only species was first described by Annandale (1917) and hitherto this species was reported to from only two places in India - Barkudia Island, Chilka Lake, Orissa and Andhra University Campus, Visakhapatnam by Rajyalakshmi (1954), Ganapathi and Rajyalakshmi (1955), Subba Rao (1982), Subba Rao and Nageswara Rao (1996).

MORPHOLOGY

Description of the Body

The Indian limbless scincid, *Barkudia insularis* has a snake like body with a smooth scaly skin (Fig. 5.1a and b). The round, slender body has its girth as wide as the little finger while the length of the lizard reaches a maximum of 25 cm, which can conveniently be divided into three regions : (*i*) Head, (*ii*) Trunk or Body and (*iii*) Tail.

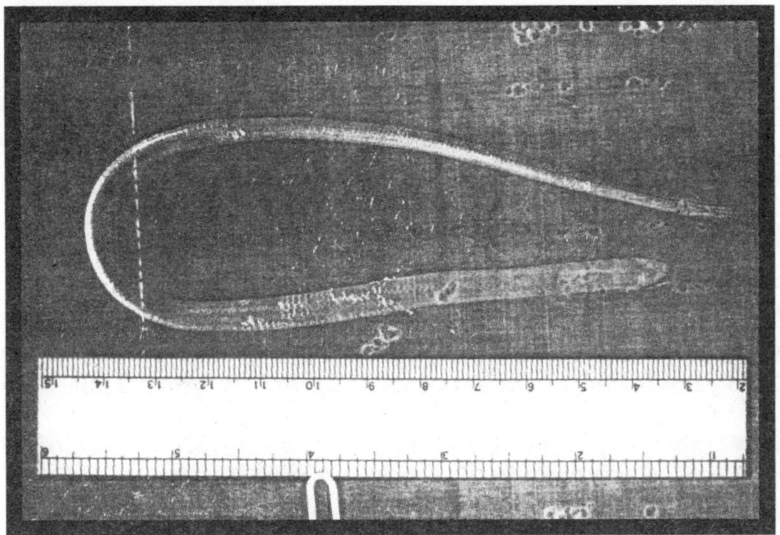

Fig. 5.1 (a). Limbless lizard, Barkudia insularis (Dorsal view)

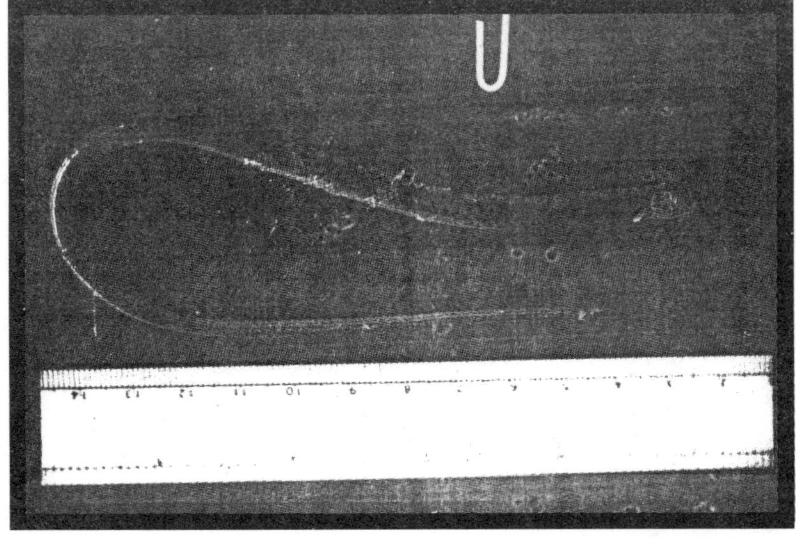

Fig. 5.1 (b). Limbless lizard, Barkudia insularis (Ventral view)

The head has an obtusely pointed snout; and was flattened dorsoventrally. The head was slightly broader than the trunk and the rest of the body. Small eyes and minute ear openings were present on the dorso-lateral side. Ear opening was at the posterior end of the head behind the parietal shields while eyes were well enterior to the ear opening. Nostril was in between the rostral and nasal shields (Fig. 5.1).

The trunk or body was separated from the head region by not so distinct neck. The region did not show any vestiges or traces of the limbs or any other organs. The region showed distinct variation from bright dorsal side to pale ventral side. This region was extended from the head to the anterior of the cloacal opening while the tail region started from the cloacal opening to the posterior tip of the body (Fig. 5.1).

The tail was cylindrical, rounded at the tip and was shorter than the trunk region. The tail was highly fragile and the lizard was capable of regenerating the broken tail. Few individuals have dark pigmented tail caps (Fig. 5.1).

Size and Weight

The total length of the limbless lizard had a range from 100 to 270 mm with a body girth of 6-14 mm. Usually, a 2/3rd of the length constituted the snout-vent region which had a range from 76 to 182 mm, while the lengths of the tail in the specimens whose tails were unbroken or fully regrown had a range between 24 and 99 mm (Table 5.1).

Table 5.1. Morphometry of the Limbless Scincid Lizard, *Barkudia insularis* in the Andhra University Campus, Visakhapatnam

Sl.No.	Character		Minimum	Maximum
1.	Total length	(mm)	103	269
2.	Snout-venti length	(mm)	76	182
3.	Head length	(mm)	5	12
4.	Tail length	(mm)	24	99
5.	Head width	(mm)	5	11
6.	Girth	(mm)	6	14
7.	Weight	(gm)	1.008	10.273

Habitat

The limbless scincid, *Barkudia insularis* inhabited in very selected areas of the Andhra University Campus. The lizard occurred in two vegetation types and at varying depths. The characteristics that were found to be common in all these areas have been delineated below :

(*i*) Red, sandy loamy soils (Table 5.2)

(*ii*) Ground was covered with dry litter and mostly, moist under the shade of old trees

(*iii*) The soil was loosely packed and undisturbed for considerably longer periods.

Table 5.2. Data of Soil Analysis at Andhra University Campus,Visakhapatnam

		Physical
Colour	:	Reddish brown
Texture	:	Sandy loamy
Particle Size	:	0.007-0.018 cm
pH range	:	6.9-7.1
Organic Carbon	:	0.51%
Conductance	:	0.9839 Mbos /cm
		Chemical (g/m^2)
Nitrogen	:	29.8
Phosphorus	:	14.3
Calcium	:	294.8
Magnesium	:	138.9

An analysis of the occurrence/collection of the lizards in different sites, types of soils and vegetation types are as follows:

Occurrence in Vegetation Types

At the outset, the occurrence of the limbless lizards was slightly higher in the patches of natural vegetation. However, the lizards were never recorded in the areas where managed vegetationwere not connected with the natural patches. About 52.74 per cent of the occurrences were recorded in the areas with natural vegetation while the remaining account for the occurrence in the managed vegetation.

Within the each vegetation type, the occurrences associated with tree type; shrubby type and herbacious type plant species were analysed aiong with those on bare ground. The results indicated that the lizard's presence in the areas with tree type and shrubby type of plant species was relatively higher than the other combinations. Both these types account for 70.89 per cent of the total occurrences in both the vegetation types.

Occurrences in Soil Types

The occurrence of the limbless lizard with species reference to three moist gradients with varying levels of organic contents (Table 5.3).

Table 5.3. Occurrence of Limbless Lizard, *Barkudia insularis* in Soils of Varying Organic and Moist Content

Organic Content	Moist type			
	Moist	Sub-moist	Dry	Total
Rich	10.96	34.02	0.00	44.98
Normal/Moderate	10.04	23.06	7.99	41.09
Less/Moderate	07.08	05.94	0.91	13.93
Total	28.08	63.02	8.90	100.00

Of the tree moist gradients Moist (M_1), Sub-moist (M_2) and Dry soils (M_3), 63.02 per cent of the occurrences were recorded in the sub-moist soils followed by moist soils (28.08%) and dry soils (8.90%). On the other hand, the lizards occurrence in the soils with rich organic content was 44.98 per cent of the total occurrences while in the soils of moderate and little quantities of organic contents, the occurrences recorded were 41.09 per cent and 13.93 per cent respectively.

The matrix of the moisture and organic contents of the soil versus occurrence indicated that the lizard's occurrence in the moist soils (M_1 and M_2) with moderate to good level of organic contents was very high.

Occurrence of Limbless lizards at Various Depths

The limbless lizards, B. insularia showed that the varying age-size groups occurred at different depths, (Table 5.4). These depth ranges were distinct in their constitution and were classified as below :

Table 5.4. Occurrence of Different Snoul-Vent groups of Barkudia Insularis in the Three Soil Layers

SV Group (mm)	Occurrence at soil layers					
	Top (No.)	Layer (%)	Middle (No.)	Layer (%)	Bottom (No.)	Layer (%)
Below 100	18	37.50	30	62.50	00	00.00
101-125	27	32.53	49	59.04	07	08.43
126-150	08	07.92	65	64.36	28	27.72
151 and above	23	11.17	109	52.91	74	35.92
All groups	76	17.35	253	57.76	109	24.89

(*i*) ***Top layer*** **:** This layer consisted the litter cover on the ground surface along with the surface layer of 3-5 cm of the soil, usually dry.

(*ii*) ***Middle layer*** **:** The layer beneath the top layer up to a depth of 20 cm constitute the middle layer, usually from sub-moist to moist.

(*iii*) ***Bottom layer*** **:** The layer below a depth of 20 cm and up to the level where the compactness of soil remains little changed (usually up to 40 cm depth) was the bottom layer of the habitat of the limbless lizard, usually moist.

On the whole, all the age-size groups of the limbless lizards have preferred the middle layer as their first choice. However, the lizards of below 125 mm SV group has their second preference to the top layer while the larger ones choose the bottom layer as their second preference (Table 5.4).

FOOD AND FEEDING BEHAVIOUR

The limbless lizard, *Barkudia insularis* was an insectivorous lizard and fed on small insects in the soil and litter. The stomach contents of these lizards revealed that the lizards staple diet is termites and ground dwelling beetles.

Termites have been found in 64.56 per cent of the stomachs examined in one year, while the ground dwelling beetles were found in 43.04 per cent of the stomachs examined. Apart from these several unidentified animal remains and soii particles were also present. About nine per cent of the stomachs examined were empty or without any solid contents (Table 5.5).

By volume, termites ranked high in importance with 42.2 per cent v/v followed by the unidentified group with 37.6 per cent v/v; ground dwelling beetles with 16.8 per cent v/v and soil particles were the least with 3.4 per cent v/v. The stomach contents of an average adult lizard had a volume range from 0.02 ml to 0.3 ml.

Table 5.5. Analysis of Stomach Contents by Volumetric Estimation of *Barkudia insularis*

Season	Isoptera	Coleoptera
Winter (n=21)		
Percentage volume	52.38	23.81
Frequency of occurrence	11.00	5.00
Summer (n=24)		
Percentage volume	45.83	38.10
Frequency of occurrence	11.00	08.00
Monsoons (n=34)		
Percentage volume	85.29	61.76
Frequency of occurrence	29.00	21.00
Annual (n=79)		
Percentage volume	64.56	43.04
Frequency of occurrence	51.00	34.00
Mean	69.69	50.61
±SD	18.02	14.80

BREEDING ECOLOGY

Brakudia insularis showed little sexual dimorphiam and is often very difficult to sex without dissection. However, by probing the cloaca, some of the large adult males could be identified with the presence of hemipenis.

Size at Maturity

The mean size at maturity was 130 mm SV (snout-vent), the greatest number of adults falling into the 140-160 mm SV group for both the sexes. Smallest female containing eggs was 138 mm SV length.

Breeding Seasons

The limbless lizard showed no variation in its appearance even during the breeding seasons. However, gonadal examination was made in order to understand the breeding season or reproductive cycles.

Lizards of snout-vent length exhibited marked seasonal variation in the length of testis. Individuals of the same age-size class have testis atleast one mm longer in the summer than in winter (4.2 to 5.8 mm for summer and 3.3 to 4.7 mm for winter). Testis reached maximum size (5.8 mm) in June and were smaller by April in the individuals of same age-size class. The first oviduct eggs appeared in June and July had eggs in the oviduct. The number of oviduct eggs appeared more in greater SV groups. Juveniles of below 90 mm SV appeared only during August and September months.

CONSERVATION AND MANAGEMENT

In view of the above important characters and endangeredness of its status, it is proposed to implement the following management techniques for the conservation of this species with immediate effect :

(*i*) Further constructional activities or other activities that alter the habitat or act as barriers for the disposal of *Barkudia insularia* are to be banned with immediate effect;

(*ii*) *Barkudia insularia* is to be declared as a threatened species and should be protected under Indian Wildlife (Protection) Act, 1972, until its distributional range and the status is established authentically;

(*iii*) Constant monitoring of the habitats by trained researchers will help in protecting and developing the habitat;

(*iv*) Exchange of breeding adults from the separated patches of habitats are to be undertaken manually to avoid the problems of inbreeding due to broken populations. However, the survival of such new releases are to be monitored carefully;

(*v*) Intensive surveys in all similar habitats along the Indian East coast are to be carried-out to investigate the distributional range of the species;

(*vi*) Simultaneously, detailed studies have to be made on the species to understand its biology and ecology, without causing any harm to the existing known population.

ACKNOWLEDGEMENTS

Sincere thanks are due to Prof. Carl Gans of Michigan University and Dr. H.R. Bustard of Man of Isle for their encouragement in exploring the truths about this rare and threatened species. We thank the authorities of Andhra University for providing us an excellent facilities and the University Grants Commission, New Delhi for financial support (Prof. MVS Rao).

REFERENCES

Annandale, N., 1917. A new genus of limbless skinks from an island in the Chilka lake. *Rec. Ind. Mus.*, 18: 17-21.

Ganapati, P.N. and Rajyalakshmi, K., 1955. Bionomics and some anatomical popularities of the limbless lizard, *Barukudia insularis.* Annandale. *Indian Museum.,* 53: 279-292.

Rajyalakshmi, K., 1954. Studies on the anatomy of *Barkudia insularis*, Annandale, M.Sc. Dissertation, Andhra University, Waltair, Visakhapatnam.

Subba Rao, M.V., 1984. Biology of the limbless lizard, *Barkudia insularis.* Annandale. UGC Res. Project, Final Technical Report, Andhra University, Waltair, Visakhapatnam.

Subba Rao, M.V. and Nageswara Rao, B., 1991. Niotes on the biology of the limbless skink, *Barkudia insularis. Proc. NESA Symp..* Waltair, Visakhapatnam, 1996.

CHAPTER

6

CAPTIVE PROPAGATION OF AN ENDANGERED SEA TURTLES, *LEPIDOCHELYS-OLIVACEA* (ESCHSCHOLTZ)

M.V. SUBBA RAO AND P.S. RAJA SEKHAR

Of living reptiles, chelenians are the eldest reptiles, which have existed forever a hundred million years. The world's seven species of sea turtles have been placed in the IUCN Red Data Book of the threatened or endangered species. Five of the world's seven species of sea turtles found in the Indian ocean were placed under Schedule I of the Indian Wildlife (Protection) Act, 1972 for legal protection. These species are (Subba Rao, 1997):

1. *Dermochelys coriacea* (leatherback)
2. *Caretta caretta* (logger heads)
3. *Eretmochelys imbricata* (Hawks bill)
4. *Chelonia mydas* (green sea turtle)
5. *Lepidechelys oliavacea* (Olive ridley).

Of these, the most common and abundant one is the Olive (pacific) ridley. In India, on the East Coast, ridleys have their major rookery largest mass nesting called *"Arribadea"*.

In the winter months (November-February), large numbers of ridleys migrate from Indian ocean to Gahirmatha for nesting. Some of the nesting turtles are observed to be sporadically lying their eggs on the beaches of the Northern Andhra Pradesh (Latitudes: 16° 50-' 18° 35' and Longitudes: 82° 10' -84° 10'). In recent times; human interference with the breeding olive ridleys while they are in courtship or in nesting, and disturbances to the nests, eggs and hatchings by domestic and natural predators are mainly responsible for the decimation of new recruitment into the dwindling population.

These days, the nesting turtles, nesting beaches and rookeries are given good protection, but still the turtle population seems to be very low as has been evident from recent studies.

In natural conditions, the hatching success is from three per cent to 40 per cent. However, under will protected conditions or where human and predatory disturbances are less, the hatching percentage may increase. Hendrickson (1958) has estimated that only 1.7% of the hatchings survive the first week after their emergence into the sea and altogether only 0.1% of the eggs laid will survive at the end of one year. The reason can be assumed to be that the young ones below one-year old are easily preyed upon as their shell is soft and completely defenceless.

To avoid greater damage to the migratory nesting turtles, to the nest, eggs and the hatchings, protection of the nesting beaches, captive propagation of the Olive ridleys has been undertaken over a period of 4 years (1983-1987) along the Northern Andhra coast, India.

STUDY AREA AND THE SOCIAL STATUS OF THE FISHERMEN

The coastline between Kalingapatnam in the North and Hope Island in the south is 286 km of shoreline and quite near the Gahirmatha Island where the mass nesting (Arribada) is held. This area has diverse shore conditions ranging from rocky to shallow sandy shores with several extensions of hill ranges projecting into the sea. Seven rivers with their major tributaries from the estuary in this area and a number of creeks, backwaters and streams also merge into the sea.

A total of 53 villages, most of which belong to fishermen tribes are present along the shoreline and the population was around 63,000. Most of their activity is fishing with nearly 4000 small dugouts (Catamarans) operating along the shoreline. The other activities are backwater fishing, salt harvesting, cattle rearing, piggery, etc. Only a few fishermen are involved in the sea turtle hunting and the percentage of literacy varied from 3.3 to 6.8 per cent.

CAPTIVE PROPAGATION OF THE OLIVE RIDLEYS

This programme involves three main phases: (*i*) Collection of eggs and transportation to the hatcheries; (*ii*) Maintenance of the hatcheries; (*iii*) Captive rearing of the newly born hatchlings have grown sufficiently big and tough enough to protect themselves atleast from small predaters.

A knowledge of the breeding ecology is essential before initiating the captive propagation programmes.

BREEDING SEASONS

The breeding season of the Olive ridleys begins with courthsip around mid-November and ceases with the emergence of hatchlings into the sea around the end of May. The time intervals between mating, nesting and hatching have been one and two months respectively.

Courtship takes place in the water over long periods, often more than two hours. Both the participants float with little movement, the male atop the female. Nesting takes place on the sandy beaches during night, mostly on the moon-lit nights. A majority of the nests are located at a distance of 16-45 metres from the hightide water mark.

NESTING HABITAT

The nesting beaches of the Olive ridleys were fine sandy areas with a gradual slope and often edged with small patches of ground vegetation at the high beach platform. The nesting areas are mainly dominated by a grass species, *Spinifex littoreus*; a creeper, *Ipomoea pescaprae*; a mangrove plant, *Pandanus fasicularis*; while shore fauna consists of mainly crabs, like ghost crabs, *Ocypoda* sp., *Uca* sp., some species of insects like mites, ants and insect larvae (maggots), birds like cranes, *Grus communis*; sea gulls, *Larus brunnicephalus*; cattle egrets, *Bubulicus ibis coromandus*; pond herons, *Ardeola grayii grayii*; and domestic crows, *Corvus splendens*, were most dominant.

Mammals like jackals, *Canis aureus;* foxes, *Vulpes bengalensis;* and hyenas, *Hyaena striata*; were most common in the areas edged with dense vegetation, while domestic dogs and pigs were common in the areas where human habitation is more.

NESTING

The complete process of nesting, between the time of the arrival of nesting turtles and the time of their return after nesting lasts for 2-4 hours. The arrival and departure forms crawl tracks on the sandy beaches. Three types of crawl tracks of Olive ridleys are observed: crescent shaped, conical shaped and false nesting crawls. The last showed more than one false nest sites, which often mislead the pedators and beach combers. The clutch size ranges from 80-145 eggs arranged in 3-6 rows or layers.

Systematic turtle walks along the nesting beaches have been conducted during night times at regular intervals for eggs. Soon after the nests are identified, the nests are opened carefully and the eggs collected and transported to the hatcheries.

Collection and Transportation of Eggs

Soon after the nests are identified, they are excavated by hand until the top layer of the eggs is exposed. Well ventilated wooden boxes are used to carry the eggs and the nest sand was used to cover the inter-spaces between the eggs and egg layers. Each row of eggs in the nest was numbered when they were exposed while opening the nest. The marked eggs are placed in the container in the same position and axial orientation as they had been in the nest. The eggs are transported by road to the central hatchery as early as possible.

Incubation of Eggs

Incubation of eggs under complete captive conditions is of two kinds :

(*a*) Nest hatching and

(*b*) Incubator hatching.

(a) Nest hatching

These hatchries are located on the beaches in suitable locations that are far from human habitation and are least susceptible to erosion, flooding, tidal effects etc., as they are the ideal sites for a nest hatchery. In such places, a piece of sandy beach above the hightide mark is to be selected and should be protected with a fence of 1-2 metres in height depending upon the number of nests to be hatched in the hatchery. This should be calculated on the basis of 1.25 sg/m/nest *i.e.*, per a hatchery of 100 nests capacity an area of 12 sq. m of sandy beach is required.

A total of 23 nests were protected individually. The clutch size of the nests had a range of 80-145 eggs with an average size of 118 eggs per clutch. Of these 10.54% of the eggs were infertile or met with early embryonic death and spoiled before the first week of their incubation. Another 34.36% of the eggs have spoiled before 45 days, while 10.21% of the eggs did not hatch but contained discernible embryes.

Nearly 45% of the eggs hatched, but of these, 23.72% of the hatchings were dead in the nest before they could merge. These hatchings were found infested with ants. On the whole, the hatching success was 34.24% of the total eggs. Hatching period was between 51 and 62 days while most of the nests hatched by the 57th day.

(b) Incubator hatching

Soon after the eggs were brought to the Central hatchery (Visakhapatnam) the eggs were placed in sterile petri dishes in-between moistened cotton layers. The cotton layers were moistened with distilled water, petri dishes arranged with eggs were placed in BOD incubators in which the required temperatures were maintained (29.5°C, 30.5°C and 31°C). As the sex of sea turtles is dependent on the incubation temperature, it is essential that every care is taken before fixing the temperature of the incubators.

A total of seven clutches (891 eggs) were incubated under artificial conditions of which 127 were infertile and the rest of the fertile eggs were kept for artificial incubation. Out of 764 fertile eggs kept for hatching, 11.26% (86) were dead in pipped eggs. This occurred between 20 and 45 days of incubation, while 52 eggs (6.80%) were unhatched but contained discernible embryos, these were seen after the sixth week of incubation. Most of the unhatched eggs with discernible embryos were observed during the seventh and eighth week of incubation.

On the whole, 626 eggs, out of 764 fertile eggs of seven clutches have been successfully hatched under complete captive conditions. The hatching time varied between 56 and 60 days, the overall hatching success was 81.94 per cent).

HATCHINGS

Immediately after hatching from the eggs, the hatchings are black in colour and weigh between 15 and 18 g and had a size range of 36-41 mm in carapace length and 30-40 mm of carapace width. The hatching have a single claw on all the flippers. Hatchings, soon after their emergence from the nest, enter the sea and live on their own.

Captive Rearing

Freshly hatched young ones in the captive rearing programme, should be released into small tubs or hatchling pools. Before the hatchlings are released into the tubs/pools, a knowledge of the water maintenance is a prerequiste. Since sea turtles are aquatic in their habits, water is an essential component of the captive rearing programme. It is not an easy task to construct pools for hatchlings on the beaches 100 or 200 metres away from the hightide water line is an ideal place for constructing the hatchling pools. Further, a location close to a backwater channel will be very helpful for long run.

The space for each hatchling depends on the number of hatchlings kept together. However, it is ideal if a hatchling is provided about one cubic ft of water, young ones of more than one-month old are very aggressive and repeatedly bite each other's soft parts, if crowded. It is desirable to have separate tanks for hatchings of one nest with a minimum size of 3 × 2, 5 × 5 metres (1 × w × d). All the tanks together should have facilities for :

(a) Good sea water supply.

(b) Protected with wire enclosure to avoid predators.

(c) Shade a part of the tank from the Sun.

(d) Smooth and curved corners on the tank walls.

Thus, for a 100-nest hatchery, the rearing centre requires 100 small tanks for which a minimum area of 1000 sq. m is required. On small scale, the turtle hatchlings can be reared in small plastic tubs (basing on the size of the tubs) individually, or in pairs or in groups.

Sea turtle hatchlings are very sensitive to salinity and temperature. It is good if the hatchlings are reared in clean flowing sea water. Flushing and refilling the tanks once or twice a day is an acceptable alternative. Where estuarine water is used for captive rearing, the salinity should be monitored and it is not desirable to keep the hatchlings in water with a salinity of less than 20 parts per thousand.

Floating vegetation and some smooth submerged rocks are to be provided in the tanks so that the hatchings can have different hideouts and resting places in the tanks.

FOOD AND FEEDING

The food and feeding habits of the hatchlings in wild conditions is still a mystery and the feeding grounds also are not known definitely. Thus, providing a balanced diet to the turtle hatchings in captive rearing has been a difficult task.

On rearing sea turtles, the kind of animal food provided is less improtant than the continuity of the supply. The diet might be successfully pieced out by combing fish, molluscans and crustaceans of various kinds or by some variety of sorted garbage.

The new born hatchlings of Olive ridleys did not feed on any of the food items provided, until they are 5-6 days old and later attempted feeding on marine alage. *Gracillaria* sp. However, a few hatchlings which appeared to be weak and inactive were forced fed with vitamin drops and glucose water.

On the whole, the following food types are provided to the hatchling during the captive rearing :

(*a*) Marine algae

(*b*) Polychaetes

(*c*) Crustaceans

(*d*) Molluscans

(*e*) Marine fish.

During the first two months, the hatchlings were fed mainly on the marine algae and molluscans. They rarely relished over varieties of artificial food though boiled eggs and finely chopped meat are eaten on rare occasions. From the fifth month, the feeding on marine algae gradually decreases while feeding on molluscans ranks high throughout the rearing period.

The food consumed by an individual hatchling increase with increasing age and the consumption of 0.75 g of food by a 19.5 g hatchling on the seventh day increased to 103 g at the end of one year by which time the hatchlings weighed 712.5 g. The increase in age and weight of the hatchling with the increase of the food consumption of hatchlings was observed.

The efficiency of captive rearing reflects in the general health and growth of the hatchlings. Growth is measured in two ways, length of the carapace and weight of the hatchling. It is more reasonable to consider the both. However, it is necessary that every rearing centre record the growth of selected individual hatchlings and develop their own references for growth with special reference to food types and area of the pools by the number of hatchlings.

Wide deviations from the set growth rate and the mortality occurrence warn the rearers of the errors in the captive rearing. A few common health problems are delineated below along with their identification and remedies:

(*i*) Injuries and infections
(*ii*) Digestive problems and
(*iii*) Excretory problems.

Injuries and Infections

In group rearing, Olive ridley hatchlings became aggressive if they are ever crowded and food and hiding places are short of the requirements. Under such circumstances they violately bite each other and cause lesions on the soft parts such as snout, flippers, nest, etc. Sometimes these lesions may cripple the hatchling, causing it to die of starvation.

Bacterial and fungal infections occur commonly if the hygiene and sanitation conditions are not maintained properly. Such infections spread rapidly from the individual to another in the pool. Infections can be seen with naked eye as patches of yellow or white colour. As the infections are spreading malady, all the infected individuals are to be separated. Infected individuals can be given a bath in 5 ppm potassium permanganate ($KMNO_4$) and should be kept in shade, dry and cool conditions for 3-4 hours. The process is to be repeated every day until the patches have disappeared and the hatchlings are active.

Digestive Problems

Some individuals show very little activity and float in the corners of the tank for longer periods showing little interest even for food. Such individuals may be suffering from digestive problems which include indigestion, malnutrition or gas formation. When fed forcibly they eject the food spontaneously. They exhibit a rapid decrease in their body weight. Such individuals should be given digene syrup and multi-vitamin syrup with glucose + sea water, normally they recover in a couple of days.

Excretary problems

Some hatchlings exhibit loss of balance and strive hard to dive into the water. Mostly their abdominal regions get bulged and these symptems indicate excretary problems. Such individuals are to be kept out of water under dry, cool and shade conditions and examined for excretions. If the bulging does not reduce, the abdominal region should be gently massaged and checked for excretions. These hatchlings can be fed as prescribed for the hatchlings suffering from digestive problems.

Finally, the captive propagation programmes along the Northern coast of Andhra Pradesh are viable and helps in conserving the Olive ridley turtles. However, it is imperative that the captive propagation programmes supported with other aspects like protection of nesting habitats, nests, nesting turtles and live turtles so as to reduce the mortality at the producing centres and implement a better Management Programme. The following points are considered to be very important in the management of the Olive ridley turtles of the Northern coast of Andhra Pradesh (Subba Rao, 1997).

(*i*) *Subsistence hunting* can be avoided through intensive extension programmes in all the 53 villages of the study, area and to bring out an awareness of the status and improtance of sea turtles.

(*ii*) *Starting of beach hatcheries* in all the zones with technically trained personnel supported with several poor fishermen tribes who after training could feed the hatcheries with eggs, provide information on nesting turtles, and protect the nesting habitats as guards. This type of involvement reduces the factor of human interference and on the other hand provides employment to several poor fishermen.

(*iii*) *A central sea turtle farm* has to be organized which will be fed with the new born hatchlings from various beach hatcheries of different zones to rear the hatchlings until they are one-year old and cross the most crucial stage of their life.

(*iv*) Starting of a *Sea turtle Farming and Management Training Institute* which may also serve as a research centre to develop sea turtle farming as one of the cottage industries in the fishermen villages so as to utilize the turtle resources in a rational way.

(*v*) Strict implementation of the Indian Wildlife (Protection) Act, 1972 and impose severe punishment on the commercial exploiters of the sea turtles. Declare *Hope Island* near Kakinada as *Sea turtle Sanctuary* and ban all fishing and other maritime activities that are harmful to the sea turtles.

ACKNOWLEDGEMENTS

The authors are gratefully akcnowledge the University Grants Commission, New Delhi for financial assistance and the Andhra Pradesh State Forest Department for given permission to collect the eggs. Finally our grateful thanks to Shri. D.S. Gangakhedkar, D.F.O. (Wildlife) A.P. Forest Department for his unrelenting co-operation.

An adult female sea turtle, *Lepidochelys olivacea* at Visakhapatnam Coast

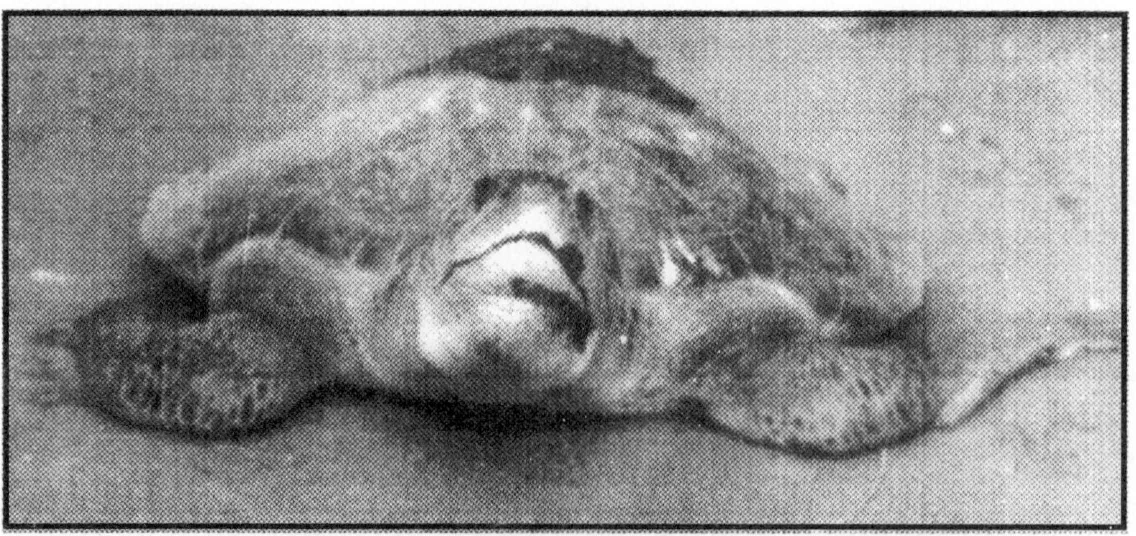

An adult Olive ridley rurtle caught in gear and was half dead before it was brought to shore

An Olive ridley digging the nest hole with the hind flippers

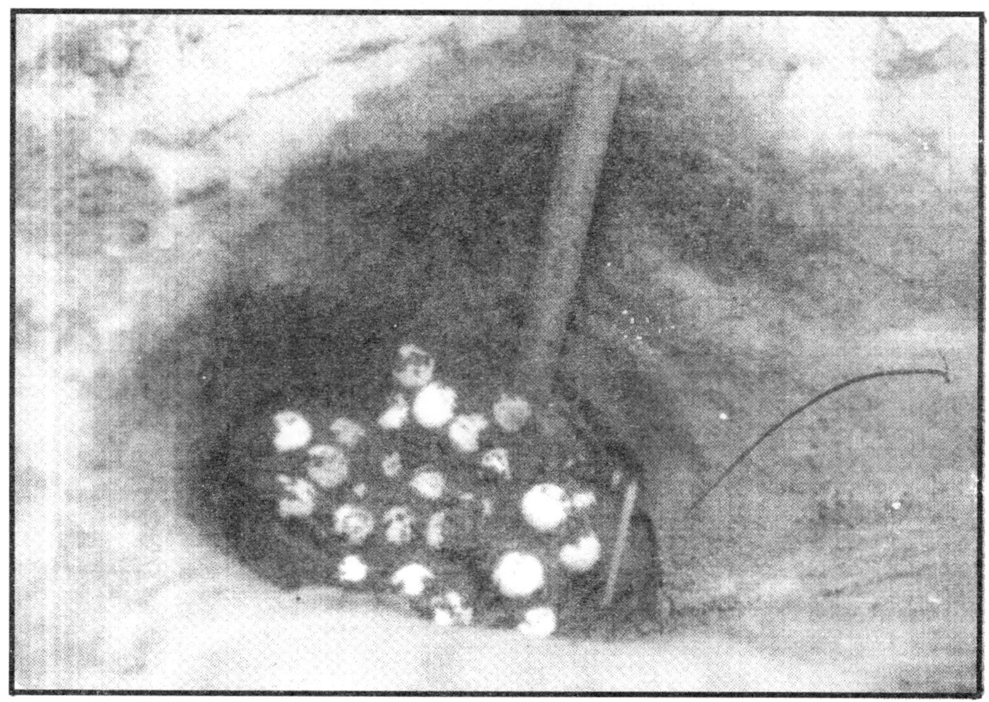

An Olive ridley nest.

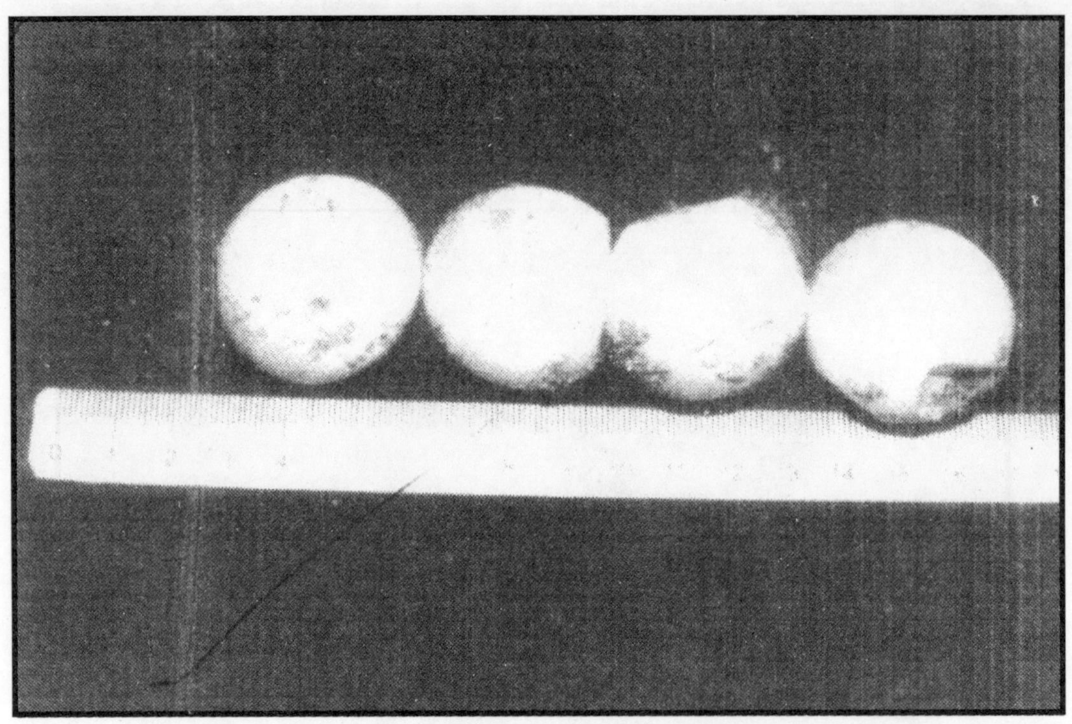

One day old Olive ridley turtle eggs (Different sizes in a same clutch)

FURTHER READING

Subba Rao, M.V. 1997, Ecology and Management of Indian Sea Turtles. EnRA Publication, 1997, 1-60 pp.

CHAPTER

7

CROCODILES - ECONOMICALLY VALUABLE NATURAL RESOURCES

M.V. SUBBA RAO

ABSTRACT

Out of 22 species of Crocodiles are present in the World, only three species are present in India. They are gharial, *Gairalis gaugeticus*; Salt water or estuarine crocodile, *Crocodylus_perosus* and the mugger or marsa crocodile, *C. palustris*. The population of crocodiles is about 100 in 1974 and increased to 10,000 in 1994 after farming. There are two types of farming - Battery or Artificial farming and Free sauge management or Natural farming.

They are cold blooded amplitions and carrivorons animals. They are best scavangers. They are economically natural resources. The eggs are milky white oval, blunt, at both *White* ends and double milled. Depending upon the size of the crocodile, they lay 8 to 97 eggs per clutch per year. They hatch themselves before Monsoon (i.e. July) after hatching, the young oves are kept in year pools for two years. On third year, they will be distributed in gazetted sancturies in India.

INTRODUCTION

Crocodiles are known to us since the down of civilization and are described in several ancient Hindu mythologies. It was described that the river Goddess, Ganga used crocodile as her *vahana* (the vehicle). The strength of a crocodile when it is in water was clearly described in "*Gajendra Moksham*", wherein a white elephant "Airavatha" was caught by a crocodile and was ultimately saved by Lord Vishnu.

The skin of the crocodiles is expensive (Subba Rao, 1993). At present, in European markets, one centimetre around the belly of crocodile costs Rs. 100 and hence pouching of crocodiles exherbantly.

The crocodiles are economically valuable natural resources and they are significantly important to maintain the balanced ecosystem (Subba Rao, 1982a).

The population of crocodiles has dwindled because of their exploitation at alarming rates (Subba Rao and Bustard, 1982a). Their commercially valuable skin, meat, eggs and oil made them vulnerable (Subba Rao, 1993). Fear of spoiling the nets and vast consumption of fish, have made them enemies of fishermen. But with their protection under Indian Wildlife (Protection) Act, 1972 and special projects launched for their conservation and management enabled to protect crocodiles (Bustard, 1974). Establishment sanctuaries and special captive breeding centres at a various places, now their populations have been restored in some places (Subba Rao and Bustard, 1982a). The effects of reintroducing crocodiles into the wild are being strongly protected by the public. Educating the public on the environmental awareness and ecological significance of crocodiles to remove the misconceptions is of much importance.

DISTRIBUTION

In all, 22 species of crocodiles are present in the world (Webb *et al.* 1988) of which only three species are represent in India. They are the gharial, *Gavialis gangeticus* . the fresh water long snorted riverine crocodile; *Crocodiles porosus*, the salt water or estuarine crocodile; *Crocodilus palustris*, the mugger or marsh crocodile.

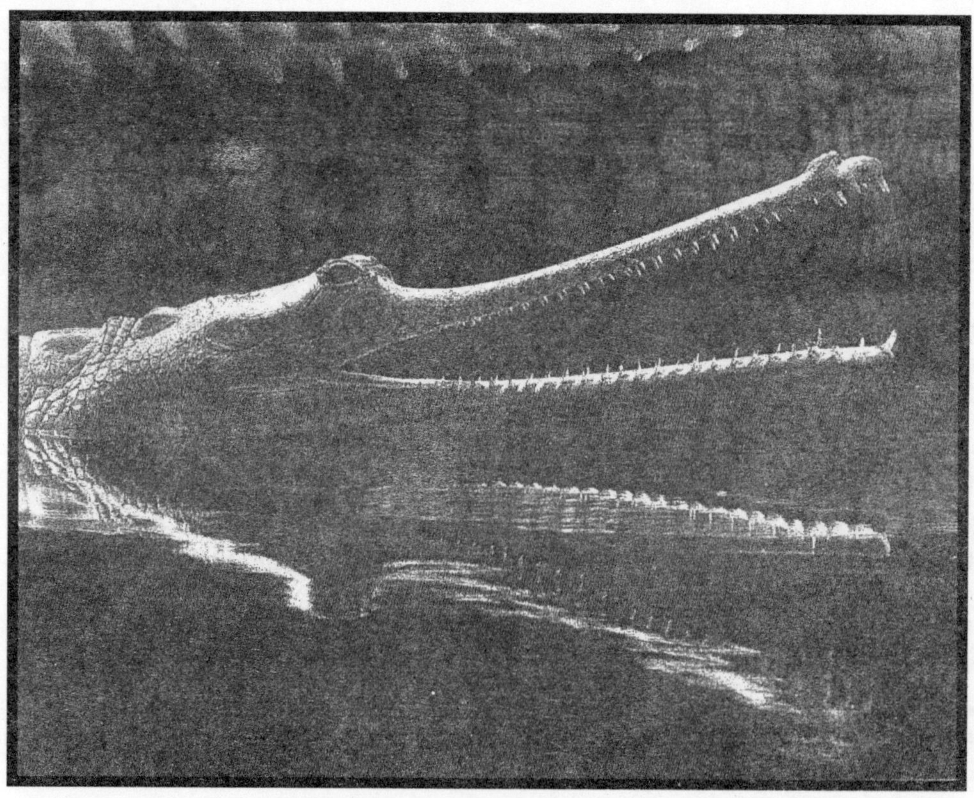

A Gharial enjoying in the pool in its enclosure at the Indira Gandhi Zoological Park, Visakhapatnam

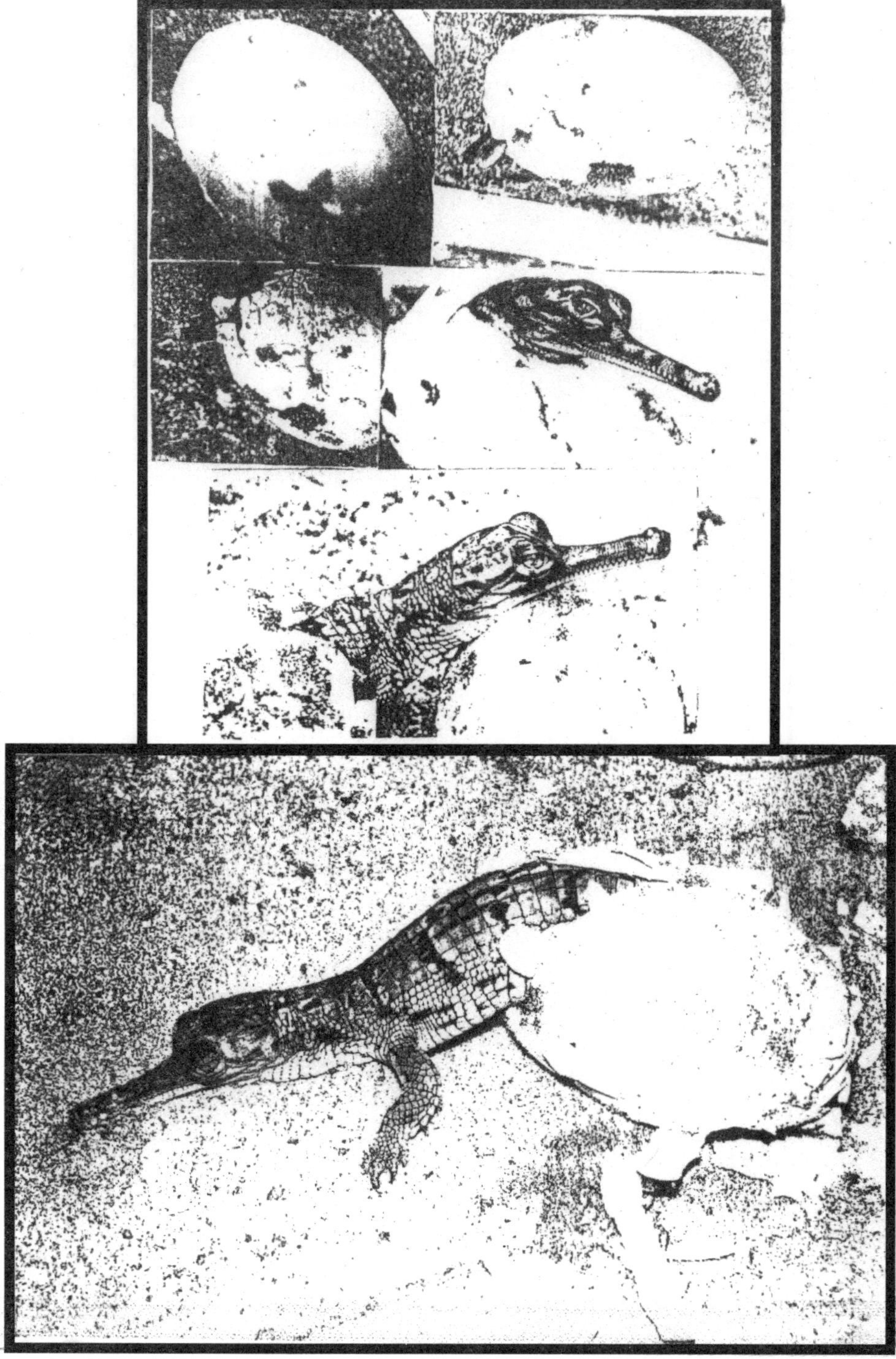

Hatching sequence of an endangered gharial, Gavialis gangeticus in captivity at Tikerapara, Orissa

1. Gharial, *Gavialis gangeticus* (Fig. 7.1) : These are disturbuted in north Indian rivers especially in Ganges, Brahmaputra, Mahanandi, Kosi, Narayani and their tributaries.They also found in neighbouring countries like Nepal, Pakistan, Myanmar, Bangladesh and Bhutan but their number is meagre.

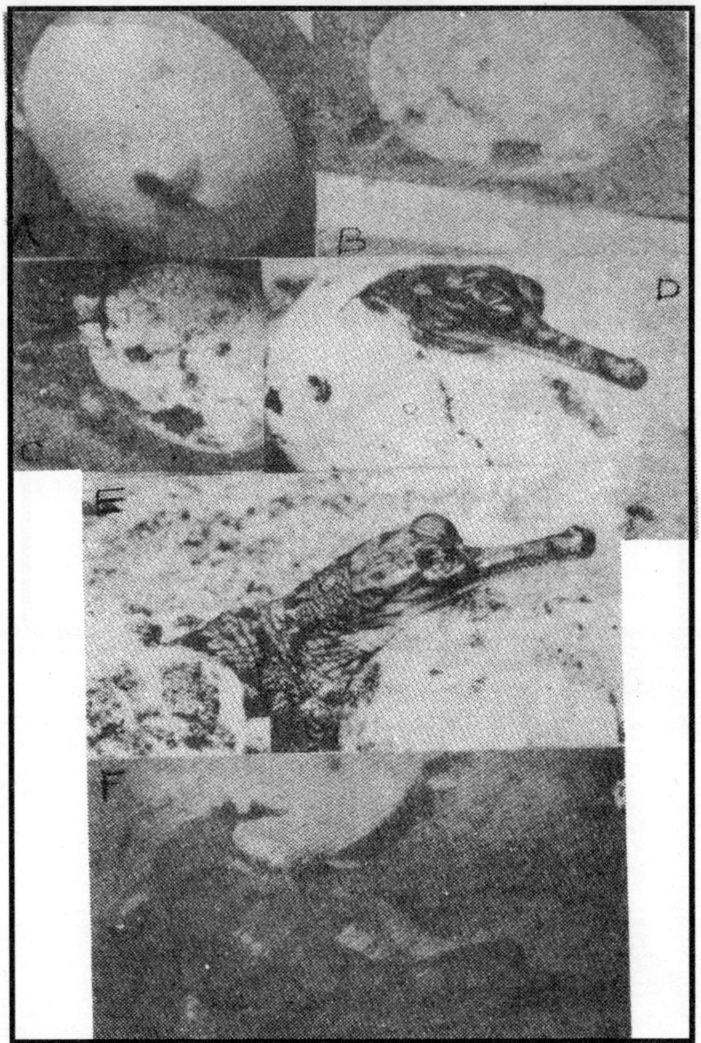

Fig. 7.1. Sequence of hatching of gharial, *Gavialis gangeticus*.

(A) Slit appearance on the egg surface

(B) Snout protruded out

(C) Emergence of the snout and eyes

(D) Emergence of head and neck region

(E) Hatching emerged with body and fore limbs

(F) Young one emerged with umbilicus (first day old gharial)

2. Salt water or esturine crocodile, *Crocodilus porosus*: They are traced in Bhitterkanika of Orissa State, Sunderbans of West Bengal and Andaman and Nicobar Islands where mangroves are present. Outside India, they are present in Sri Lanka, Indonesia, North Australia (Darwin) and Fiji Islands.

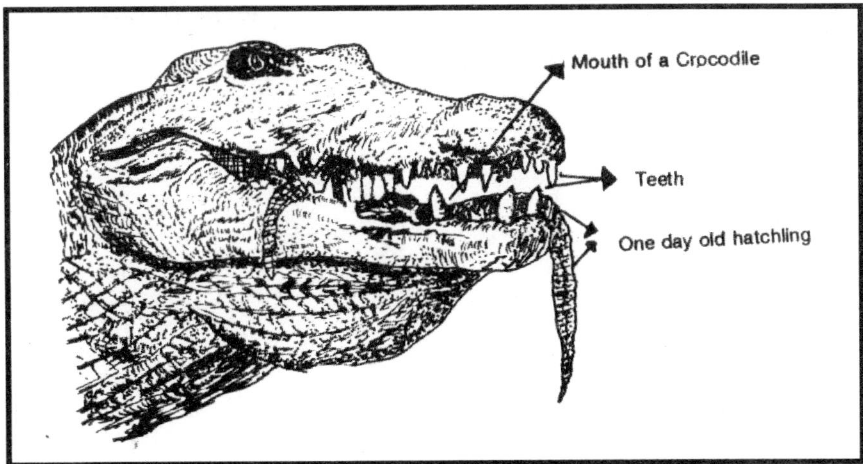

Fig. 7.2. Parental care by a saltwater crocodile : Hatclings carried upto the water by mouth, in between teeth without harm.

3. Mugger or Marsh Crocodile, *Crocodilus palustris*: They are present in rivers, pools, ditches, canals, nallahs, ponds, lakes and marshes etc., throughout India except in the desert areas of Rajasthan. They are also present in Sri Lanka, Myanmar and Malay, Peninsula, Larger Islands of Malay Archipelage.

Fig. 7.3. Crocodile skins and its Economic values : making belts, purses, stuffed animals, chains, keys, and foot wear, high market values in European Countries.

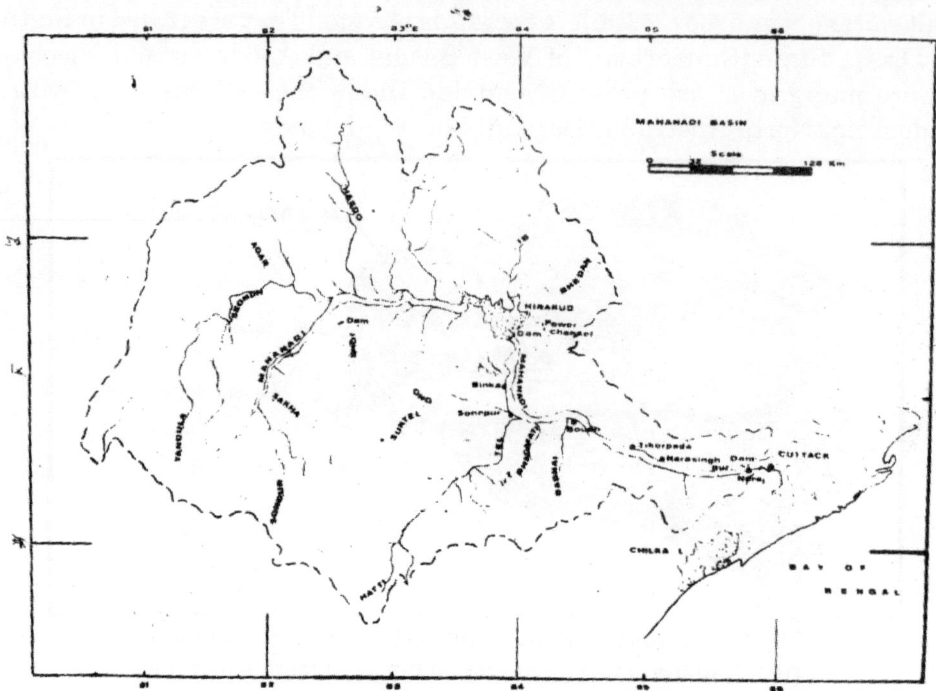

Fig. 7.4. Map showing the distribution of gharials, Gavialis gangeticus in Mahanadi and its tribuataries, a stronahold

An adult feruale gharial, gavialis Gangeticus, Gmelin.

Crocodiles are not found in Europe due to cold climatic conditions.

Differences Between Crocodiles, Alligators and Caimans

Characters	Crocodiles	Alligators	Caimans
Snout	Narrower	Broader & Rounded	Triangular Blunt
Nostrils	United	Separate	Separate
Lower Jaw teeth	Exposed when mouth closes	Not exposed	Not exposed
4th tooth of lower jaw	Exposed when mouth closes	Not exposed	Not exposed
Distribution	Present troughout World except Europe	Only America and China	Only South and Central America

BIOLOGY

Crocodiles appears like lizards. The tail is literally compressed and used for swimming and also as a weapon of offence and defence. Limbs are short with five digits on the fore limb and form on the limd limb. The three liner digits in each limb bear clows. The body of a Crocodile covers with thick harry epidermal scales below the scales, there are bony seates on the back. Tail with sisi scutes arranged in rings with crests on the dorsal side. The joins are long so the gape of the month is wide. The external nostuls lie dorsally at the tip of the snont. They are procided with values which can be closed when the crocodile is in water. Labial glands in upper and lower jaiws; Nasal and premabillary glauds in upper jaw; and lacrimal glauds in eyes are present in crocodiles. Each eye has two eye lids and a mictitating membrane. The open-ing of the ears can also be closed by folds of K. skin. Teeth are the codont. The tonngue is broad and non protractile. There is a faap (throat valve) attached to the hind end of the tongue which directs the passage of air or food. The kidneys are rnetareplnoi and no urinary bladder. The colaca is a lengitudival scit and there is a median unpaired copulatory orgom in the male. Two pairs of scent glauds are present. They are active during the breeding season in the males. One pair lies in the region of throat and the other pair in the lips of the cloaca. The crocodiles are oviparous (egg laying) animals.

They are cold blooded (Pockilothermic) animals. Amphibious, Basking like lizards. Like mammals four, they have four chambered heart; the codont dentition and the presence of diaphragm. Like fishes, they have an air bladder.

Their main food is mostly dead organisms and hence they are best scavangers. Cannibolism (takes their own young ones as food) is also observed in crocodiles.

The teeth are useful to grip of food only. They takes small amount of food and swallows. Usually they shed their teeth by a dozen per week.

The crocodile are unisexual. One male crocodile can mate 3 or 4 females. Mating takes place in water during December to February in every year. They have diffinate parental care. Depending upon the size of female crocodile, they lay 8 to 97 eggs in each clutch per year. Mugger crocodiles matures at the age of six .uhereas the salt water crocodile matines at the age of eight and the gharid at the age of the tenth year. Eggs are laid in March to May, 5 to 10 meters away from the share, Digs a hole (ghanal and mugger crocodile) or specially prepared a nest like bird (Salt water or estuarine crocodile). Eggs are milky white,oval, blunt at both ends, double shelled (2 to 2½ times of Hen's egg) immediately after laying the size of the egg is 40 × 65 to 50 × 30 mm and weighs 65 to 95 gm. During incubation, the size of the egg is increasing upto 45 to 50 days. The incubation period is 65 to 84 days. During incubation, the preferable temperature is 30°C ± 1°C and the range of us temperature is 28° to 34°C + 1°C. Depending upon the temperature the sex is determined. At higher temperature (34°C), all hatches to males and at lower temperature (28°C), all becomes female crocodiles (Subba Rao, 1986). Hence manipulate the sex of crocodiles as per the incubation temperature.

The fully developed embryo have with egg tooth.

Immediately after hatching, the size of the young ones are 30 to 35 cms in length and weighs 60 to 90 gm.

The predaters are monitor lizards, wild dogs, jackals, cats, big crocodiles. First two years are vulnerable period in a crocodile life.

FARMING, CONSERVATION AND MANAGEMENT CAPTIVE BREEDING OF CROCODILES (SUBBA RAO.1977)

Though the life span of the crocodiles are about 100 years, they are becoming scace not only in India but also in abroad. This is mainly due to :

1. Habitat destruction
2. Urbanisation
3. Industrialisation
4. Deforestation
5. Pesticidal Pollution
6. Introduction of exotic species
7. Collection of eggs for food
8. Destruction of both juveriles and adults by Nylon set nets used for fishing
9. Extensive hunting for their extremely valuable skin.

In conse of time, the crocodiles may became totally extinct if uncared for (Bustard,1974). AS early as 1974, the author, Dr. Subba Rao with Dr. Bustard, Man of Isle, Scotland has surveyed the population of all three species of crocodiles in India. Their number was about 100 during 1974. It was then suggested that the conservation of India's three endangered species of crocodiles must be ensured by extensive conservation and management in National habitat area and their population must be stepped up though crocodile farming.

There are two types of crocodile farming :

1. Battery farming or Artificial farming.
2. Free Range Management or Natural farming.

1. Battery Farming or Artificial Farming

With the help of fisherman and tribals, to keep watch on the crocodiles egg laying sites. Generally mating in crocodiles takes place in water during December to February. The eggs are laid in shore, 5-10 meters away from the shore live. Before premansoon, *i.e.*

June-July, they hatch themselves with the help of egg tooth. These young crocodiles are reared for two years (in first year and second year crocodile pools). Finally, they let into the Gazetted sanctuaries (protected areas) during third year (Subba Rao, 1993). At present, Andhra Pradesh have 15 Gazetted Sanctuaries and more than 10,000 crocodiles (2008).

2. Free Range Management or Natural Farming

The crocodiles of an area, which could be a lake or reservior or section of a river or tidal creek are managed freely as it is and should be a protected area. In this type of natural farming, the costs of maintenance will be meagre.

STATUS AND PRESENT POSITION

All the Indian Crocodiles have been catagorised in schedule of Indian (Protection) Act, 1972 along with tiger, black buck and sea turtle.

Starting about 100 crocodiles in 1974 and increased their population for about 10,000 crocodiles after successful completion of artificial farming in different sanctaries of crocodile centres and Zoos in India.

The crocodiles are great importance to the balanced ecosystem and they are economically valuable natural resources.

ACKNOWLEDGEMENTS

Thanks are due to my good friend and crocodile lover, Dr. H.R, Bustard, Formerly FAO expert on crocodiles and instrumental in involving me in the farming, conservation and management of Indian crocodiles. I am also thankful to Mr. Sripal Jee, IFS, Ex Principal CCF, Govt. of Orissa and Mr. Pusp Kumar, IFS, former CCF, Govt. of Andhra Pradesh for helping *me* during survey work, cooperation and encouragement.

REFERENCES

Bustard, H.R. 1974 : Preliminary survey of the prospects of crocodile farming, India. FAO Report, IND 71033, Rome.

Indian Wildlife (Protection) Act,1972 : Government of India publication, New Delhi.

Subba Rao,M.V.1977 : On breeding Crocodiles, *Science Today 12(4), 29-33.*

Subba Rao, M.V.1982a : Rearing, Farming, Conservation and Management of the Indian crocodiles,*Gavialiis gangeticus* (Gmelin) , *Crocodilus_palustris* (Lesson). VI International Reptile Symposium, Washington DC(USA).

Subba Rao,M.V.1986 : Incubating eggs of the ghacial (*Gavialis gangeticus*) for conservation purposes. Wildlife Management: Crocodiles and Alligaters (Eds. GJW webb; S.C.Manolisand P.J. Whitehead). Surrey & Beaty sons Put.Ltd., Austrialia, 503-505.

Subba Rao,M.V.1993 : *A Hand book of Indian Crocodiles.* Andhra University Press, Visakhapatnam, India.

Subba Rao.M.V. and Bustard,H.R. 1982 : Studies on the Conservation and Management of Indian Crocodiles *J. Environ Biol.*, 3(2):83-90.

Webb, G.W., Manolis, S.C. and Whitehead,P.J 1988 : *Wildlife Management; Crocodiles and Alligators.* Surrey & Beaty sons Pvt.Ltd., Australia.

CHAPTER

8

A SYSTEMATIC SURVEY OF SEA TURTLES ALONG NORTHEAST COAST OF ANDHRA PRADESH

M. RAMA MURTHY AND C. PRUDHVI RAJ

INTRODUCTION

Dolphin Nature Conservation Society is a registered non-government, ecofriendly, student based voluntary organization committed for the cause of Nature Conservation, environmental protection, education and awareness. It had a strength of about 200 students from different institutions in an around the city. The society came to existence on *March 5, 2001* and right from the day of its inception has been striving towards the aim of nature conservation and environmental protection mainly in three spheres of activities like Environment Pollution Prevention, Wildlife Conservation and Awareness, Tree Plantation and Maintenance. Over the past 10 years the organization is actively involved in the conservation of sea turtles along the coastline of Srikakulam and Visakhapatnam districts of northeast cost of Andhra Pradesh, with a coastline of about a 300 km, is one of the most important maritime zones of the country. Since it is just south of Orissa, it has particular significance for the thousands of turtles annually migrate through its coastal waters each year to reach their mass nesting grounds along the Orrisa coast. Northern Andhra, particularly is historically significant, as it has a unique temple dedicated to *kurma avatar,* the incarnation of Vishnu as a turtle. There is significant trawling related mortality in the State, with over a 1000 turtles being killed each year along its coast.

The aim of the present study is to document the present ground status of sea turtles and other marine mammals along the Northeast coast of Andhra Pradesh. So as to create to create awareness about these endangered sea turtles in general and Olive ridleys in particular among people especially among fishermen, students in particular, people whose livelihood is indiseparably dependent on the sea and to the general public so to mobilize people's participation in protection and carry out 'in-site' protection activity if necessary.

The surveys had be carried out on foot along the entire coast. Each zone had been allotted a group of student volunteers whose task is to report the mortality and nesting sites. Each zone had been thoroughly visited once in a week to avoid ambiguity in counting of dead turtles, the carapace of the dead turtle had been marked with paint and given a number specifying the sex of the individual. The carapace length (cl) and the carapace breath (cb) had been taken for all most all the turtles .To access the turtle nesting behaviour many turtle walks had been undertaken during night time by the volunteers of the society. Fishermen and local people were interviewed regarding sea turtle occurrence in their localities. Species of turtle nesting/ sighted in offshore waters were confirmed by showing them photographs of different species of sea turtles. They were also interviewed on the number of dead turtles found on their beach, cause and peak season. Other information collected included incidental catch of turtle in artisanal gear, type of net used, etc. Besides, developmental activities along the beach such as plantations, industries, land-use pattern, socio-economic status and consumption of turtle eggs and meat by local villagers were also taken into account.

Study Area

Visakhapatnam is one of the busiest maritime city along the east coast has a total of about 100 km approximately. The coast line extends from Annavaram in the north to Pentacota in the south. There are 16 fishing villages and one major landing centre (fishing harbour) and a number of minor landing centres.

The coast starting from Annavaram in the north to Pudimadaka down to south had been covered under the study area. The whole area accounts to over 70 km of the Visakhapatnam coast and where most of the fishing villages are present. The whole area had been divided to about five zones each comprising out of an average of about 12 km. The zones are as follows :

1. Zone A= Annavaram to Totlakonda
2. Zone B= Totlakonda to Appugarh
3. Zone C=Appugarh to Coastal Battery
4. Zone D= Coastal Battery to Mutyalammapalem and
5. Zone E= Mutyalammapalem to Pudimadaka.

METHODOLOGY

March to May 2001 : A preliminary survey was carried out on the Visakhapatnam coast to identify the Topography feasibility, key nesting areas, to assess trawling related mortality and identify the main anthropogenic pressure on the sea turtles.

October 2002 to May 2005 : Every year the survey was started from the last week of October and ended on the last week of May.

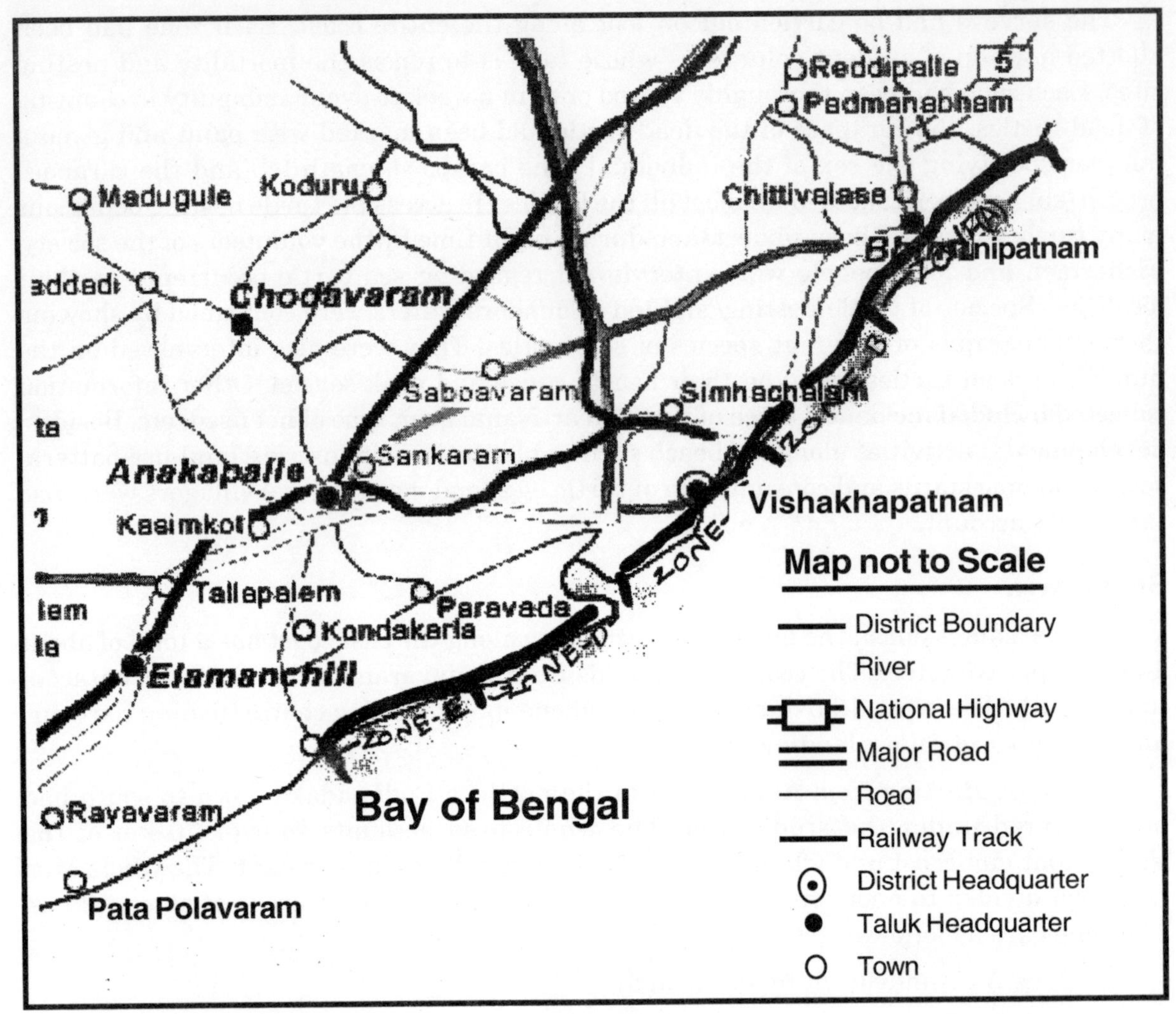

RESULTS

Of the five species of sea turtle occurring in the eastern Indian Ocean and coastal waters of India, four species Olive ridley *(Lepidochelys olivaced),* Green turtle *(Chelonia mydas),* Hawksbill *(Eretmochelys imbricata)*, Leatherback *(Dermochelys coriaced),* have been reported from the Andhra Pradesh coast. In the present survry only two species Olive ridley and Green turtle had been reported from the coast. According to some fishermen, Leatherback and Hawksbill are also seen in the off shore waters but are very rare. A brief summery of the two species and their status along the coast had been explained briefly below:

Olive Ridley Turtles

The olive ridley is the most commonly seen and present along the entire coast of

Visakhapatnam.. Local fishermen and workers on trawlers reported their presence, as the turtles get entangled in their fishing nets. According to them they are seen in post-monsoon and pre-monsoon period of the year. The Olive ridley accounted to almost 98 per cent (Table 8.1) of the turtle mortality along the Vizag coast during the present survey. Deaths has been reported as early as the month of October, but most of the mortality is seen from Mid-December to Feburary month end.

Table 8.1. Olive Ridley Sea turtles (*Lepidochelys ovivacea*) : Mortality Survey, 2002-2005

Zone	Sex	2002		2003		2004		2005	
		No.	CCL/CCB Avg	No.	CCL/CCB Avg	No.	CCL/CCB Avg	No.	CCL/CCB Avg
Zone A	M	18	69/68	15	69/69	21	69/67	19	68/68
	F	11	68/66	12	69/67	29	68/67	17	69/67
	O	9	68/66	10	69/68	12	68/68	8	68/66
Zone B	M	9	67/67	15	68/67	22	68/68	17	69/67
	F	17	69/66	16	69/68	27	68/66	20	69/68
	O	3	67/68	2	70/72	16	69/66	11	69/68
Zone C	M	12	67/66	16	69/66	19	67/65	23	69/65
	F	13	69/66	15	68/68	17	69/67	11	69/67
	O	4	71/69	7	68/67	12	68/66	9	68/66
Zone D	M	21	67/66	23	68/67	32	68/66	21	68/67
	F	16	68/66	21	69/67	11	66/65	22	67/67
	O	12	69/66	7	68/67	19	67/66	12	67/66
Zone E	M	17	69/68	15	68/67	32	69/66	26	68/67
	F	18	69/68	18	69/66	21	67/66	26	68/68
	O	13	68/67	17	68/65	19	68/66	13	69/67
Total	M	77	68/67	75	68/67	126	68/66	106	68/67
	F	75	69/66	82	69/67	105	68/64	96	68/67
	O	39	67/67	43	69/68	78	68/66	43	68/66
G. Total		191	68/67	210	69/67	311	68/66	245	68/67

Nesting of only Olive ridley turtles had been reported in the present survey and this had been confirmed by other reports. Interview results reveal sporadic Nesting of olive ridley all along this coast which had also been conformed by our study during turtle walks.

Though the beach substratum is predominantly rocky in the coast of Visakhapatnam, There are a few nesting beaches present along the coast mostly in zones of A, C, D, E nesting had been recorded. On an average around 5-10 nesting per night can be seen along the entire coast. Peak nesting had been reported in the months of Febuary and March.

Green Sea Turtles

The occurrence of this species has been reported from the coast of Visakhapatnam. It is sporadically seen and its occurrence is rare and is reported only in few locations by the fishermen where ocassionally they get entangled in their nets. The present study had also reported their presence by few dead specimens washed ashore and the number had been dramatically gone up over the years (Table 8.2). Their sightings are mostly reported by fishers on trawlers and according to them it is associated with rocks and feeds on algae.

Table 8.2. Green Sea turtles (*Chelonia mydas*) : Mortality Survey 2002-2005

Zone	Sex	2002		2003		2004		2005	
		No.	CCL/CCB Avg	No.	CCL/CCB Avg	No.	CCL/CCB Avg	No.	CCL/CCB Avg
Zone A	M								
	F								
	O	1	59/55	1	54/53	1	49/47	4	54/51
Zone B	M								
	F								
	O	1	47/55	2	54/53	3	5250	2	53/52
Zone C	M								
	F								
	O					2	54/52	1	58/57
Zone D	M								
	F								
	O	1	57/53	2	53/51	1	49/48	1	50/49
Zone E	M								
	F								
	O	3	54/52	6	54/52	7	51/49	8	55/51
G. Total		3	54/52	6	54/52	7	54/49	8	55/51

No nesting of green turtle had ever been observed or reported all the reported turtles were sub adults.

The members on their survey recorded may spinner and bottle nose Dolphins, a Grey Dolphin,Porpoise and three whales dead and stranded on the coast.

DISCUSSION AND CONCLUSION

The present survey field visits and secondary information from local people, fishermen and other institutional personnel shows that Olive ridleys nest sporadically all along the Visakhapatnam Coast. Likewise there had been large incidental capture related turtle mortality along the coast. Though there is no commercial market, consumption of turtle eggs and meat still continues in some coastal villages.

Threats

1. **Egg poaching :** The main threat to the population of sea turtle on the coast of Visakhapatnam is from egg poaching and by predation by feral animals. The eggs are consumed by humans along the Southern part of coast. The locals informed us that the eggs are consumed by stray dogs, foxes etc. About 4 to 5 years ago, eggs were sold in the market but nowadays as the nesting has decreased the eggs are consumed by the person who collects them. Around 80 to 85 per cent of the nest are lost every year due to the above reasons and an *ex-suite* consevation strategy plan had to urgently worked out.
2. **Problems regarding management of coastal areas :** The beaches in and around Visakapatnam are good solitary nesting grounds for Olive ridleys, though the population has been affected by the usual problems attendant with urbanization, namely lighting, sand-mining, predation of eggs and hatchlings by dogs, crows and so on. There should be no violation of *CRZ* (Coastal Regulation Zone) rules and their concerned area.
3. **Incidental catch:** Fishing is intensively carried out all along the Visakhapatnam coast. There are records of turtles getting in the nets but in most of the localities they are released immediately by local fishermen.The mortality rate of sea turtles is on the rise and every year the number of dead turtles had been ever increasing. The decrease in the average *Mean value* of ccl/ccb of the carapace of dead turtles is of a concern and awareness campaigns are to be carried out to create awareness about these endangered species and to mobilize people's participation to protect them and if possible carry out 'in-site' protection activity in the vulnerable pockets along the coastline. The use of T.E.D in trawl nets is to be implemented strictly

To bring awareness about the consevation of "OLIVE RIDLEYS" is the need of the . hour. A co-ordinated efforts by all valunteers, N.G.Os, government institutions and especially fishermen is essential for future survival of the species.

CHAPTER

9

PRESENT-DAY THREATS AND PERSPECTIVES FOR CONSERVATION AND MANAGEMENT OF SEA TURTLES ALONG EASTCOAST OF ANDHRA PRADESH, INDIA

M.V. SUBBA RAO

INTRODUCTION

Sea turtles are ancient group of reptiles, which have inhabited oceans for over a hundred million years. These oldest reptiles become valuable resources for many people of coastal region with their nutritional, economic and cultural significance.

However, despite the long-standing values of these resources, its future is in jeopardy. Many sea turtles populations have been declined to the point, where they are no longer significant resources either materially or culturally. This is mainly due to indiscriminate exploitation mainly at breeding stages (Friezer, 1982) and threats (Subba Rao, 1997).

Presentation and exploitation of marine turtles is an international problem. All the seven species of sea turtles cross-boundaries of ocean and some of them commute over a quarter of the world (Carr, 1968).

A World Conference on Sea Turtle Conservation was held in Washington, D.C., U.S.A. in November 1979 and annual meeting of sea turtle biology and conservation is organizing by IUCN Marine turtle specialist group at U.S.A. during February-March, every year emphasized the need for conserving these valuable resources and developed a conservation strategy of world-wide scope (Pritchard *et al*, 1983).

India with its 6100 km of coastal line representing five species of sea turtles. They are the leather back, *Dermochelys coriacea :* the logger head, *Caretta caretta :* the green turtle, *Chelonia mydas;* the Hawk's bill turtle, *Eretomochelys imbricata* and the Olive Ridley, *Lepidochelys olivacea* (Eschscholtz).

There are three species of sea turtle mainly the green turtle, Hawk's bill and the Olive Ridley in East coast of Andhra Pradesh (960 km).

All the five species of sea turtles in the Indian Ocean are facing depletion of their population mainly due to pouching of the breeding turtles and their eggs. Now most of the nesting colonies of these sea turtles have disappeared from the East coast of Andhra Pradesh beaches. The Olive Ridley sea turtle, *Lepidochelys olivacea* is the most common Indian sea turtle and the worst victim of human depredation.

The present study mainly deals with the present-day threats and perspectives for conservation and management of sea turtles along the East coast of Andhra Pradesh, India.

Study Area

The study area is extended from Kalingapatnam of Northern Andhra Pradesh to Tada of Southern Andhra Pradesh with a coast line of 960 km and situated between 15° 50' and 18° 50' Latitude 79° 10' and 84° 10' Longitude.

This area has diversified shore condition ranging from rocky to sandy shores with several extensions of hill ranges projecting into the sea. Nine rivers with their major tributaries discharge their water in this area and a number of creeks, backwaters and streams also merge into the sea.

A total of 153 hamlets, most of which belong to fishermen communities and their population is around two lakhs. A total of 650 to 700 fishing craft including mechanized boats and catamarans operate along this coastline. Visakhapatnam is a major port and the headquarters of the Eastern Naval command of India.

Nesting

Olive Ridley sea turtles lay their eggs on the sandy beaches by making nest pits dug by them. Nests and nesting habitat of the Olive Ridleys are recorded by examining the shorelines at regular intervals during nights with the assistance of a few fishermen by observing crawl tracks of the sea turtle. A total of 121 nests of Olive Ridleys were located during 1999-2000.

Nesting Habitat

The beaches selected by the nesting Olive Ridley were fine sandy areas with a gradual slope and often edged with small patches of ground vegetation at high tide level. The nesting regions of sea turtles were mainly dominated by gross species, *Spinifex littoreus*; a creeper, *Ipomea pescapme;* a mangrove plant, *Pandanus fascicularis;* shore fauna mainly consists of ghost crabs, *Ocypoda* spp., *Uca* spp. Several other species of insects like mites, ants and insect larvae (maggots). Birds like cranes, *Grns communis:* Sea gulls, *Larbis brunnicephalus;* Cattle egrets, *Bubilcus ibis coromandaus;* Pond herons, *Ardela grayic;* and domestic crows, *Corvus splendis* were most dominant. Of mammals, jackals, *Canis aureus;* foxes, *Vulphus bengalensis;* and yaenas, *Hyacna striata* were common in most of the areas where the areas are edged with dense vegetation. Domestic dogs and pigs were common in the areas where human habitation is more.

Nesting Times

Basing on the crawl tracks of Olive Ridley sea turtles, the time of nesting was arbitrarily determined. Olive Ridley usually nest during nights mostly on the moonlit and nights between dusk and dawn. The successful nesting occurred mostly during spring tide 2200-2400 hr. Most of the nests were located at a distance of ranging from 16 to 45 metres from high tide watermark.

Nest and Clutch Size

The depth of the nest of Olive Ridley ranged from 40 to 90 cm while the maximum number of nests have a depth of range between 50 to 60 cm. The clutch size of the Olive Ridley has a range from 80 to 145 eggs. The eggs were arranged in 3 to 4 rows.

Eggs

The eggs of the Olive Ridley turtle are white in colour and round in shape with a diameter ranging from 3.7 to 4.6 cm and weight ranges from 22.4 to 37 g. The shell was porous and delicate and slightly flexible.

Incubation and Temperature

The incubation temperature is 28-31°C and incubation period is 60 days.

Hatchlings

Immediately after the emergence from the eggs, the hatchlings of sea turtles were dark black in colour and weighted between 15 to 18 g and had a size range of 3 to 4.1 cm of carapace width.

Nesting Behaviour

The time lapsed between the nesting from 127 to 232 minutes. After the nest hole dug by sea turtle, the eggs were laid one by one and at times 2 or 3 together. Soon after the egg laying, the nest hole was filled moist sand by the sea turtle with the help of her flippers and later the body and finally covered the pit hole by using all the four limbs and left no trace of the activity.

THREATS

Human Interference

Along the defined coastline of study area around 2 lakh population inhabitance (153 fishing-hamlets), the literacy rate comprises 5 to 8 per cent. The activities of shore inhabitants are mainly fishing crabs, hunting, shell collection for lime, ornamental knitting, drying of fish and preparation of fishing nets. Of these fishing is the major activity.

At present, the fishing activity has become intensive all along the coast. Extending deep-sea fishing with modern trawlers is being employed now-a-days. Due to the above, the adult sea turtles are entangled with trawlers, fishing nets and the knife like keel. The indiscriminate exploitation of Olive Ridley Sea turtles by fishermen for subsistence economy is resulting massive migration tendency of these endangered species. The depletion of sea turtles population is mainly from the following threats.

1. Incidental mortality at off-shore waters from trail fishing
2. Consumption of eggs and meat of sea turtles.
3. Poaching of eggs and live sea turtles.
4. Marine pollution and distance due to high intensive lighting along beaches (disorientation of both adults and hatchlings).

Predatory Disturbances

The eggs of Olive Ridleys are distributed either by predators or human for consumption. In urban areas, the eggs are spoiled by dogs and pigs at any time during incubation period (55-65 days). Besides, shore crabs and rodents are great menace to the nests and hatchlings of Olive Ridleys.

Extension Programmes

Since the major threat to the Olive Ridley and collection species of sea turtles is ignorant and innocent activity of fishermen. It is proposed to educate them on the significance of sea turtles and also to involve them in the conservation movement. A pilot extension programme is organized to bring out importance of sea turtles as to avoid or reduce the decimating impact of the human factor and to protect the sea turtles. Educating local fishermen to protect the Sea turtle nests from wild predatory mammals.

Extension programme were conducted at each village and the villages were educated through Audio-visual aids, slides, charts, pamphlets, displaying boards in local Telugu language on the significance of the sea turtles, as *kurmavatara* and need to conserve and to save the sea turtles as our national heritage and also create awareness among the fishermen.

Suggestions and Recommendations

Basing on the present study, the following recommendations are considered very importance in the conservation and management of the Olive Ridley sea turtles:

1. **Subsistence Hunting :** It can be avoided through intensive extension programme in all 153 villages of the study area and to bring out an awareness of the status and importance of sea turtles.
2. **Starting of Beach Hatcheries :** In all the fishermen villages of the East coast of Andhra Pradesh should have sea turtle hatcheries with eggs. The fishermen who, after due training regarding information of nesting sea turtles in their jurisdiction should be appointed as guards for conservation of sea turtles.
3. **Starting of Sea Turtles Farming and Management Training Institute :** It may also serve as a research centre to develop sea turtles farming as one of the cottage industries in the fishermen villages so as to utilize the turtles resources in a rational way.

4. *Strict Implementation of the Indian Wildlife (Protection) Act, 1972*: Impose severe punishment on the commercial exploitation of the Sea turtles. Declare the Hope Island, near Kakinada, Andhra Pradesh as sea turtle sanctuary and ban all fishing and other maritime activities, which are harmful to the Sea turtles.
5. Use TED (Turtle Exclusive Deviser) to all the trawlers for survival of Turtles.

Acknowledgements

Thanks are due to the authorities of the Andhra University especially the Vice-Chancellor, Prof. R. Radhakrishna, the Registrar, Prof. J.M. Naidu for their encouragement. Greatful thanks are due to the Principal Chief Conservation of Forests, Chief Wildlife Warden, Government Andhra Pradesh and their staff for the help rendered during the Sea turtle survey work in East coast of Andhra Pradesh.

REFERENCES

Carr, A.F. 1968. *So excellent a Fish: A Natural History of Sea turtles.* Cox and Wyman Ltd., Cassel, London.

Frazier, J. 1980. Sea turtles faces extinct in India. Crying Wolf or Saving Sea turtles. *Environmental Conservation,* 7(3): 239-240.

Frazier, H. 1982. Subsistence hunting in the Indian Ocean. *Proc World Conference on Sea turtles Conservation.* K.A. Bjorndal, (Ed). Smithsonian Institution, Washington, D.C., 391-396.

Pritchard, P.C.H., Bacon, P and Carr, F. 1983. Manual of sea turtles research and conservation Techniques. K.A.Bjorndal and G.H Balazas (eds). Center for Environmental Education, Washington, D.C., 1-107.

Subba Rao, M.V. 1997. *Ecology and Management of Indian Sea turtles.* EnRA Publication, Visakhapatnam, India.

CHAPTER

10

MUNICIPAL AND INDUSTRIAL WASTE : UTILIZATION IN AGRICULTURE

ANKALA RADIKA AND M.V. SUBBA RAO

Every day billions of gallons of wastes irom cities ana nousmy settlement, industries and agriculture are thrown in to fresh waters. In Class I and Class II cities in India, 8209 and 1226.32 MLD waste water is generated. Out of which, 59% and 15.54% are collected and only 37% and 5.44% respectively get some kind of treatment. In a survey done by Central Pollution Control and Prevention Board, out of about 1700 large and medium industries polluting the water resources, only 460 had effluent treatment plants. The others were simply discharging their waste, as it is, into fresh water sources.

Sewage has been utilized on land throughout the world for several decades as a method of its final disposal. Recent investigations have established the feasibility of waste water reuse on land as a method of treatment for pollution control. The advantages of this system are (i) the water component and nutrient components of sewage are recycled through crop irrigation, (ii) Pollution of water sources can be eliminated and (iii) if there is higher crop yield, economic benefits increase. The prime objective of sewage farming is to achieve the purification of sew-age effluent for control of water pollution simultaneously with the cultiva-tion of crops at a very low cost in comparison to the conventional sew-age treatment methods. The mechanism involved in the purification in-clude complex physical, chemical and biological interaction operating together. The physical factors include filtration, absorption, adsorption, photo-oxidation, evapo-transpiration, osmosis etc. The chemical fac-tors are ion exchange, precipitation, solubilisation, oxidation, reduction etc. The biological factors include carbon assimilation, proteolysis, enzymatic hydrolysis, respiration, catalytic decomposition, ammonification, nitrification, denitrification and phosphate mobilisation (Loehr, 1979). The successful operation and efficient management of a waste water reuse system for crop irrigation depends upon the effluent quality (volume, organic load, nutrient content, total suspended solids, salinity, pH, pathogens etc.), soil properties (texture, permeability, sub-soil drainage, water-table depth, cation exchange capacity, exchange-able sodium percentage) and nature of crop species (tolerance capacity, nutrient and oxygen uptake requirement, duration).

In developing countries, industrial development and urbanization is increasing the discharge of sewage. In India, there are about 80 cities and towns having complete or partial sewage system while majority of the towns have surface drainage system. The sewage in many towns in disposed off by discharge into nearest river or streams throughout the year. There are about 145 cities and towns in India where sewage farm-ing is practised covering about 13,000 hectares. Farmers at Aurangabad frequently irrigate waste water for sugarcane, pigeon pea, ground nut, tomato, fodder crops and vegetables throughout the year due to scarcity of rains in the area.

However, the use of raw sewage continues to be a health hazard. Domestic sewage may transmit diseases like Salmonellosis (Salmonella typhimurium), Shigellosis (Shigelladysentriae), Leptosprosis (Leptospira australis), Taulermia (Bacterium tularense), Cholera (Vibrio cholerae), Tuberculosis (Mycobacterium tuberculosis), Amoebiasis (Entamoeba hystolitica), Parasitic worms (Taenia saginata, Ascaris, Lubricoides) and many enteric viruses (poliovirus, coxvirus, ECHO virus, hepatitis *B* etc.). Use of microbial and chemical methods in controlling these orgainsms are necessary before sewage is applied in agriculture. Microbial ap-proach includes the use of predator antagonists and bacteriophages which help in reducing pathogenic population. The chemical approach leads to the use of chemicals which can eliminate pathogens but are also not toxic to human beings.

The utilization of sewage and waste water produced by human community in fish culture is practised in China. However, it has not found wide acceptance in our country because of aesthetic and hygienic con-siderations. Purifying waste water by means of large scale production of algae is getting into use more and more now. In India, West Bengal is perhaps the pioneering state where sewage is extensively utilized for fish culture in about 2500 ha fish ponds. A fish yield of 28,000 kg/ha/year has been reported frorTi aWest Bengal sewage farm (Tapiador, 1973). In addition to commercial fishery, a few trials on sewage application in fish culture are now available from different states.

Of the three locations i.e. surface water, atmosphere and land for the disposal of industrial wastes, land represents not only an appropriate disposal medium for many industrial liquid effluents but also an opportu-nity to manage wastes with minimum adverse environmental effects. Industrial waste water from sugar industry, paper mills, distillery have been tried by several workers for irrigation of rice, maize, sugarcane and other cereals with satisfactory results. Based on these observations. The following for the utilization of waste water in land treatment and agri-culture :

1. Land treatment of sewage through sewage farming can be a very effective method for the purification of primary and secondary ef-fluents.
2. Prior treatment of raw sewage (physico-chemical and biological) is very essential upto either primary or secondary level before its use for growing crops.
3. The organic loading on land must be limited to keep the soil sys-tem predominantly aerobic.

4. The waste water load on soil should be judiciously worked out based on water requirement of the crops and soil permeability.
5. The nutrient loading of the crop should be balanced and agro-nomic practices of either dilution or nutrient fortification may be adopted whenever necessary.
6. Sewege purification rather than crop yield should be the prime objective.
7. It must have the community participation and acceptance to meet the socio-economic needs.

CHAPTER

ENVIRONMENTAL EDUCATION : MONITORING AND MANAGEMENT

M.V. SUBBA RAO, A. RADHIKA AND Y. AVASN. MARUTHI

As concern for environmental protection and conservation of environment have increased world-wide, the detrimental impacts of pollution and human dominance on natural ecosystems have become increasingly important for resource management. There is no doubt about the progress and prosperity brought about by industrialization, however, the materialistic progress posing has ruthlessly demolished the very natural surroundings and is posing threat to environment. Deforestation has led to destruction of wildlife, soil erosion, loss of soil fertility, floods and formation of deserts. Urbanization and improper planning expansion of cities have created the problem of waste disposal, sanitation and provision of pure water and clean air, use of synthetic chemicals, as pesticides in agriculture are also intensifying the problem of water pollution. Pollution of water, air and soil is formidable problem at globally.

The environmental problems of developing countries are not just the side effects of excessive industrialization and also due to man's incomplete knowledge of the possible impact of scientific development. Progress has become synonymous with an assault on nature. Industrialized countries witnessed much more acute environmental pollution and began realizing its adverse impact of the lives of the people, which were sought to be enriched through industrial production. The United Nations Conference on Human Environment held at Stockholm in June, 1972 proved very timely with it began an era of increasing consciousness world timely with it began an era of increasing consciousness world-wide regarding the urgent need for protection of the environment.

It was fortunate that our country took up this matter in right earnest. To make people aware of environmental protection constitution was amended. Article 48(A) & 51 (A) (G) were added to the constitution there by imposing duties on Government as well as citizens for protection and improvement of the environment. The aim of this paper is to discuss about various problems arising in the course of environmental management and their possible solutions.

Strategies of Environmental Management

Environmental management is a process which, by taking into account the overall ecological, cultural, economical, social, technological and other factors, attempts to ensure that the human environment is developed in an integrated and systematic manner. It aims at the best use of existing and potential resource base in such a way as to maintain for now and in the long term, the best possible sustained yield from the biosphere. Its ultimate objective is to provide greater personal and social opportunities and to improve overall human well being for present as well as future generations. Some of the objectives of environmental management are :

- Environmental Planning,
- Environmental status evaluation,
- Environmental Impact Assessment and
- Environmental Legislation and Administration.

To be successful, environmental management requires first the availability of particular parameter data to assess its present status. Data can be obtained by a monitoring system designed to measure at different points of space and time, various selected parameters and these can be consolidated into appropriate indices which characterize the quality of environment. Secondly, to identify the consequences due to alteration in the environment quality, on existing both biotic and abiotic components of ecosystem including human response do it. The third action involves the projection of the proposed action and the presentation of the results in a manner that the analysis of probable environment consequences can be incorporate or used in the decision making process.

Government of India in 1972 constituted the National committee on Environmental Planning and Coordination (NCEPC), some of the objectives of the committee were to advice on environmental problems and make recommendations for their improvement. To carryout these objectives, the NCEPC is to review, formulate and promote policies and programmes covering development projects, Physical Planning Legislation, Administrative procedures, Education and public information and research. Department of Environment was created with effect from November 1980 under the charge of Prime Minister. It is function as a promoting research in environmental problems, pollution monitoring, conservation of natural resources and marine ecosystems. Various plans have been formulated for environment management in India.

Plans for Conservation of Forests

It is clear that for the last long years there has been vast decrease in deterioration and denudation of forests. Forests are one of the valuable natural resources and they are very basis of our survival maintain the proper balance of organisms, chemicals in the environment by producing or absorbing them and preventing soil erosion, floods, droughts, etc.

The Government of India revised the old forest policy of 1952 in December 1988. The major objectives of the new National Forest Policy are :

1. To maintain ecological stability by adopting appropriate measures of environmental protection, conservation and restoration,
2. To implement social forestry project on large scale,
3. Protection of existing floods,
4. Protection of Wildlife and Biodiversity.
5. To meet basic requirement of rural people & tribals for fuel, fodder and shelter purposes.

Protection of forest cannot be possible unless a person volunteers himself or herself to co-operate. Therefore, it is necessary to create awareness about protection and development of forests among the people.

Environmental Protection, Water and Air Pollution

Water and Air are important for life. Control over sewage and industrial discharge into rivers and disposal of waste is so fragile that all most no pollution control is possible. Air pollution has become a great menace to life and it causes severe health hazards. For the control of water and air pollution, there are three main acts.

- ➢ The Water (prevention and control of pollution) Act, 1974.
- ➢ The Air (prevention and control of pollution) Act, 1981.
- ➢ The Environmental (protection) Act, 1986.

The Government agencies must play a constructive role to provide guidance and advice to the industry in understanding the requirement of the laws and ensuring their faithful compliance.

To make people aware of environment protection, environment education should be made compulsory in primary school level onwards.

Environmental Education

Since pre-historic time, man developed certain tools and techniques to fulfill his basic needs. But time to time changes in the human society, civilization and technological development. Man is the creator and consumer of so many things. Now the increased unethical activities of man are responsible for the present state of environmental crisis.

The pressure on resources increased with the increasing rate of population. The rapid industrialization, urbanization, deforestation, desertification, threatened wildlife nature, over grazing, shifting cultivation, dwelling process, soil erosion, climatic changes, increased rate of pollution in air, water and land. The loss of Biodiversity and so on are responsible for the present environmental disasters like "Bhopal Gas Tragedy". "Chernobyl incident" and other accidents threatening the life of man.

The following are a few examples to estimate the environmental crisis :

1. At present the world forest cover is decreasing by 18-20 million hectares per year. India is losing 1.5 million hectares of forest cover every year. The recent Satellite survey is showing the forest cover is not more that 10% in the total geographical area in our country.
2. It is estimated the flood damage cost is about 1,000 crore per year in the country.
3. Soil erosion is taking place at an accelerated phase, more than 6000 million tons of fertile top soil is eroding every year. The cost in the economic point of view is more than 12,000 crore.
4. Desertification is also taking place at an accelerated phase, during the last 50 years 65 thousand million hectares of productive land in southern parts of Sahara region has converted into desert and nearly 14 percent of the world's population is living in the threatened dry lands.
5. The use of "non-renewable" resources, such as coal, petroleum, minerals etc. has increased in recent times.
6. The loss of "Biodiversity" will effect the balanced ecosystem.
7. Pollution causing severe damage to the environment.
8. Climatic changes are expected in the early part of 21st century.
9. Environmental refugees.
10. Sustainable development and so on.

The above mentioned issues are only examples. Besides these there are so many environmental problems. Now the question with us, how to over come these problems and what can be done to resolve these issues? The only good approach is promoting environmental education at all levels.

Environmental education is to promote an understanding about the sensitive nature and man's interaction with physical, biological, economic, political, social, cultural aspects of environment and to awaken human societies to safeguard the only life supporting system in the universe.

Environmental education is a process to bring awareness, knowledge, skill development, attitude, motivations and commitments to work individually and collectively to solve the present environmental problems and to prevention of new one's.

The biosphere is the central theme of environmental education to build up environmentally literate citizens with responsibility. The environmental education curriculum should be based on the present environmental trends and should reflect the man's inter-relationship with nature. It must be a remedy measure to the present situation.

Environmental education at global level was discussed in the Stockholm conference in 1972 and then Belgrade Charter in 1975. The first International conference on environmental education held in Tbilisi 1977. The first environmental education conference was held in New Delhi 1981. The International workshop on development and biosphere stability, in New Delhi 1985 adopted a declaration to protect the nature and stressed the need of "Environmental awareness".

Environmental Awareness Through

1. Both formal & non-formal education.
2. National parks, Sanctuaries, Botanical gardens, Monuments, etc.
3. Future articles, Interviews, News time.
4. News papers.
5. Radio & Television.
6. Slogans, Cartoons, Drawings, etc.
7. Awareness campaigns, field visits, demonstrations, meetings, seminars, exhibitions.
8. Books, Journals, Reports, etc.,
9. Charts, Posters, Films, Slides, etc.
10. Folk media.
11. Organizing Eco-camps and Eco-clubs.
12. Science clubs, essay writing, debate drama and other extra curricular activities.

The following organizations working at International level to promote environmental education and to conserve nature. The WWF, ISEE, NAEE, IUCN, WCMC, FAO, SCOPE, GEF, FEC, WMO, WHO, SACEP and other organizations were involved in the field of environment.

In India more than 908 Non-Governmental Organizations (NGOs) are working in the field of environment. The union Government has launched a NEAC campaign to buildup environmental awareness. Finally the opinion is that, the peoples participation is very important for the success of any program. Hence the approach should attract the people to involve in the environmental education program for quick results.

Environmental Monitoring and Environmental Issues

Environmental monitoring is the systematic collection of physical, chemical, biological and related data pertaining to environmental quality, pollution sources and other factors that influence or influenced by environmental quality. Environmental quality data are vital components for one or more of the following uses :

- Establishments of or revisions to standards.

- ➢ Demonstration that adequate progress is being made for that attainment of the standards, in the scheduled time frame.
- ➢ Providing assurance that compliance with standards has been attained.
- ➢ Information regarding maintenance of standards.
- ➢ Determine if control of high pollution episodes or spills is adequate and provide guidance on choice of actions.
- ➢ Definition of environmental pollution problems for periodic determination of priorities for resource allocations and the development of control programs.

OBSERVATIONS

The main goal of the monitoring program is designed to sample the environment for pollutants for which national environmental standards has been promulgated. An example of such standards is the National ambient air quality standards for particulate matter, Sulfur dioxide, Nitrogen dioxide, Carbon monoxide and Photochemical oixidants.

Results and Discussion

Environmental monitoring related activities are divided into the following categories: Trend monitoring, Ambient-source linked monitoring and exposure monitoring. Monitoring of trends involves the measurement of pollutants or the effects of pollutants in air, water, soil and biological matter over extended periods of time. Ambient source linked monitoring involves relating the ambient environmental quality to sources through modelling, considering other pertinent supporting data such as meteorology, hydrology, demography, topography and so on. Exposure monitoring involve the measurement of pollutant concentrations in air, water and food at the location where exposure may occur.

The present day monitoring of the Nations environmental quality is a cooperative effort involving local, state and federal agencies as well as industry. Most monitoring efforts are in the area of air and water. There are also monitoring programs such as the National Pesticide Monitoring Program. The atmospheric monitoring program conducted by local and state agencies is directed towards those pollutants for which National Ambient Air quality standards have been promulgated, namely particulate matter, Sulfur dioxide, Nitrogen dioxide and Photochemical oxidants. Table 11.1 provides a list of atmospheric pollutants currently being measured by EPA (Environmental Protection Agency).

Water quality monitoring is also carried our by many different agencies of groups. Most local municipal water treatment facilities monitor raw water quality daily. Many municipal wastewater treatment programs and country agencies also routinely monitor receiving waters upstream and downstream from treatment plant discharges. Many universities regularly collect water quality data. Table 11.2 shows a list of parameters presently used in the evaluation of water quality.

Table 11.1. List of Atmospheric Pollutants

Element	Radicals	Gases	Others
Antimony	Ammonium	Carbon monoxide	Aeroallergens
Arsenic	Fluoride	Methane	Asbestos
Barium	Nitrate	Nitric oxide	Benzene
Beryllium	Sulphate	Nitrogen dioxide	-soluble organic compound
Bismuth		Ozone	Benzene(a) Pyrene
Boron		Pesticides	Pesticides
Cadmium		Reactive hydrocarbons	Radionuclides
Chromium		Sulphar dioxide	Respirable particulates
Cobalt		Total hydrocarbons	Total suspended particulates
Copper			
Iron			
Lead			
Manganege			
Mercury			
Molybdenum			
Nickel			
Selenium			
Tin			
Titanium			
Vanadium			
Zinc			

Table 11.2. Parameters used in the evaluation of the water quality

Dissolved oxygen, pH, Coliform, Temperature, Floating solids, settlable solids, Turbidity or Colour, Taste-Odour, Toxic substances, Radioactive substances, Total dissolved solids, Methylene blue active substances, Zinc, Salinity, Chlorophyll, Arsenic, Barium, Cadmium, Chromium (hexavalent & trivalent), Lead, Selenium, Silver, Suspended solids. Chloride, Copper, Nitrate, Phenols, Phosphate, Sulfate, Cyanide, Electrical conductance, Ammonia, Acidity, Alkalinity, Carbon chloroform extract, Fluoride, Hydrogen sulfide, Pesticides, sodium, Iron, Plankton, Foaming substances, Boron, Manganese, hardness, Biological Oxygen Demand.

Monitoring Sensors and Methods

Assessing the quality of the environment depends to a considerable degree upon sensor availability and applicability. Until recently, most of the available pollutant sensors capable of providing quantitative or qualitative information were in situ or contact type instrumentation. Such sensors are restricted to assessing some chemical, biological or physical parameters of the environment at a specific point or when mounted on a mobile platform, at sequential points as a function of time. Presently the use of remote sensors came into existence, which are capable of very rapid measurement of an array of points in space and time. The use of remote sensing is not a new concept. Many Federal agencies, including the EPA, the National aeronautics and Space Administration and the Department of Transportation have sponsored extensive development of such sensors. Initial work in air monitoring concentrated on measure of temperature, water vapour and ozone primarily from satellites using the upwelling infrared radiation from the earth. Photographic techniques have been refined in the water and land media. They provide information on location of pollution outfalls, extent of oil spills, vegetal stress, impact of urbanization on water bodies and the presence of sedimentation or other water plumes.

An example of such remote system developed by the environmental monitoring and support laboratory at Las Vegas, which has recently become available for field use is the air craft mounted light intensity detection and ranging system (LIDAR). This instrument uses a pulsed laser and telescope arrangement to detect and range atmospheric particulate matter. The laser mounted on an aircraft flying 10,000 feet is periodically fired towards the ground. The telescope collects the returning reflective signal from the ground and from particulate matter in the air and the information's stored on tape for subsequent analysis. There are also present individual exposure sensors. These have only been perfected in a practical sense in the field of radiation. These devices, placed on an individual, measure for integrated exposure to specific types of irradiation regardless of this time-spatial relationship to sources. Such devices are developed to measure the integrated exposure of an individual to a variety of air-borne pollutants.

Environment Problems where Priority Action is Needed

Population stabilization, Planning of integrated land use, Betterment of crops and Land use, Revegetation of Marginal Lands, Biological Diversity Conservation, Control of air and water pollution, Development of non polluting renewable energy systems, Recycling of wastes and residues, Human settlements, Environmental awareness and Education, Updating Environmental Legislation.

CONCLUSIONS

Historically, environmental monitoring has been conducted more in a reactive fashion than in a planned systematic way. Furthermore, regardless of the purposes for which the monitoring began, there is usually considerable resistance to change any existing network once a substantial body of data has been collected. It is now time to reevaluate all existing environmental monitoring from a more systematic and analytic point of view. Precise answers to the following questions must be provided.

- For what purpose is the monitoring being done?
- Does it satisfy that purpose as performed?
- Can alternate means be used?

Until answers to these questions are provided, it is not possible to design minimum adequate monitoring networks that optimize cost effectiveness.

CHAPTER

12

ENVIRONMENTAL MONITORING AND ENVIRONMENTAL ISSUES

M.V. SUBBA RAO AND M. ARUNA KUMARI

INTRODUCTION

Environmental Monitoring is the systematic collection of physical, chemical, biological and related data pertaining to environmental quality, pollution sources and other factors that influence or are Influenced by environmental quality. Environmental quality data are vital components for one or more of the following uses :

➢ Establishment of or revisions to standards.

➢ Demonstration that adequate progress is being made for the attainment of the standards, in the scheduled time frame.

➢ Providing assurance that compliance with standards has been attained.

➢ Information regarding maintenance of standards.

➢ Determine if control of high pollution episodes or spills is adequate and provide guidance on choice of actions.

➢ Definition of environmental pollution problems for periodic determination of priorities for resource allocations and the development of control programmes.

OBSERVATIONS

The main goal of the Monitoring programme is designed to sample the environment for pollutants for which National Environmental standards have been promulgated. An example of such standards is the National ambient air quality standards for partlculate matter, Sulphur dioxide, Nitrogen dioxide, Carbon monoxide and Photochemical oxidants.

RESULTS AND DISCUSION

Environmental monitoring related activities are divided into the following categories : Trend monitoring, Ambient-Source linked monitoring and Exposure monitoring. Monitoring of trends involves the measurement of pollutants or the effects of pollutants in air. water, soil and biological matter over extended periods of time. Ambient source linked monitoring involves relating the ambient environmental quality to sources through modeling, considering other pertinent supporting data such as meteorology, hydrology, demography, topography. Monitoring exposure involve the measurement of pollutant concentrations in air, water and food at the location where exposure may occur.

The present day monitoring of the Nation's environmental quality is a cooperative effort involving local, state and federal agencies as well as industry. Most monitoring efforts are in the area of air and water. There are also monitoring programmes such as the National Pesticide Monitoring Programme. The atmospheric monitoring programme conducted by local and stale agencies is directed toward those pollutants for which National Ambient Air quality standards have been promulgated, namely particulate matter. sulphur dioxide, carbon monoxide, nitrogen dioxide and photochemical oxidants. Table 12.1 provides a list of atmospheric pollutants currently being measured by EPA (Environmental protection Agency).

Table 12.1. Atmospheric pollutants currently being measured by EPA

Element	Radicals	Gases	Others
Antimony	Ammonium	Carbon monoxide	Aeroallergins
Arsenic	Fluoride	Methane	Asbestos
Barium	Nitrate	Nitric oxide	Benzene - soluble organic compounds
Beryllium	Sulphate	Nitrogen dioxide	
Bismuth		Ozone	Benzone (a) Pyrene
Boron		Pesticides	Pesticides
Cadmium		Reactive hydrocarbons	Radionuclides
Chromium		Sulfur dioxide	Respirable particulates
Cobalt		Total hydrocarbons	Total suspended particulates
Copper			
Iron			
Lead			
Manganese			
Mercury			
Molybdenum			
Nickel			
Selenium			
Tin			
Titanium			
Vanadium			
Zink			

Water quality monitoring is also.carried out by many different agencies or groups. Most local municipal water treatment facilities monitor rawwater quality daily. Many municipal wastewater treatment facilities also monitor raw water quality daily. Many municipal wastewater treatment programmes and country agencies also routinely monitor receiving waters upstream and downstream from treatment plant discharges. Many universities regularly collect water quality data. Table 12.2 shows a list of parameters presently used in the evaluation of water quality.

Table 12.2 Parameters used in the evaluation of water quality

Dissolved	Selenium	Boron
pH	Silver	Manganese
Coliform	Suspended Solids	Hardness
Temperature	Chloride	Biochemical Oxygen Demand
Floating solids (Oil grease)	Copper	
Settleable solids	Nitrate	
Turbidity and/or Colour	Phenols	
Taste - Odour	Phosphate	
Toxic substances	Sulphate	
Radioactive substances	Cyanide	
Total dissolved solids	Electrical conductance	
Methylene blue active	Ammonia	
substances	Acidity	
Zinc	Alkalinity	
Salinity	Carbon Chloroform extract	
Chlorophyll	Fluoride	
Aresenic	Hydrogen sulfide	
Barium	Pesticides	
Cadmium	Sodium	
Chromium (hexavalent &	Iron	
trivalenl)	Plankton	
Lead	Foaming substances	

Monitoring Sensors and Methods

Assessing the quality of the environment depends to a considerable degree upon sensor availability and applicability, until recer.dy, most of the available pollutant sensors capable of providing quantitative or qualitative information were in *situ* or contact type Instrumentation. Such sensors are restricted to assessing some chemical, biological or physical parameters of the environment at a specific point or when mounted on a mobile platform, at sequential points as a function of time. Presently the use of remote sensors came into existence which are capable of very rapid measurement of an array of points in space and time. The use of remote sensing is not a new concept Many federal agencies, including the EPA, the National Aeronautics and Space Administration and the Department of Transportation have sponsored extensive development of such sensors. Initial work *In* air monitoring concentrated on measure of temparature, water vapour, and ozone primarily from satellites using the upwelling infra red radiation from the earth. Photographic techniques have been refined In the water and land media. They provide information on location of pollution outfalls, extent of oil spills, vegetal stress, Impact of urbanization on water bodies and the presence of sedimentation or other water plumes (A Citizens Report, 1982).

An example of such remote system developed by the Environmental Monitoring and support Laboratory at Las Vegas, which has recently become available for field use is the air craft mounted Light Intensity Detection and Ranging System (LIDAR). This instrument uses a pulsed laser and telescope arrangement to detect and range atmospheric particulate matter. The laser, mounted on an aircraft flying at 10,000 feet, is periodically fired toward the ground. The returning reflective signal from the ground and from particulate matter in the air is collected by the telescope and the information stored on tape for subsequent analysis. There are also present individual exposure sensors. These have only been perfected in a practical sense in the field of radiation. These devices, placed on an individual, measure his integrated exposure to specific types of irradiation regardless of his time spatial relationship to sources. Such devices are developed to measure the integrated exposure of an individual to a variety of air borne pollutants (Environmental Research; 1990).

CONCLUSIONS

Historically, environmental monitoring has been conducted more in a reactive fashion than in a planned systematic way. Furthermore, regardless of the purposes for which the monitoring began, there is usually considerable resistance to change any existing network once a substantial body of data has been collected, it is now time to reevaluate all existing environmental monitoring from a more systematic and analytic point of view. Precise answers to the following questions must be provided.

- For what purpose Is the monitoring being done?
- Does it satisfy that purpose as performed?
- Can alternate means be used?

Until answers to these questions are provided, it is not possible to design minimum adequate monitoring networks that optimize cost effectiveness.

CHAPTER

13

ENVIRONMENTAL ACTS

M.V. SUBBA RAO

The public liability Insurance Act, 1991, has been promulgated in the interest of humanity and the environment as a whole, to provide immediate relief to persons affected by accidents occurring while handling hazardous substances, or for that matter, connected there with or incidental thereto.

Management of Hazardous Substances, 1986

The rules under the Environment (Protection) Act, 1986, serve to control the personal risks involved in the handling of hazardous substances and to mitigate their adverse effects on the environment. They cover a set of regulations governing manufacture, storage and import of hazardous chemicals, management and handling of hazardous wastes, manufacture, use, import, export release and storage of hazardous micro-organisms, genetically engineered organisms or cells. These rules are not limited to providing legal action in case of non-implementation, but also indicate a set of measures necessary for handling of hazardous substances. They do not over-ride any existing regulations like the Explosives Act, Petroleum Act, Factories Act etc.

Water Act, 1974

The Water (prevention and control of pollution) Act, 1974, provides for the prevention and control of water pollution and maintenance/restoration of wholesomeness of water in wells, streams, water courses, inland water, subterranean water and sea/tidal waters to an extent of 5Kms from the shore-line. It is obligatory on the part of industries and local bodies to seek and obtain the consent of Pollution Control Board, to discharge trade effluents/domestic sewage within the quality/quantity standards set up, as measured by various parameters. In the event of failure to do so, the parties are punishable under certain provisions of the act, irrespective of their size or pollution potential.

Water Cess Act, 1977

The Water (prevention and control of pollution) Cess Act, 1977, once amended in 1991, broadly states that any person carrying on any specified industry, or any local authority consuming water for domestic purposes, is liable to pay cess complying with certain provisions of the Water (prevention & control of pollution) Act, 1974, or any of the standards laid down by the Central Government under the Environment (Protection) Act, 1986. The list of specified industries and rates .applicable are mentioned in schedule I & II respectively of the Act. The cess payees are to furnish returns in a form prescribed, to the authority, i.e Pollution Control Board. Any amount due under the act (including any interest or penalty payable) may be recovered by the Central Government in the same manner as an arrear of land revenue.

Air Act, 1987

The basic functions under the Air (prevention & control of pollution) Act, 1987, are to provide for the pollution control, or abatement of air pollution, from industrial establishments, automobiles and all other sources, so as to ensure air quality is maintained. All industries are required to obtain consent from Pollution Control Board under the provisions of the act.

Environment Protection Act, 1986

Important decisions were taken at the United Nations Conference on the Human Environment held at Stockholm in 5th June, 1972, (1st World Environment Day) in which India participated, to take appropriate steps for the protection and improvement of the human environment. Wherever it is considered necessary further to implement the decisions aforesaid in so far as they relate to the protection and improvement of environment and the prevention of hazards to human beings, other living creatures, plants and property.

- Persons carrying on Industry, operation, etc., not to allow emission or discharge of environmental pollutants in excess of the standards.
- Persons handling hazardous substances to comply with procedural safeguards.
- Furnishing of information to authorities and agencies in certain cases.

Forest Conservation Act,1980

With holding of renewal valid - absence of declaration under Sec.20 of the Indian Forest Act, 1927, Immaterial.

It is well known that breaking up of the soil or the clearing of the forest land affects seriously reforestation or regeneration of forest and therefore such breaking up of the soil can only be permitted after taking into consideration all aspects of the question, such as, the overall advantages and disadvantages to the economy of the country, environmental conditions, ecological imbalance, that is likely to occur, its effects on the flora and the fauna in the area, etc. It was therefore thought that the entire control of forest areas should vest in the Central Government. The argument that a notification under Sec. 20 of the Forest Act, 1927 declaring the forest in question as "Reserved Forest" had been issued prior approval of the Central Government was not required, is not acceptable.The explanation includes "any purpose other than reforestation". Mining operation is definitely a purpose other than reforestation. For this purpose, no permission or approval of the Central Government is required under Section.

CHAPTER

14

ECO-FRIENDLY NON-TOXIC COLOURS

B.P. DAS

INTRODUCTION

Colours are an integral part of our life and the usage of colour has undergone a process of evolution and is still doing so. The concept of colour and colouring is prehistoric and, has been practiced since time immemorial. Egyptian tombs has colorings of saffron, indigo, safflower and madder. The primitive people of Britain decorated their skins with a blue dye. .

Magic word today is *'eco-friendly' i.e.*, use products, which are ecologically safe and do not harm the natural balance of the environment. They are produced totally free of pesticides and potentially harmful chemicals. These dyes are considered to be environment friendly as they cause no pollution and are safe in use, India is main advantageous position since, this country holds a rich reservoir of natural resources with potential products. Also, it provides employment for rural people and preserves our traditional craftsmanship.

A worldwide interest for dyes from flora and fauna has encouraged comercialization of natural dyes. Naturally dyed food, cosmetics, drugs and textile have already captured a large share in the market and the demand for them is increasing.

Small quantities of dyes are being used for colouring paper, shoe-polish, leather, wood, cane, candles etc. Realizing the fascination and commercial reality of ecoproducts manufacturers and exporters are emphasizing this character of their product. To meet this new challenge the goods carry labels indicating the fulfillment of recognized eco-standards. Various institutions like National Handloom Development Corporation (NHDC), Weaver's Service Centers (WSCs), NGOs etc. are making several efforts to revive the ancient art of colouration with Natural dyes.

In the beginning, there were dyes derived only from natural sources *i.e.*, a plant, mineral or animal. After the accidental synthesis of Mauveine by William Henry Perkin in 1856, heralding the advent of coal tar dyes, the use of natural dyes receded.

The Limitations of the Natural dyes that were Responsible for their Decline are

- Availability
- Colour yield
- Complexity of dyeing process
- Reproducibility of shade

Besides these, Following are the Perceived Technical Drawbacks of Natural Dyes

- Limited number of suitable dyes.
- Allow only wool, silk, linen and cotton to be dyed.
- Great difficulty in blending dyes.
- Non-standardized.
- Inadequate degree of fixation.
- Inadequate fastness properties.
- Water pollution by heavy metals and large amounts of organic substances.
- Limited number of suitable dyes.

Use of synthetic dyes involves release of enormous amount of hazardous chemicals in the environment during the production and subsequent use. Realizing this fact, eco-friendly trend has made man return to nature leading to a revived interest in the use of natural dyes.

The Following Properties are Often Considered to be Advantages of Natural Dyes

- No health hazards, sometimes they act as health cure.
- Practically no or mild chemical reactions are involved in their preparation.
- No disposal problems.
- They are unsophisticated and harmonized with nature.
- Lot of creativity is required to use these dyes judiciously.
- They are obtained from renewable sources.

The research effort devoted to natural dyes is negligible. As there is much catching up to do after 150 years of neglect, there is plenty of scope for rapid development.

Stake Holders of Natural Dyes

The use of natural dyes has increased substantially during the last couple of years. They are mainly used by :

- Hobby groups.
- Designers.
- Traditional dyers and printers.

- NGOs.
- Museums.
- Academic institutes and Research associations.
- Industry.

The use of natural dyes particularly by women has continued as a hobby. Many guilds have been formed in the US to discuss about these dyes and organize workshops. Interest has given fillup to this activity. Some schools have introduced natural dyeing as a co-curricular activity. Many companies have come out with hobby kits for beginners. In India, Alps Ind. Ltd. have designed a large range of do it yourself kit.

Designers have very efficiently and effectively used natural dyes as a design tool. The non-reproducibility and non-uniformity of shades makes each creation a unique piece. Various kinds of design production methods such as tie and dye, stitching, resist printing, stencilling, Batik, Indian Ajrak, Kalamkari, Ikat etc are being practiced even today.

Source of Natural Dyes

Natural dyes are obtained from Vegetable, Animal and Mineral sources.

Vegetable Dyes

Vegetable dyes are obtained from every part of the plant *viz.*, Leaves *(Lawsonia inermis)*, Flowers *(Carthamaus tinctorius)*, Fruit *(Terminalia chebula)*, Bark *(Ventilago madraspatna)*, Wood *(Pterocarpus santalinus)*, Seeds *(Bixa orellana)* and Roots *(Curcuma longa)*.

Animal Dyes

This class of dyes is extracted from the animals.

Lac dye is an example of this class.

The following insects and insect groups may be the possible dye producers.

- Cochineal scales (*Dactylopius sp*), found on *Opuntia.*
- Lac insect. (*Laccifer lacca*) found on lac hosts.
- Gall-like coccids (*Kermes sp*) found on oak.
- Mealy bugs, especially the red bodies. Many garden plants are host to mealy bugs.

Mineral Dyes

Various inorganic metal salts and metal oxides Mineral colouring oxides are represented mainly by the khaki dyeing on cotton obtained by the use of mixtures of iron and Chromium salts.

Classification of Dyes

Bancroft classified natural dyes into two groups :

1. Substantive dyes
2. Adjective dyes

In this classification the colourants that dye the fibres directly are classified as substantive dyes. The adjective dyes are nothing but mordant dyes which are applied on material, mordanted with metallic salts.

The above classification was later replaced by an equivalent classification :

1. Direct dyes
2. Mordant dyes

- **Direct dyes :** The untreated cellulosic fibres absorb these dyes. *Turmeric, Annato* and *Carthamus* (from safflower) are examole of direct dyes.
- **Mordant dyes** : Mordant dyes are defined as those dyes, which have affinity for mordanted fibres. All dyes which form complex with mordants are grouped under mordant dyes.

Mordants

Mordants are considered as an integral part of the natural dyes or, to be more precise, the natural dyeing process by the most dyers of natural dyes. A close look at the chemical structures of natural dyes will show that these dyes like synthetic dyes, also consists of vat dyes, acid dyes, basic dyes, disperse dyes, direct dyes and mordant dyes (dyes that are capable of forming complex with metals). Many dyes fall under more than one class of dyes. For instance, in the case of mordant dyes, there are dyes which have affinity for the fibre; however, their uptake as well as hue can be modified by pretreatment or post treatment with so called mordants. Hence, they can be placed in more then one class of dyes.

Tannins such as a hard tannic acid etc. are considered natural mordants. Since some of the natural dyes can from metal complexes and thereby give different colours, there is a tendency to use all types of metal salts for this purpose. The restrictions to the use of metal salts have been put by the famous *'German Ban'*. Accordingly, the indicative maximum permissable quantities of different metals in the ultimate product are as follows : As-1.0 ppm, Pb-1.0 ppm, Cd-2.0 ppm, Cr-2.0 ppm, Co-4.0 ppm, Cu-50.0 ppm, Ni-4.0 ppm and Zn-20.0 ppm.

There is no upper limit on Al, Fe and Sn. Upper limit on Cu is fairly high. Hence, salts of these metals could be safely used for complexing and mordanting. Their quantity should be optimized to minimize the pollution load.

SOME IMPORTANT NATURAL DYES

Indigoid Dye

Two very important dyes have indigold structure namely, *Indigo* and *Tyrian purple.* Indigo is perhaps the oldest natural dyes used by man. It occurs as the glucoside indican in the plant *Indigofera tinctoria.*

Anthraquinone based Dyes

Madder dyes are Hydroxy- anthraquinones which are extracted from the root bark of various Rubiaceae family eg. from madder root *(Rubia tinctorium).*

Lac dye is obtained from scale of the insect *Laccitera.*

Kermes and *Cocchineal* is obtained from the insects.

These dyes are the mordant dyes.

Alpha - Naphthoquinones Dyes

The most important member of this class of dyes is lawsone or *Henna.* It is ' obtained from the leaves of *Lawsonia inermis.* Lawsone has been identified as 2-hydroxy 1-4 naphthoquinone. Another similar dye is *Juglone,* obtained from the shells of unripe walnuts.

Flavone based Dyes

Flavone is a colourless organic compound. Most of the natural yellow dyes are derivatives of Hydroxy and Methoxy substituted flavones or isoflavones. It is obtained from *wild, Reseda luteola.*

Dihydropyran based Dyes

It is closely related to flavone and are substituted dihydropyrans eg. Haematin and its leuco form. This is obtained from *Haematoxylon campechianum, Caesalpinia.*

Anthocyanidin based Dyes

The naturally occurring members of this classt include **Carajurin** obtained from the leaves of *Bignonia chia.*

Carotenoid based Dyes

This dye is obtained from orange pigment ot carrots. The colour is due to long, conjugated double bonds.

The major chemical constituent of *Saffron* is crocetin. It is obtained from the pistils of the *Crocus cstivas.* The name of the colouring matter comes from the Arabic *Zafrein* meaning yellow.

SOURCES OF NATURAL DYES ON THE BASIS OF COLOURS

Sources of natural red dyes			
Botanical name	Common name	Parts used	mordant
Carthamus tinctorius	Safflower	Flower	-
Caesalpinia sapan	Caesalpinia	wood	Alum
Sanguinaria canadensis	Blood root	Roots	Alum
Rubia Tinctoha	Madder	Roots	-
Coccus lacca (Insect)	Lac	Twigs inhabited by this insects	

Botanical name	Common name	Parts used	mordant
Source of Natural Yellow dyes			
Pinus roxburghii	Chir	Bark	Alum
Terminate chebula	Harda	Fruits	Alum
Tagettus species	Marigold	Flower	Chrome
Tectona grandis	Teak	Leaves	Alum
Equisetum	Horsetail	Leaves/Stalk	Tin
Punica granatum	Pomegranate rind	Fruits	Copperi
Curcuma longa	Turmeric	Root	
Chrysanthemum species	Corn marigold	Flowering tops	-
Source of Blue color dye			
Indigofera tinctoria	Indigo	Leaves	
Nymphaea alba	Water lily	Rhizomes	
Acacia nilotica	Sunberry	Seed pod	
Sources of Black color dye			
Annona reticulata	Custard apple	Fruits	
Acacia arabica	Babla	Bark	Alum
Terminalia chebula	Harda	Fruit	iron
Sources of Brown color dye			
Impatiens balsamina	Balsam	Flower	Chrome
Acacia catechu	Catechu	Wood	iron
Ficus religiosa	Asund chhal	Bark	Alum
Sources of Green color dye			
Urtica dioica	Stinging	Leaves/stalks	Alum
Convalbria majalis	Lily	Leaves/stalks	Iron
Sources of Orange color			
Dhalia species	Dhalia	Flowers	Alum/ Chrome
Bixa Orellana	Annatto	Seeds	

COMPOSITE COLOURS OR MIXED COLOURS

These colours can be obtained by mixing dyestuff in the same dye bath or different dye stuffs can be boiled separately and mixed in various proportions Some examples are:

- Green colour can be obtained by adding blue and yellow colours
- Blue- black colour can be prepared by combining blue and black grey
- Purple, violet, crimson, Lilac, Lavender can be obtained by red and blue

TECHNOLOGY FOR PRODUCTION OF NATURAL DYES AND COLOURANTS

For the production of natural dyes for the use in the dyeing of textiles products the aqueous extraction with alkalis is the most economical method.

Flow Chart

Raw Material → Size Reduction → Batch Extraction Phase Separation → Eine Filteration → Evaporation Spray → Drying → Finishing → Packing

NATURAL COLOURS AND THEIR APPLICATIONS

(*a*) Food and Medicines

	Ingredients	Shade	Applications
Turmeric colors	Turmeric oleoresin, polysorbate 80, propylene glycol	Bright yellow at neutral pH and below	Dairy Products, Sugar confectionary, Salad dressings, Water Ice relishes etc
Powdere Turmeric color	Turmeric oleoresin	Bright Yellow	Bakery Products, Sauces confectionary, Pickles, fish, compressed vitamin tablets, snack food
ANNANTO COLOURS Water-soluble Annatto Colors			
Annatto Extract	Extracts of annatto annatto, water and potassium hydroxide	Yellow Orange	cheese,ice cream Bakery Products
Annatto Powder	Extracts of Annatto with sodium carbonate	Yellow Orange	cheese,ice cream Bakery Products
OIL - SOLUBLE ANNATTO COLORS			
Annatio Oil Soluble	Extracts of annatto vegetables oil, mono- and glycerides propylene glycol, potasium hydroxide	Yellow Orange	Butter, oils, margarines Processed cheese, Fat based system
Annatto Suspension	Extracts of annatto in vegetable oil	Yellow Orange	Bakery, oils, margarines, Processed cheese, Fat based systems
ANTHOCYANIN - BASED COLORS			
Black Carrot	Carrot juice, propylene glycol	Pink to Red	Low PH systems such as beverages, fruit fillings, candy and confections

	Ingredients	Shade	Applications
	BEET ROOT JUICE BASED COLORS		
Beet Powder	Red beet juice and maltodextrin	Bluish-red	Condiments, gelatin products, fruit preparations, sauce candies, certain powered beverage products
	TAGETES EXTRACT (LUTEIN - XANTHOPHYLLS)		
Marygold (tagetes erecta)	Lutein, vegetable oil	Egg Yellow	Chiken Feed, pet foods
	LYCOPENE		
Lycopene	Tomato extract Vegetable Oil	Orange Red	Snacks, butter, Margarine, vegetable oils/fats, Pasta, Soup gravies, sauces
	SPINACH EXTRACT		
Copper Chlorophyll	Spinach Oleoresin, Vegetable oil	Green	Bakery, soups, vegetable Oil. Fat based application

RECENT RESEARCH WORK ON NATURAL DYES

With the World Trade Organization (WTO) on the verge of implementing reforms in global trade, all nations are gearing up to exploit their specialization and create a rich market for themselves. This would be imperative to make a dent in the highly competitive global trade scenario then. Natural dyes have been a part of our cultural heritage and evidence of use of these dyes in India dates back to thousands of years. With the world moving back to nature and green products being considered upmarket, natural dyes can give us a unique platform. Today natural dyes have found applications on not only natural fibers (cotton, linen, wool, silk etc) but on synthetics and then blends as well.

Readymade garments and home furnishings dyed and printed with natural dyes are considered as hi-fashion: a novel way of achieving value addition of such products.

AVAILIBILITY OF NATURAL DYES

From the information available on the internet, it is observed that there are over a dozen of companies offering natunl dyes. Some of the prominent among them are Michelle Wiplinger, Carol Todd, Carol Leigh and Trudy Van Stralen.

- Alps Industries is one of the major natural dye producing company. This company has a production capacity of around 300 tons per year
- Indian companies are : Satal Kathga, Sam & Ram, Amma Herbal, D. Manohar Lal, etc.

COMPANIES SELLING NATURAL DYES THROUGH INTERNET ARE:

- Jane's Fiber works http://qreene.xtn.net/-fibre/dyes.html
- The mannings Catalog http://the-mannings.com
- Carol Leigh's Fiber Studio http://www.hillcreek.com
- Louet Sales http://www.cybertap.com
- Mawia Handprings http://wvyw.mawia.com
- Misty Mountain Farm http://www.mistvmountainfarm.com
- La Lana Wools http://www.mistymountainfarm.com
- The Spinnery http://www.thespinnery.com
- Alps Industries http://www.alpind.com
- Alexandria Textiles http://www.alextex.com
- Earth Guild http://www.earthguild.com

CONCLUSION

Azo dyes may cause allergic reactions, twenty-two of the degradation products - called aromatic amines are carcinogenic. Their degradation products may be toxic to aquatic animals and plants and can accumulate in soil and sediments. Azo dyes are probably released into the environment, particularly into water and soil, for example, be discharged into water metalation to the production of azo pigments or when the dyes are used in production. About 1,200 tonnes of dyes are placed in landfills each year.

Pigments and certain dyes can accumulate in soil and in water sediments, partly because the substances have very strong binding properties and partly because they will only degrade in environments v.'hich are deficient in oxygen. Degradation products may also accumulate in the environment if they are not released in an environment rich in oxygen.

Azo dyes may accumulate in living organisms. There may be several reasons for this, one reason being that the dyes consist of large molecules and are difficult to dissolve in water. As a result, the degradation products of azo dyes accumulate.

In this scenario, the only ecologically safe option available to mankind is the use of 'Biodegradable Natural dyes'.

REFERENCES

Natural Dyes and their Application to Textiles, edited by M.L. Gulrajani and Deepti Gupta, (IIT, Delhi), 1992.

M.L. Gulrajani, *Proceedings of Convention on Natural Dyes*, IIT, Delhi, December 9-11, 1999.

M.L. Guirajani, *Proceedings of Convention on Natural Dyes;* IIT, Delhi, December 17-18, 2001.

Proceedings of Conference on *'Natural Dyes-Contemporary Perspective*, Lady Irwin College, Delhi, December 13, 2003.

B.C. Mohanty, K.V. Chandramouli and H.D. Naik, *'Natural Dyeing Processes of India*, '1987, published by Calico Museum of Texitiles, *India*.

Trotman, E.R., *Dyeing and Chemical Technology of Textile Fibres* 6th edition, B.I. Publications Pvt. Ltd., New Delhi, 1994.

The Wealth of India, Raw materials, CSIR, 1990.

Gahlot, M. and Kaur S. (1996) *Rebirth of Natural dyes; Eco-friendly Textiles.* The Indian Textile Journal, 106(2) pages, 46-48.

Gupta D., *Natural Dyes and their application on Textiles.*, ed., Gulrajani, M.L., and Gupta D. Department of Textile Technology, IIT, Delhi.

'The Useful Plants of India'. Publication & Information Directorate, CSIR, New Delhi.

R.S. Prayag, '*Vegetable Dyes*', Journal of Indian Institute of Handloom Technology, Alumini Association, 2000.

The Merck Index, *'An Encyclopedia of Chemicals, drugs and biologicals,* 12th edition, Merck Research Laboratories, Whitehouse Station, New Jersey, 1996.

CHAPTER

15

WILDLIFE CONSERVATION AND MANAGEMENT

PUSP KUMAR, IFS (Retd.)

Wildlife

To the common man the term 'wildlife' means the wild undomesticated annuals living in their natural habitats such as a forests, deserts, grasslands etc.

Wesbsites Dictionary defines wildlife as being tungs that are neither human nor down domesticated but which are specially mammals, birds and fish united. However, a report entitled 'Wildlife conservation in India' (1970) by the India Board for wildlife defines wildlife as the entire native uncultivated flora and fauna of the country. The wildlife (protection) Act, 1972, also defines wildlife as any animals, bees, butterflies etc. including aquatic and land vegetation which form part of any habitat. However, an ecologist includes both, the naturally occuring animals (fauna) as well as plants (flora) in wildlife.

Thus a comprehensive definition of wildlife may be given as any or all cultivated and non-domesticated life including both, plants and animals.

Importance of Wildlife

The wildlife resources provide acstheic, reactional and economic benefits and at the same time are ecologically important. In nature, flora and fauna go hand-in-hand and one cannot exist without the other. Birds and insects are necessary for the cross pollination of flower and these with other animals also serve for dispersal and propogation of vegetation. Not only this, the health of vegetation are also depends on natural browsing and grazing. One can mention that animals directly depend on green plants for their food. Food plants are also provide shelter to a variety of animal species. Early important are the relation among animal population. If many herbivous are killed, the predation, deprived of their natural food, will leave forest and prey upon domestic live-stock or even man. On the other hand if too many carnivores are killed, the herbivores *because of release of* predation pressure with become too numerous and acquire the status of pest for agricultural crops.

Thus most important is the balance of nature for which wildlife in an integral and important part.

Wildlife of India

The wildlife *i.e.*, the flora and the fauna are mentioned according to the ecological sub-divisions of India, India is divided into three ecological sub-regions.

1. The Himalayan mountain system : There are altitudinal as well as East-West variation in this region. There are three district sub zones, each with its characteristics flora and fauna.

(*a*) **Himalayan foothills :** These extend form eastern frontiers of Kashmir to Assam.

(*b*) **The Western Himalayas :** It includes the higher altitudes in Himalayas from Kashmir including *Ladakh to Kumaon.*

(*c*) **The Eastern Himalayas :** It includes regions of Sikkim and extends to the east upto Nepal.

2. Peninsular-Indian sub region : This is the *raised* plateau land of the Deccan extending upto the flood plains of the Indo-Gargetic basin westwards into the Great Thar desert of Rajasthan *Tropical Evergreen forests or Indo-Malayan forests sub-region*. This is the region of heavy rainfall. It comprises of the north-eastern India and the Western Ghats in South including Malabar Coast.

Himalayan Mountain System

Wildlife is typical of both the oriental and *paleoarctic* regions. Altitude affects the wildlife distribution. Besides, altitude, east-west variation also occur due to decrease in monsoon rainfall towards the west. The west Himalayas have low rainfall, heavy snowfall, whereas in east Himalayas there is heavy rainfall, snowfall only at very high altitudes, and at lower altitudes conditions are like tropical rain forests. Flora and fauna of both the Himalayas are different.

1. Himalayan foot-hills : These have characteristics bhanbar and tarai formation and the siwalik ranges in the South.

Flora : Natural monsoon evergreen, and semi-evergreen forests, dominant species are sal, silk, cotton trees, giant bamboos, tall greasy meadow with *Savannahs* in tarai.

Fauna : Big mammals of North India like elephants, **sambar**, swamp deer, cheetal, long deer, barking deer, mil boar, tigers, panther, wild dogs, hydena, black bear, sloth bears porcupine, Great Indian one houred rhinoceras, wild buffaloes, Gangetic glavial, golden longur are present.

2. Western Himalays : (Highests Altitude Region) Flora : Coniferous pine forests, Rhododendnons, dwarf hill bamboo and bird forests mixed with alpine pastures.

Fauna : Wild assess, wild goats (*thar, marbhor, ibex*) and sheep (Nayan, blue sheep), antelopes (China and Tibettan gazelle), deer (hangul or Kashmir stag), smaller mammals like marmots and pikas, golden eagles, snow cocks, snow patriages, snow leapords, wolfs, wixen, cats, back and brown bear, birds like Himalayan monal pleasant, western Erogopean Griffox vultures, lammergiers, choughs.

The Eastern Himalayas

Flora : Oaks, magnolias, larvels and birches covered with moss and ferns, coniferous forest of pine, fir, yew and jumpes with made growth of sumbly epiphytes dominant (due to higher humidity and high rainfall).

Fauna : Red panta, hog bodger, fenet badge crestless psorsepines, goat, antelopes (Seroni, Goral, Talins).

II. The Peninsular-Indian Sub-Region

This is the real time house of Indian wildlife. It has two zones (*i*) Pensular India and its extension into the drainage basin of Ganges river system, and (*ii*) The desert region of Rajasthan-the Thar of Indian desert region.

1. The Peninsular India : It is the house of tropical *deciduous to tropical dry deciduous and sub* vegetation depending upon the variation in rainfall and humidity.

Flora : Sal in north and east extensions (higher rainfall), and teak in southern plateau are dominant trees. Western Ghats have evergreen vegetation (flora and fauna similar to evergreen rainforests of northeastern India). In dry areas of Rajasthan desert and Aravalli hills, trees are scattered and thorny scrubs species predominate. The forests give way to more open savannah habit.

Fauna : Elephants, wild bear, deers (hog, deer, swamp deer, sambar, muntjak deer, antelopes (four-horned antelope, nilgai, black buck, chinkara gazelle), wild dog, tiger, leopard, cheetah, lion, wild pig, monkey, striped hyaena, jackal, gaur (a bull).

2. Indian desert : That desert of Rajasthan has unqiue flora and fauna.

Flora : Thorny trees with reduced leaves, reacti, other succelents are the main plants.

Fauna : Animals are mostly barrowing ones. Among mammals, rodents are the largest group. The Indian desert gerbils are mouse like rodents. Other animals are wild ass, desert cat, black buck, desert cat, repteles (snakes, lizards and tortoise). Agamids, lacertids and geckos include the desert lizards. Among birds is the Great Indian bustard.

III. Tropical Rain Forest Region

Flora : Extensive grassy stands interspread with densely forested garges of evergreen vegetation known as sholas occur in the Nilgiris. Sholas also occur in Annamalai and Palni hills. The rain forests of the Western ghats brave dense and lofty trees having large variety in species diversity. The diverse habitat consist of the mosses, ferns, epiphytes, orchids etc. The predominate type in these forests is the Dipterocarpus species. Different varities of tropical orchids are also found. Stratification in rain forests is key district. Three horizontal layers are destinguished. The lower slopel has seedlings of palms, vardaman and ginger.

Fauna : It is very rich with all kinds of animals. There are wild elephants, gaur and other larger animals. Most species are tree dwellers. The most common are horlock gibbon, golden larger, capped langur, Assam macaque and the pig tailed macaque, bats, gaint squirrels. Nilgiri-langur, mongoose, spiny mouse, flying squirrels.

1. Andaman-Nicobar Islands

Flora : These are home of tropical rain forests. Gaint Dipterocarpus, Terminatian and Larger-straemia are dominant. There are mangroves on coastal areas.

Fauna : Mammals of (about 35) species, a numer of reptiles and marine animals occur in this area. Among mammals are the bats and rats (3/4th of the total mammals on islands), Andaman pig, deers (barking deer, sambar, spotted deer, hog deer), palm civet. Among marine mammals there are dugongs, dolphin, false killer whale. Among birds (about 250 sp. and sub species) are rare warcardum hornbill, Nicobar pigeon and megapode. There are also other birds like white-bellied sea eagle, white-brkasted surftlet and several fruit pigeons.

These are also salt water crocodiles, a number of marine turtles, coconut crab, lizards (the largest being water monitor), 40 species of snakes, including cobra, viper, viral and sea snakes, pythons.

2. Mangrove Swaps of Sunderbans : Sunderbans are delta regimes of the Ganges, where both the Brahmaputra and Ganges join and drain into the Bay of Bengal.

Flora : The lower tidal zones have pioneer trees like Sonneratia and Avicennia. Above this zone (middle level), there are philophora, Bungunia and Excaecaria - Cereaps forests (covering nearly 70% of the mangrove forests). Above this level (high land level), there are supporting forests of Phoenix, pure of in association with Excaecaria. There are Heriteria forests in the highest portion with thick undergrowth of Phonix and Neepa palms.

Fauna : Fish (mud skippers or semi-terrestinal Gobies), small crabs, (land crabs, fiddler crabs), and the Dorippe, the one that has unusual association with sea anemones. Other animals are weaver ants. In the higher regions of mangroves, there are spotted deer, pigs, monitor lizards, monkeys etc. The most interesting animals is the man eater Sunderbans tiger.

ABUSE AND DEPLETION OF WILDLIFE

We curve across the headless in newspapers like 'dragon downfall' in rhino population, save golden langur Tragedy which strikes the sea turtles, '1st of the blue whales', 'Great Indian bustard on the road of extinction ... etc. levels the sad story of abuse and depletion of on wildlife heritage.

According to the statistics in last 2002 years the world has lost, by way of extension about 160 species of mammals and 88 species of birds.

India is endowed with rich biological heritage. Her various varieties and epics are full of and beautiful account in wildlife. Over 500 mammalian and 1,200 avian species contribute to the rich of the wealth. Unfortuantely, today, the Indian wildlife as that in many other parts of the world, is threatened because of main unprecedented intervention with nature. Nearly 134 plant species have been declared threatened as against 71, 45 and 15 species of mammals, birds and reptiles respectively. (Khosboo, 1984). For example the Great Indian bastard, Charitias migiceps which is confined to the semi-acid region of Rajasthan and Gujarat, and the white-minded wood duck, Cairina scutalata inhabiting the Brahmaputra, swamps and the flood plains of Assam are both on the brink of extinction.

REASONS FOR DEPLETION OF WILDLIFE

Man is his zeal for progress facts to realize that his own existence is being jeeparadized "progress", as he says, has made him contaminate air and pollute streams, lakes and occeans, chain swamps and wetlands, burning the water table, rape prairies and forests, spray pesticides over water and land, kill animals excessively for immediate profit or on false assumptions that they are noxious or for fashionable "spot". Man above of ten in combination with his live stock, is destroying the natural environment.

"Linlization", as we apply the term, is not just cities, industrial development, hills of highways, enormous airfields and nervous other technological convencies. By destroying wildlife for civilization and culture, we are only nagating the meaning of the words.

If he does have to charge habits, then he must be able to manage them properly in order to maintain a rich and varied wildlife. Man has to think of the dangerous trap he a setting up for himself by human overpopulation.

In short, we can say that the basic reasons of extinction of wildlife are :

(*a*) Destriction of them natural habits due to expanding agriculture, urbanisation and industrialisation.

(*b*) Overgrazing by domestic animals that convert the area into deserts.

(*c*) Packing for meat, skin, fur, ivory Rhino horns etc.

(*d*) Export of some species.

So, it is man's ability to think that formulated idea of conservation. Conservation is applied ecology and also may be regarded as bioeconomy. In other words, conservation is defined as sound preservation, managment and sensible use of the available renewable natural resources.

CLASSIFICATION OF SCARCE WILDLIFE

There are three major categories of wildlife that are facing extention.

(*a*) Endangered species : They face the most severe threat of extinction and require direct human protection for survival.

(*b*) Threatened species : They are abundant in certain areas but are facing serious dangers nevertheless. Dangers being carried due to unfavourable environmental conditions, extensive hunting, fishing, trapping or even collecting by hobbyists.

Table 15.1. Indian Endangered Flora

Himalayas and Eastern India

1. *Abies delavayi* (Pinaceae)
2. *Acanthephippium sylhetense* (Orchidaceae)

3. *Aconitum deinorrhzum* (Ranunculaceae)
4. *Adinandra griffithii* (Theaceae)
5. *Aglaia perviridis* (Meliaceae)
6. *Amblyanthus multiflorus* (Myrsinanceae)
7. *Anacolosa ilicoides* (Oleaceae)
8. *Anocciolchilus sikkimensis* (Orchidaceae)
9. *Angiopteris erecta* (Angiopteridaceae)
10. *Aphyllorchis montana* (Orchidaceae)
11. *Arachnanthe cathcartii* (Orchidaceae)
12. *A. clarkei* (Orchidaceae)
13. *Artenisia amygdolina* (Asteraceae)
14. *Arundia grammifolia* (Orchidaceae)
15. *Astrogalus strobiliferus* (Papilionaceae)
16. *Atropa acuminata* (Solanaceae)
17. *Balanophora dioica* (Balanophoraceae)
18. *Botrychium virginianum* (Ophioglossaceae)
19. *Brainae insignis* (Blechnaceae)
20. *Camellia caduca* (Theaceae)
21. *Catamixis baccharoides* (Asteraceae)
22. *Colchicum luteum* (Liliaceae)
23. *Captis teeta* (Ranunculaceae)
24. *Cyathea gigantea* (Cyatheaceae)
25. *Cymbidium macrorhizon* (Orchidaceae)
26. *Cypripedium cordigerum* (Orchidaceae)
27. *C. elegans* (Orchidaceae)
28. *C. himalacicum* (Orchidacessae)
29. *C. macranthon* (Orchidaceae)
30. *Dendrobium densiflorum* (Orchidaceae)
31. *Dianthus coschernircus* (Caryophyllaceae)
32. *Didiciea cunningnamii* (Orchidaceae)
33. *Dioscorea deltoidea* (Dioscoreaceae)
34. *Dipteris wallichii* (Dipteridaceae)
35. *Dischidia benghalensis* (Asclepiadaceae)
36. *D. raflesiana* (Asclepiadaceae)
37. *Drosera indica* (Droseraceae)

38. *D. burnanni* (Droseraceae)
39. *Dlaeocarpus prunifolius* (Elaceocarpaceae)
40. *Eremostachys superba* (Lamiaceae)
41. *Eria crassicaullis* (Orchidaceae)
42. *Galcola lindleyana* (Orchidaceae)
43. *Gastrodia exilis* (Orchidaceae)
44. IGentiana kurroo (Gentianaceae)
45. *Hedysarum cachemirianim* (Papilionaceae)
46. *Helminthostachys zeylanica* (Helminthostachyaceae)
47. *Helwingia himalaica* (Helwing inaceae)
48. *Ilex embelioides* (Aquifoliaceae)
49. *Iodes hookeriana* (Leacinaceae)
50. *Lavatera kashmiriana* (Malvaceae)
51. *Lespedeza elegans* (Papilionaceae)
52. *Loropetalwn chinese* (Hamamelidaceae)
53. *Magnolia grifithii* (Magnoliaceae)
54. *M. gustavi* (Magnoliaceae)
55. *Mpterooarpa* (Magnoliaceae)
56.
57. *Nardostachys grandiflora* (Valerianaceae)
58. *Nepenthes Khasiana* (Nepenthaceae)
59. *Olax nana* (olaceae)
60. *Omnosia glauca* (Papilionaceae)
61. *Osmunda regalis* (Osmundaceae)
62. *Par hiopedilum druryi* (Orchidaceae)
63. *P. fairleanum* (Orchidaceae)
64. *P. hirsutissimum* (Orchidaceae)
65. *P. insigne* (Orchidaceae)
66. *P. spicerianum* (Orchidaceae)
67. *P. venustum* (Orchidaceae)
68. *P. villosum* (Orchidaceae)
69. *P. villostachys bambusoides* (Poaceae)
70. *Picea brachyrla* (Pinaceae)
71. *Platycerum wallichii* (Polypodiaceae)
72. *Pleione humilis* (Orchidaceae)

73. *Podophyllum hexandrum* (Podophyllaceae)
74. *Populus gamblei* (Salixaceae)
75. *Potameia paradoxa* (Lauraceae)
76. *Psilotum nudum* (Psilotaceae)
77. *Rauvolfia serperutina* (Apocynaceae)
78. *Renanthera inschootiana* (Orchidaceae)
79. *Rheum nobile* (Polygonaceae)
80. *Rhododendron arizelum* (Ericaceae)
81. *R. dalhousiae* (Ericaceae)
82. *R. edgeworthii* (Ericaceae)
83. *R. nivale* (Ericaceae)
84. *R. nutallii* (Ericaceae)
85. *R. Santapaui* (Ericaceae)
86. *R. stenaulum* (Ericaceae)
87. *Rhus hookeri* (Anacardiaceae)
88. *Sapria himalayana* (Rafflesiaceae)
89. *Saussurea bracteata* (Asteraceae)
90. *S. gnaphalodes* (Asteraceae)
91. *S. lappa* (Asteraceae)
92. *Schizaea digitata* (Schizaeaceae)
93. *Tetracentron sinense var himalense* (Tetracentraceae)
94. *Thylacospermum rupifragrum* (Caryophyllaceae)
95. *Vanda coerulea* (Orchidaceae)
96. *V. purmila* (Orchidaceae)
97. *Vanilla pilifera* (Orchidaceae)
98. *Viola falconeri* (Violaceae)
99. *Zanthoxylum scandens* (Rutaceae)

Rajasthan and Gujarat

100. *Commiphora wightii* (Burseraceae)
101. *Helichrysum Cutchicum* (Asteraceae)
102. *Hyphaene dichotoma* (Arecaceae)
103. *Meconopsis betonicifolia* (Papaveraceae)

Gangetic plain

104. *Aldrovanda vesiculosa* (Droseraceae)

Peninsular India

105. *Anemia tomentosa* (Schizaeaceae)
106. *Apama barberi* (Aristolochiaceae)
107. *Bentinkia condapanna* (Arecaceae)
108. *Ceropegia fantastica* (Asclepiadaceae)
109. *Cycas beddomei* (Cycadaceae)
110. *Dioscorea wightii* (Dioscoreaceae)
111. *Entada pursaetha* (Mimosaceae)
112. *Frerea indica* (Asclepiadaceae)
113. *Gnetum ula* (Gnetaceae)
114. *Hoya wightii* (Ascleoiadaceae)
115. *Lilium neilgherrense* (Lobeliaceae)
116. *Lobelia nicotianaefolia* (lobeliaceae)
117. *Loeseneriella bourdillonii* (Hippocrateaceae)
118. *Manisurius devergens* (Poaceae)
119. *Piper barberi* (Piperaceae)
120. *Podocarpus wallichianus* (Podocarpaceae)
121. *Pterocarpus santalinus* (Papilionaceae)
122. *Pterospermum obtusifolium* (Sterculiaceae)
123. *Santalum album* (Santalaceae)

Andaman and Nicobar Islands

124. *Ailanthus kurzii* (Simaroubaceae)
125. *Canarium mannii* (Burseraceae)
126. *Dipterocarpus kerrii* (Dipterocarpaceae)
127. *Hippocratea nicobarica* (Hippocrateaceae)
128. *Lagerstroemia hypoleuca* (lythraceae)
129. *Myristica andamanica* (Myristicaceae)
130. *Ophioglossum pendulum* (Ophioglossaceae)
131. *Podocarpus neriifolius* (Podocarpaceae)
132. *Psilotum complantum* (Psilotaceae)
133. *Symplocos odoratissima* (Symplocaceae)
134. *Uvaria nicobarica* (Annonaceae)

Table 15.2. List of Endangered Fauna (1986)

Order	Family Name	Zoological Name	Common Name	Status	Habitat
Primates	Cercopithecidae	Macaca	Lion	E	Southern
	Class	Silenus	tailed		Western
	Mammalia		Macaque		Ghats
Lagomorpha	Leporidae	Caprolagus	Hispid	E	Assam
		hispidus	Hare		
Catacea	Platanistidae	Platanista	Indus	E	India
Carnivora	Viverridae	India	Dolphin	E	Southern
		Viverra	Malabar		Western
		Megaspila	spotted		Ghats
		Civetina	civet		
	Felidae	Pantheraleo	Asiatica	E	Gir
		Persica	Lion		Forest
		Panthera	Tiger	E	India
		Tigris			
		Penthera	Snow	E	Himalayas
		uncia	leopard		
Probascidae	Elephantidae	Elephas	Asiatic	E	South
Periossodactyla	Equidae	maximum	elephant	NE	India
		Equus	Indian	E	Gujarat
		henionus	wild ass		
		khur			
	Rhinoceridae	Rhinoceros	Great	E	Assam
		unicornis	Indian		North
			Rhino		Bengal
Artidocatyla	Suidae	Sus	Pygmy	E	NE India
		Sulvanius	hog		
	Cervidae	Cervus	Hungal	E	Terai
		duvaucelli			Kashmir
		Cervus	Swamp	E	Central
		elaphus			
		hungal	deer		India
		Cervus	Manipur	E	Manipur
		eldi eldi	deer		
	Bovidae	Bubalis	Wild	E	Assam
		bubalis	asiatic		Bastar
			water		
			buffalo		
Galliformes	Phasianidea	Tragopan	Cobot's	E	NE India
		caboti	Tragopan		
		Tragopan	Western	E	Western
		malano	Tragopan		Himalayas
		cephalus			

Order	Family Name	Zoological Name	Common Name	Status	Habitat
Gruiformass	Otidadae	Ardeotis nigricepe	Great Indian Bustard	E	Rajasthan MP
	Class Reptilia				
Testudines	Crocodylidae	Corcodylus Porosus	Estuarine crocodile	E	East coast
	Garialidae	Garialis	Gharial gangetius	E	N Indian river
	Class Insecta				
Anoplura	Haematopinidae	Haematopinus oliveri	Pygmy hog sucking louse	E	Assam

They have shall populations. They live in protected areas or environments and then numbers are not deceasing.

ENDANGERED FLORA AND FAUNA OF INDIA

I. Indian Endangered Flora

In India, nearly 450 plant species have been identified as endangered, threatened or rare. A list of some species in different parts of the country. (Table 15.1).

II. Indian Endangered Fauna

The IUCN maintains a Red List of endangered species. This list is updated annually. A 1986 list of some endangered species (Table 15.2).

IMPORTANCE OF WILDLIFE CONSERVATION

When we talk about the conservation of wildlife, a question arise in the mind, *i.e.*, why should we care about the disappearing annuals? The answer to this question can be answered with many reasons because of the following :

(*a*) Survival value : Every species play an important role in maintaining an ecological balance among the beco system of the earth. These systems must continue to function of life is to survive. Loss of many species threatens the survival of several species including man. The survival depends upon his willingness and ability to co-operate with the long environment Human beings term to nature and wildlife for spiritual, psychological, physical and cultural benefits.

(*b*) Scientific value : The study of wildlife provides valuable knowledge about life process which has helped scientists understand the functioning and behaviour of the human body. Scientists have also gained medical knowledge and discovered important medical products by studying wildlife. By studying the effects of environmental pollution on wildlife, it is possible to learn how pollution affects human life.

(*c*) Economic value : Wild species of animals provide meat for food and skin for form the financial value of wild species is the region of importance in the economics of many nations.

(*d*) Beauty : Wildlife includes a diversity of species that contributes in a special way to the beauty of the nature. Such beauty enriches life and increases the enjoyment of camping and outdoor recreation. On all continents, wildlife is becoming an increasingly important recreational asset and tourist attraction.

WILDLIFE MANAGEMENT

Concept of Wildlife Management

Wildlife management is a part of wildlife conservation.

Most wildlife management is directed towards birds and mammals. Fish management has also developed which is done quite separately. Amphibians, reptiles and plants have received little attention in wildlife management until the recently increased concern for endangered species.

Wildlife management is the art of making land produce valuable populations of wildlife. It is implied that this definition includes the control of post populations to limit negative value of wildlife. Wildlife management involves direct population management (control of harvest, transplanting etc.) and indirect management of populations through habitat manipulation to favour or inhibit target species.

The principle of wildlife management include some that are specific of the profession and many that are shared with other professions and sciences. Therefore, the education of a wildlife manager should include study not only of wildlife biology and management, but also of basic sciences, such as chemistry and meteorology, and applied sciences related to land use, such as forestry agriculture and economics. The Figure 15.3 below shows the principles of wildlife management.

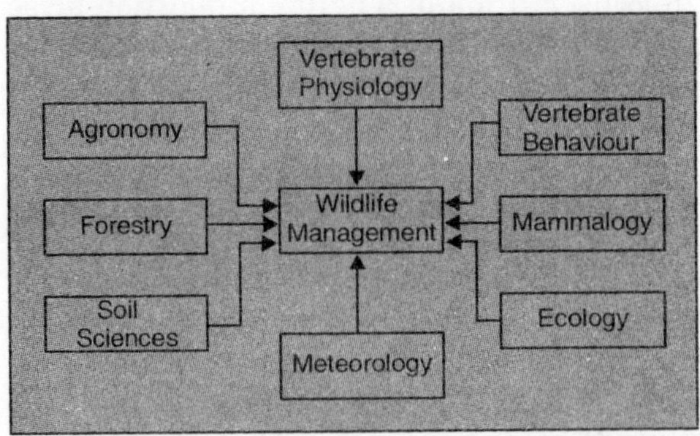

Fig. 15.3. Principles of Wildlife Management

Principles of wildlife management : Most wildlife managers participate in several activities in the conservation process because some of them efforts involve administration, education, law enforcement and research.

WILDLIFE MANAGEMENT PROCESS

For wildlife management purposes, it is useful to classify the numerous and complexly inter-related factors operating in ecosystem as welfare factors, determinating factors and environmental influences. Welfare factors, the habitat requirements of wildlife species, can be defined at several lands of resolutions. At the lowest level of resolution, (*i*) all species require oxygen, food, cover types, species needs, interperson and space with increasingly greater resolution, the habitat requirements of a species can be defined, (*ii*) emprically as a list of needed habitat types, (*iii*) as a list of specific welfare factors and (*iv*) a list of welfare factors components.

Suitable habitat must supply welfare factors for both serves and all age classes of animals during all seasons and weather conditions. Detecting limiting welfare factors is basic to efficient programmes of habitat management. Two methods for detecting limiting factors are :

1. Observing correlations between trends of welfare factors and trends in population performance and
2. Observing symptoms of welfare factors deficiencies in the animals and symptoms of welfare factors overcome in the habitat.

Wildlife habitats are not stable. Much change occuring in habitats is due to biotic succession, retrogession or to rather sudden natural or man-caused substances such as by fire, logging or flooding. These changes alter food, cover and other habit resources for all wildlife species and are fairly predictable. Much wildlife habitat management is, therefore, the management of succession, retrogression and disturbances.

Weather affects wildlife directly as a cause of mortality and indirectly by restricting animal movements and influencing the abundance and availabilities of habitat resources and the abudance of competetions, predators and disease organisms.

Wildlife management consists of controlling the number, distribution, and quality of wild animals, either directly as by manipulating wildlife habitat. Selecting a data basis for a management programme is one of the management biologists most important decisions. Selection will be influenced by the availability and precision of method for measuring population and habitat characteristics and by budget constraints but the selected data base should have a meaningful relation to management objectives.

The types of wildlife measurements are :

(*i*) population indices.

(*ii*) population censuses.

(*iii*) habitat measurements, and

(*iv*) indices of ecological density including population condition and habitat-condition indices.

Wildlife management is the art of making land produce population of wildlife, for honest or other values. In simplest terms, wildlife management consists of a series of decisions. Whether to have a long hunting season or a short one, whether to plant food patches and pine trees or to manipulate food and cover with fire or herbicides, whether to spend money on a gene-check station or on a forge survey, whether to compromise biologically optimum goals with prevailing public opinion, whether to improve existing habitat or to purchase more land, and whether to feed deer during severe winters or to reduce the deer herd or to improve the natural supply of winter foods. These decisions must be made every year.

An overall scheme for wildlife management process is as follows (Fig. 19.4).

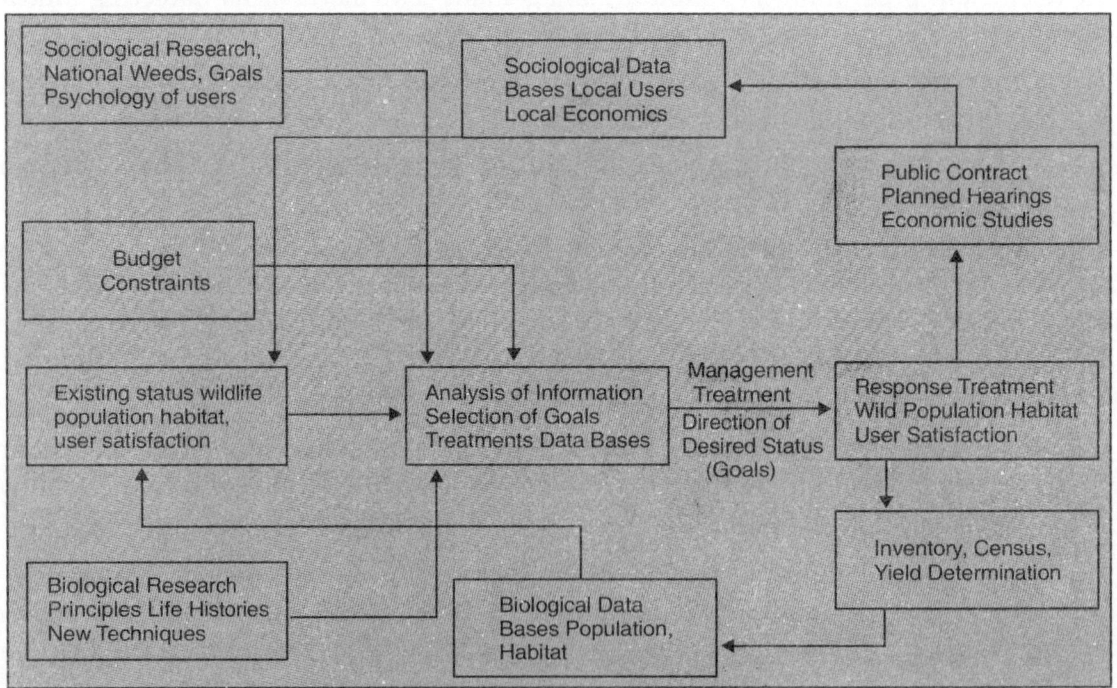

Fig. 15.4. Wildlife Management Process

Wildlife management and cyclic, inaemental process. (At each cycle, the information bases increase, permitting more intensive management. Management activities and responsibilities are mentioned within ellipses.

WILDLIFE CONSERVATION

Concept of Wildlife Conservation

Wildlife conservation is a social process encompassing both lay and professional activities that define and seek to attain wise use of wildlife resources and maintain the productivities of wildlife habitats. Wildlife managers, research biologists, administrators, extension agents and also mining company lobbigists, non-governmental clubs etc. participate in this process. The professional activities in wildlife conservation are research, education, administration, law enforcement and management Fig. 15.5.

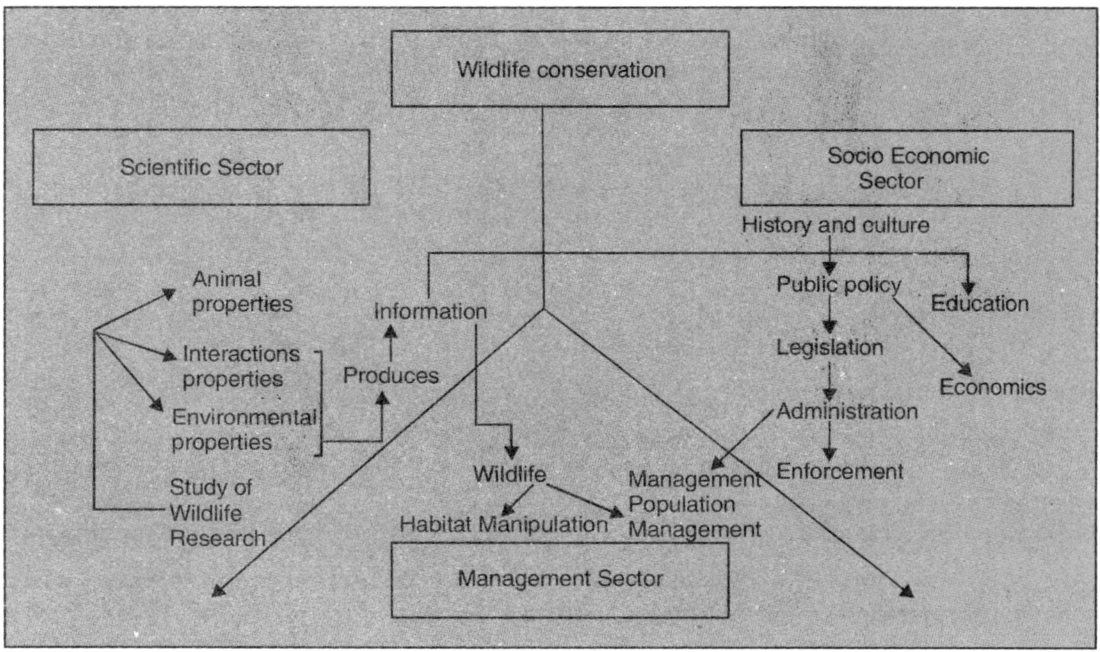

Fig. 15.5. Professional activities in the wildlife conservation process.

There are two modes of wildlife conservation process. There are named as :

I. In-situ conservation *i.e.*, on-site preservation.

II. Ex-situ conservation *i.e.*, experimental situation in monitored condition.

I. In-situ Conservation

In-situ conservation of wildlife is a comprehensive system of protected areas. There are different categories of protected areas which are managed with different objectives for bringing benefits to the society. These include (*Source-IUCN, 1985*):

(*i*) Scientific reserve (*ii*) National Park (*iii*) National Movement (*iv*) Managed nature reserve or wildlife sanctuary (*v*) Protected landscape (*vi*) Resource reserve (*vii*) Natural biotic area or Anthopological reserve (*viii*) Multiple use management area or managed resource.

Objectives of each of the above mentioned categories are as follows :

***(i)* Scientific Reserve :** Protect nature and maintain natural processes in an undisturbed state. Emphasise scientific study, environmental monitoring and education and maintenance of genetic resources in a dynamic and evolutionary state.

***(ii)* National Park :** Protect relatively large natinal and scenic areas of national or international significance for scientific, educational and recreational use.

***(iii)* National Movement :** Preserving nation's significant natural features and maintain their unqiue characteristics.

***(iv)* Wildlife Sanctuary :** Protect nationally significant species, groups of species, biotic communities or physical features of the environment when these require specific human manipulation for their perpetuation.

***(v)* Protected landscape :** Maintain nationally significant natural landscape characteristic of the harmonious interaction of people and land while providing oppotunities for public recreation and tourism within the normal lifestyle and economic activity of these areas.

***(vi)* Resource Reserve :** Protect natural resources for future use and present or contain development that could affect resources pending the establishment of managed objectives based on appropriate knowledge and planning.

***(vii)* Natural Biotic area :** Allow societies to live in harmony with the environment, undisturbed by modern technology.

***(viii)* Managed Resource :** Sustain production of water, wildlife, timber, pasture and outdoor recreation. Conservation of nature oriented to supporting economic activities (although specific zones) can also be designed within these areas to achieve specific conservation objectives.

In India, nearly 67 National parks, 394 Wildlife sanctuaries and 35 Zoological gardens have been established for wildlife management.

The different National Parks and Sanctuaries in India are as follows (Table 15.3).

Table 15.3. National parks and Sanctuaries in India

Name and District	Areas sq. km.	Species found	Good visting time
Andhra Pradesh			
Pakhal, Warangal	860	Tiger, Panther, sambar chital, nilgai.	Dec-March
Tadwai, Warangal	803	Tiger, Panther, gaur, jungle cat sambar, black buck.	Dec-March
Pocharam, Medak	129-5	Panther, chital, chinkara pea fowl and water bird.	Dec-March
Kawal, Adilabad	616	Tiger, panther, gaur, sambar, chital, black buck, wild bear, sloth bear.	Dec-March
Kolleru Pelicanary Elleru	673	Pelicans, flamingo, heron, painted storks, avocet, teals and terns.	Dec-March
Melapattu Bird Sanctuary Nellore	16	Gray pelican, heron, cormorants, teals, duck etc.	Dec-March
Kinnersani, khammam	635.40	Tiger, panther, wolf, chital, sambar, nilgai, sloth bear, gaur.	Dec-March
Papikonda, E. Godavari, W. Godavari, Khammam	591.00	Tiger, panther, wild dog hyena, jackals wolves, gaur, four horned antelope, chital, sambar and nilgai.	Nov-Jun
Coringa, E. Godawari	235.00	Esturine crocodile, otter, fishing cat, jackal, seagull, pelican, stork, heron, flamingo	Oct-May
Nagarjunasagar, Srisailam, Guntur, Prakasam, Kurnool Mahabubanagar and Nalgonda	3568.00	Tiger, panther, sloth bear, wild boar, chital, sambar, nilgai, black buck, jackal, foxes, wolves and mugger crocodile.	Oc-Jun
Pulicat, Nellore	500.00	Flamingos, Pelicans ducks teals, stork, crune, heron.	Oct-March
Arunachal Pradesh			
Namdafa, Tirap	1807.82	Tiger, panther, snow leopard, clouded leopard, golden cat, binturang, wild buffalo, wild dog, gaur, Iranian bison, sambar, hod. Deer, barking deer, elephant, sloth bear, python, king cobra, Indian cobra, monitor, lizard and, birds of many kinds.	Nov-March
Pakkui, Kameng	861.95	Elephant, gaur, Indian, sambar, hog deer, barking deer, python	Nov-April

National Parks and Sanctuaries in India

Assam			
Garampani, Diphu	430.00	Elephant, wild buffalo, leopard, common langur, hoolock	Feb-May
Kaziranga National Park, Jorhat	430	Great Indian one-hroned rhinoceros, wild buffalo, elephant, gaur, leopard cat, wild boar, civet cat, otter, swamp deer, hog deer, sambar, tiger, python, pelican, partridge, floricans.	Feb-May
Lakhawa, Nawgong	70	Rhinoceros, wild buffalo, swamp deer, water ducks, cormorants	January
Manas, Barpeta (Tiger Sanctuary)	80	Elephant, tiger, panther, gaur, wild buffalo great Indian one horner rhinoceros, goldern langur, civet cat, otter, swamp deer, hog deer, sambar, pigmy hog, water monitor, wild boar, great pied hornbill, florican.	
Sonai-Rupa, Tezpur	195	The great Indian one-horned rhinoceros, elephant, wild buffalo, sloth bear, wild dog, wild boar, sambar, barking deer, swamp deer, leopard, tiger hornbill, imperial pigeon etc.	February
Bihar			
Hazaribagh	186.25	Tiger, leopard, sambar, chital, nilgai, wild boar, wild cat, peafowl etc.	Oct-June
Bhimbandh, Mongyr	681.90	Tiger, leopard, sambar, chital, wild boar, wolf, water birds.	Oct-June
Mahudaur, Daltongung	63.25	Tiger, leopard, wolf, chital, barking deer, wild boar etc.	Nov-June
Dalma, Singhbhum	193.22	Elephant, leopard, wild boar, mouse-deer, barking deer, sloth bear.	Oct-June
Palamau, Daltongung	979.27	Elephant, panther, leopard, wild boar, barking deer, gaur, chital, sambar, peal-fowl etc.	Whole year
Gautam Budha, Gaya	259.50	Tiger, leopard, sambar, chital, baring deer, pea-fowl etc.	Oct-June
Kaimur, Rohtas	1342.22	Tiger, leopard, chinkara, sambar, nilgai and crocodiles.	Oct-June
Bamiaburu, Singhbhum	129.50	Tiger, panther, sambar, elephant, wild boar etc.	Oct-June
Kodaram, Hazaribagh	176.12	Tiger, leopard, sloth bear, sambar, chital, four-horned antelope.	Oct-June

National Parks and Sanctuaries in India

Goa, Daman and Diu			
Mollem, Goa	240	Gaur, sambar, mouse deer, barking deer, panther, flying squirrel, porcupine, civet, cats, ant-eaters, slender loris, grey jungle fowl.	Nov-May
Gujarat			
Gir National Park	140.40	Asiatic lion, panther, stripped hyena, sambar, nilgai, chital, four-horned anatelope, chinkara, wild boar, crocodiles	Dec-June
Valavadar National Park, Bhavanagar	17.83	Black buck, wolf.	Oct-June
Gir, Janagarh	1412.13	Asiatic lion, panther, stripped hyena, sambar, nilgai, chital, four-horned antelope, chinkara, wild boar, crocodiles.	Dec-June
Nal Sarovar Bird Sanctuary, Ahmedabad	115.00	Water Birds	Nov-Feb
Wild Ass Sanctuary Little, Rann of Kutch	4840.89	Wild ass, nilgai, wolf, chinkara,	Jan-June
Surendranagar, Purna, Dags	299.43	Tiger, panther, leopard cat, jungle cat, jackal, fox, four horned antelope, wild pig, chital, sambar, bonnet macaque.	Jan-June
Haryana			
Sultanpur Lake Birds Sanctuary, Gurgaon	1.2	Sarus crane, spot-bills, ruddy shel drakes etc.	Oct-March
Jammu and Kashmir			
Dachigam, Srinagar	55sq. miles	Leopard, black, bear, brown bear, babcons, serow, musk deer, hangul.	Apr-Nov
Raj Parian Anantnag	20.50	Brown bear, musk deer, serow, hangul.	Apr-Nov
Himachal Pradesh			
Rohia National Park, Kulu	178.8	Idex, musk deer, goral, serow, lynx, Himalayan brown bear, snow leopard, tragophan, snow pigeon, snow cock etc.	Apr-June
Tundah, Chamba	64.2	Goral, brown bear, black bear, musk dear, goral, serow, ibex, monal, tragopan, snow cock, Kalij, chakor and chir, snow leopard, panther, weasel, martens, civets fox, flying, fox.	Apr-June Sep-Oct

National Parks and Sanctuaries in India

Kugti, Chamba	118.3	Goral, brown bear, black bear, musk deer, goral, serow, ibex, monal, tragopan, snow cock, kalij, chakor, chir, snow leopard, panther, weasel, martens, civets, fox, flying, fox.	Apr-June Sep-Oct
Nargu and Whinch, Mandi	278.4	Goral, black bear, serow, musk deer, monal, kalij, koklash and chir, panther, snow leopard, martens, civet fox, flying fox.	Apr-June Dec-Jan
Shikari Devi, Mandi	213.5	Black bear, goral Dec-Jan barking deer, serow, Apr-June musk deer, monal, kalij, chir, chakor, partridge, panther, snow leopard, martens, civet, fox, flying fox.	
Govind Sagar, Lilaspur	100.4	Duck, teal goose, crane.	Whole year
Sri Naina Lilaspur	163.4	Sambar, barking deer, black bear, wild bear, nilgai, kalij, red jungle fowl, partridge, panther, snow leopard, martens, civet, fox, flying foxes.	Whole year
Derang Kinnaur	167.4	Goral, black bear, serow, monal, kalij, koklash, chakor, panther, civets, martens, flying foxes.	Apr-June Sep-Oct
Talra, Simla	72.2	Goral, black bear, sambar, musk deer, kalij, koklash, chakor, monal, panther, flying fox, civet, martens.	Apr-June Sep-Oct
Raksham and Chitkul	138.3	Bharat, goral, black bear, brown bear, monal, koklash, snow cock, chakor, panther, fox, martens, flying fox.	Apr-June Sep-Oct
Lipa Asrang Kinnaur	109.1	Ibex, bharal, goral, monal, koklash, snow cocks, chakor, panther, fox, martens, flying fox.	Apr-June Sept-Oct
Simbalbara, Sirmur	55.4	Sambar, goral, barking deer, wild boar, kalij, pea fowl, red jungle fowl partridge, panther, fox, martens civet, flying fox, chital and monal.	Whole year
Kanswar, Kulu	54.3	Tahr, serow, goral, black bear, kalij, koklash, chakor, partridges, chir, panther, civets, martens, flying fox.	Apr-June Sep-Oct
Karnataka			
Bandipur National Park, Mysore, (Tiger Sanctuary)	874.20	Indian elephant, tiger, samabr, chital, barking deer, wild dog, wild boar jackal, sloth bear, panther four-horned antelopes, malabar, squirrel jungle.	Mar-Aug.

National Parks and Sanctuaries in India

		fowl, partridge, green pigeon, bush quail etc.	
Bannarghatta National Park, Bangalore	104.30	Elephants, sloth bear, chital, barking deer, gray partridges, bush quail, jungle fowl, etc.	Whole year
Nagerhole National Park, Coorg	571.55	Elephant, tiger, panther, chital, samber, sloth bear, jungle fowl, partrige etc.	Oct-March
Someshwara South Kanara	844.8	Chital, gaur, sambar, panther, tiger, cloth bear, wild dog, etc.	Oct-March
Brahmagiri, Coorg	181.29	Tiger, panther, sambar, chital, barking deer, sloth bear, cobra, flying squirrel, malabar squirrel, civet cat, mouse deer.	Oct-March
Malkote, Mandya	40.82	Panther, wolf, sloth bear, black bucks, hare, cupines, wild boar.	Oct-March
Ghataprabha Bird Sanctuary, belgaum	29.785	Egret, cormorant, heron, etc.	Oct-March
Tungabhadra, Bellary	224.22	Black-buck, chinkara, panther, chital, pig, four-horned antelope, fox, sand grouse, florican great Indian bustard, sloth bear, sambar etc.	Oct-March
Ransbennur Black Buck Sanctuary, Dharwar	119.00	Black buck, chital, wolf, hare, great Indian bustard.	Whole year
Mukambika, South Kanara	247.00	Panther, sambar, elephant, wild boar, porcupine.	Whole year
Sharawathy Valley Shimoga	348.00	Indian elephant, tiger, panther, gaur, sambar, chital, barking deer, wild boar, sloth bear, four horned, antelope, partridges, green pigeon bush quail, lion, tailed monkey, tortoise, crocodile, python, cobra, krait, viper, green snake etc.	Feb-may
Biligiri Rangaswamy Mysore	324.4	Elephant, gaur, chital, barking deer, sambar, panther, sloth bear.	Feb-May
Bhadra, Chikmagalur	492.00	Gaur, elephant, panther, wild bear, sambar, chital, barking deer, sloth bear.	Jan-June
Shettimalli, Shimoga	395.60		Feb-May
Ranganthitto Bird Sanctuary, Mysore	26.70	Open hill stork, white ibis, little egret, cattle egret, darter, cormorant, pond heron, river, tern, spoon bill, crocodile etc.	July Aug
Dandeli, Dharwar	874.20	Tiger, panther, elephant, gaur, sloth bear, sambar, chital, wild bear etc.	Feb-May

National Parks and Sanctuaries in India

Kerala			
Eravikulam Rajmallay	97	Elephant, gaur, sambar, barking deer, tiger, panther, civet, jungle cat, nilgai, langur, wild boar, lion tailed macaque, malabar squirrel, wild dogs, nilgiri tiger, imperial pigeon, grey jungle fowl.	Oct-Apr
Periyar, Idukki	777	Elephant, tiger, panther wild dog, gaur, sloth, bear, nilgai, wild boar, sambar and barking deer.	Oct-Apr
Parambikulum Palghat	285	Elephant, gaur, leopard, tiger, sloth bear, nilgai, chital, sambar, wild boar, crocodiles.	Oct-Apr
Wyand, Cannanore and Kozhikode	844	Elephant, gaur, sambar, wild boar, chital, barking deer, etc.	Oct-Apr
Madhya Pradesh			
Kanha National Park Mandla and Balghat	940	Tiger, panther, gaur, barasingha, chital, sambar, black buck, chowsingha, barking deer, mouse deer, nilgai, wild dog, boar.	Mar-June
Bandhvgarh National Park, Shahdol	105	Tiger, panther, gaur, sambar, nilgai, chinkara, barking deer, bear, wild boar, and a variety of upland birds.	Nov-June
Shivpuri National Park, Shivpuri	156	Tiger, panther, sloth, bear, hyena, sambar, spotted deer, four horned antelope, black buck, nilgai, chinkara, wild boar, crocodiles etc.	Jan-June
Bori, Hoshangabad	802.89	Tiger, panther, bison, sambar, chital, nilgai, barking deer, chinkara, wild, boar, bear.	Jan-June
Kutri Wild Buffalloes Gane Sanctuary, Bastar	2273.58	Wild buffalo, tiger panther, sloth bear, nilgai, chital, sambar, wild pigs, barking deer, bison, wild dogs, chowsingha etc.	May-April
Tamor-pigle, Sorguja	608.52	Tiger, panther, gaur, chital, sambar etc.	Dec-March
Samrsot, Sorguja	430.361	Tiger, panther, gaur, chital, sambar etc.	Dec-March
Sitanadi, Raipur	1500	Tiger, panther, samber, chinkara, chital, bison, wild boar, barking deer, peacock etc.	Mar-June

National Parks and Sanctuaries in India

Nordehi, Sagar, Demoh and narsinghgart	1500	Tiger, panther, sambar, chinkara, chital, nilgai bear, etc.	Dec-March
Bagdara, Sidhi	478.900	Panther, black buck, chinkara, sambar, nilgai, wild pig etc.	Nov-June
Pachmarhi, Hoshangabad	654.49	Tiger, panther, bear, bison, spotted deer, sambar barking deer, nilgai, etc.	Mar-June
Achankmar, Bilaspur	551.52	Tiger, bison, sambar, chital, boar, peacock etc.	Nov-June
Ratapani, Raisen	530.36	Tiger, panther, sambar, chital, blue bull, chinkara etc.	Feb-June
Panch, Chindwara &Saoni	449.39	Tiger, panther, gaur, chital, sambar, nilgai etc.	Nov-June
Gandi Sagar, Mandsaur	224.65	Water birds, chital, sambar, chinkara, barking deer.	Nov-June
Maharashtra			
Todoba National Park	116.55	Tiger, panther, sloth bear, gaur, sambar, chital, nilgai, chinkara, jungle fowl and pea-fowl.	
Nawgaon National Park, Bhandara	133.884	Tiger, panther, sloth bear, gaur, sambar, chital, barking deer, nilgai, and migratory birds.	May
Borivli National Park Bombay Suburban	67.977	Panther, sambar, four horned antelope, mouse deer, wild boar, and langurs.	Jan-March
Melghat, Amraya (Tiger Sanctuary)	381.58	Tiger, panther, gaur, sloth, bear, sambar, barking deer, four horned antelope, wild boar, chital and plentiful birds.	Apr-May
Yawal, Jalgaon	177.52	Panther, jungle cat, nilgai, bonnet, Macque and common langur, wild dog, sambar, hyena, tiger, chital, and chinkara, pea-fowl, green pigeon, sand grouse and partridge, grey jungle fowl.	Apr-May
Radhanagri (Bison), Kolhapur	2072	Gaur, panther, sambar and wild boar. Bird life is fairly lavish.	May-Sep
Barnbala (Bird), Kolba	4.48	Ashy minivet, paradise fly-catchers, shama, malabar whistling thrush, racket tailed drongo, wood-pecker etc. Other life seen are the panther, four horned anthelope and common langur.	Jan-Apr
Tansa, Thane	216.75	Panther, four-horned antelope, chital, sambar, and wild boar. Bird population	May

National Parks and Sanctuaries in India

		is diverse and colourful around the Tansa lake.	
Manipur			
Reibul Lamjao National Park, Central	25	Brow antlered deer, wild goat and water birds.	
Meghalaya			
Balpakram Garo Hills	85	Elephant, gaur, chital, sambar, wild boar.	winter
Mizoram			
Dampa, Aizawl	180.00	Elephant, tiger, leopard, sambar, barking deer, Himalayan bear, wild boar, wild dog, wild-cat, gaur, leopard, cat, king cobra, python hornbill pheasant etc.	Nov-Feb
Nagaland			
Intangki, Kohima	202.00	Gaur, boar, elephant, barking deer, wild boar, clouded-leopard, panther, tiger, pangolin and various kinds of birds and reptiles.	Nov-March
Orissa			
Satkosia Gorge Dhenknal Puri, Cuttack and Phulbani	750	Gharial and muggar, tiger, leopard, jungle cat, civet, gaur, ratel, sloth bear, sambar, chital, nilgai, four horned antelope, elephants horbill, peafowl, jungle-fowl and other birds.	Summer and Winter
Bittar Kanika Cuttack	170	Salt-Water crocodile, leopard hyena, jungle cat, leopard cat, wild boar, chital, sambar, giant squirrel, water monitor, sea turtle, king cobra, python, painted stork, adjutant storks, openbilled stork, white ibis, black ibis etc.	Winter
Chilka, Ganjam and Puri	900	Black duck, chital, sea winter cow, carnes, ibis, cormorant, ergret, flamingo, and pelican.	Winter
Karlapat Kalahandi	145.	Tiger, leopard, gaur, chital, winter sambar etc.	Winter

National Parks and Sanctuaries in India

Tirunelveli Tiger Sanctuary	520	Tiger, chital, sambar, wild boar, liorn tailed macaque.	Sept-Nov
Kalakad, Tirunelveli	223.58	Lion-tailed macaque.	Whole year
Uttar Pradesh			
Corbett National Park, Nainital, Garhwal (Tiger Sanctuary)	525	Elephant, tiger, panther, sloth bear, nilgai, sambar, chital, wild boar, porcupine, peafowl, red Indian jungle fowl, partridge and both the species of Indian in land crocodiles, goral and fourhorned antelope.	Nov-May
Dudwa National Park, Lakhimpur, Kheri	500	Tiger, panther, sloth bear, sambar, swamp deer, chital, hog deer, barking deer, nilgai, peafowl and jungle fowl partridge etc.	Nov-May
Govind Pashu Vihar Uttar Kashi	953	Brown and black Himalayan bear, snow leopard, bharal, musk deer, tahr, serow, goral, panther, sambar, wild boar, monal pheasant, snow, pigeon, green pigeon.	Sept-Oct May-June
Nanda Devi Chamoli	324	-do-	
Rajaji, Sharanpur	247	Elephant, tiger, panther, sloth, bear, nilgai, sambar, chital, kakar, wild bear, porcupine, pea fowl, red Indian jungle fowl and partridges etc.	Nov-May
Kishanpur, Lakhimpur Kheri	227.12	Brown and black Himalayan bear, snow leopard, bharal, musk deer, tahr, serow, goral, panther, sambar, wild boar, pheasant snow pigeon, kokla, green pigeon, moals etc.	Nov-May
Kedarnath, Chamoli	957	-do-	Sep-Oct May-June
Chandraprabha, Varanasi (2nd home for Gir lions)	78	Tiger, panther, sambar, Indian gazelle, sloth bear, nilgai, pea fowl, partridges, sand grouse etc.	Sep-May
Katarniaghat, Bahraich	400	Tiger, panther, sambar, bear, chital, black buck.	Nov-May
Ranipur, Banda	230	Tiger, panther, wild cat, sambar, hyena, fox, jackal, chital, chinkara, black buck etc.	Nov-May
Chila, Garhwal	249	Tiger, panther, bear, elephant, chital, sambar nilgai etc.	Nov-May

National Parks and Sanctuaries in India

Ushakothi, Sambalpur	192	Elephant, gaur, tiger leopar, sambar, chital and barking deer.	Winter
Similipal, Mayurbhanj (Tiger Sanctuary)	303	Tiger, elephant, gaur, chital leopard, mouse deer, flying squirrel and mugger.	Winter
Punjab			
Abohar, Ferozepur	228	Black buck, hare, partridge, grey and black pigeon and doves.	Ist Oct. Ist March
Rajasthan			
Ranthambor Sawai-Madhopur (Tiger Sanctuary)	392.20	Tiger, panther, hyena, jungle cat, civet, sambar, chital, nilgai, bear, wild boar, partridge, geen pigeon, red spur fowl etc.	All year except July Aug-Sep
Sariska Alwar	195	Tiger, panther, hyena, jungle cat, civets, sambar, chinkara, nilgai, four horned antelope, patridge, green pigeon, red spur fowl.	All year except Jul Aug and Sept
Ghana Bird Sanctuary Bharatpur	29	Siberian crane cormorants storks, spoon bil, quails coot, heron, teal, terns etc. and sambar, chital, black duck, wild boar, civet etc.	1st Oct end of Feb
Darrah Kota	201	Tiger, panther, sambar, chital, nilgai, wild boar, hare, partridge, grouse.	All year July-Sept
Mount Abu, Sirohi	112.60	Sambar, nilgai, hare, jungle fowl partridges etc.	
Kumbhalgarh-Ranakpur Udaipur, Jodhpur distt.	500	Wild bear, sambar, panther, nilgai, wild boar, jungle fowl, red spur fowl.	
Sikkim			
Khangchandzenda National Park, Gangtok Himalayan	850	Snow leopard, clouded leopard, marbled cat, civet, binturone, Himalayan black bear, red panda, Tibetan wild ass, blue sheep serow, taking, musk deer, pheasant, partridge, green pigeon etc.	
Tamil Nadu			
Guindy National Park, Madras	2.8	Chital, black buck and a snake park.	Whole year
Mudumalai, the Nilgiris	321	Elephant, gaur, chital, sambar, tiger, panther, sloth, bear, wild dogs etc.	Feb-June
Amarmalai, Coimbatore	958	-do-	Feb-June

National Parks and Sanctuaries in India

West Bengal			
Lothian Island 24-Parganas	38.00	Wild pigs, chital, otter, estuarine crocodiles, gangetic dolphin, water birds etc.	Dec-Feb
Halliday Insland 24-Parganas	5.95	Royal Bengal Tiger chital, water birds etc.	Dec-Feb
Sajnakhali, 24-Parganas	362.40	Tiger, wild boar, chital, cormorant, openbill, storks, snake bird, white ibis, purple heron, grey heron, green bitter, pelican etc.	July-Dec
Gorumara Jalpaiguri	8.52	Rhino, elephant, gaur, tiger, sambar, hot sambar, hog deer, wild boar, varieties of birds.	Oct-Apr.
Jaldapara, Jalpaiguri	115.53	Rhino, elephant, tiger, leopard, wild boar, gaur, barking deer, hog deer, sambar and variety of birds.	Dec-May
Mahanadi, Darjeeling	127.22	Tiger, elephant, gaur, sambar, hog, wild boar, gibbons and a variety of birds.	Nov-April
Sunderbans, 24-Parganas	2585.00	Tiger, different species of deer, wild boar, estuarine crocodile gangetic dolphin.	Sep-May

Special Projects for Endangered Species

1. Project Tiger : There were about 40,000 Royal Bengal tigers in 1909-10. This number reduced to 2500 by the year 1982. As a result of the recommendations of a Task Force of the IBWL, this project was initialised as a Central Sector Scheme on 1st April 1973, with nine Tiger Reserves (Area, 13, 017 sq. km) located in different kinds of habitats in nine states. In 1982, two more and in 1983, four more and 1987, one were added to a total of 16 reserves. In 1988, 17th reserve was established in Tamil Nadu. 18th reserve was established in 1990 at Valmiki (Bihar) taking the total to 18 Tiger Reserves in the country in 13 states, covering an area of 28609 sq. km.

2. Gir Lion Project : The Gir forest in Saurashtra paninsula of Gujarat is an unique as the only surving habitat of the Asian lion. At present in whole of the Asia, this lion is found in Gir forest of Gujarat only. Clearing of forest for agriculture, cattle grazing and other factors led to the decline of the lion.

A five year plan scheme was prepared in 1972 by Govt. of Gujarat for this project. The total area of Gir Sanctuary in 1412.12 sq. km, in which the central core of about 140.40 sq. km was constituted as National Park in 1975. In 1978 an additional area of 118.13 sq. km was declared as National Park and ultimately the entire sanctuary was declared as a National Park.

As a result of this, there has been increase in lion population. 1968 there were 177 lions in the Gir whose number increased to 180 in 1974.

3. Crocodile Breading Project : The project arose from a proposal for development of a crocodile farming industry in India. Dr. H.R. Bustard, and FAO expert on crocodile breeding and management was invited as a consultant to the country in 1974. Based upon his advise, the project was initiated in 1975 in Orissa. The Gharial eggs were hatched for the first time in captivity at Tikerpada, Distt. Dhenkanal, Orissa. A small batch was also hatched at kurkrait, near Lucknow the same year. Crocodile husbandary work was undertaken with a view to sanctuary development. 11 Sanctuaries have been declared under the project, two of which among the largest sanctuaries in the country (Krishna Sanctuary, A.P. 3,600 sq. km and Chambal Sanctuary a tri-state sanctuary in U.P., M.P. and Rajasthan, 5,4.00 sq. km.). By 1981, more than 1000 crocodiles raised in captivity from eggs hatched by the project have been released in nature.

Gharial rehabilitation began in 1977 with the release of 26 crocodiles in Mahanandi river, Orissa. By 1980, 107 animals had been released in the river where wild population had declined to five in 1974. During the project, Prof. M.V. Subba Rao (Editor) has worked for conservation of gharials and associate with Dr. Bus.

There are three species of crocodiles in India (*i*) salt water or extensive crocodile (*ii*) freshwater, swamp crocodile or mugger (*iii*) gharial or gavialis.

4. Rhinos Conservation : The centrally sponsored scheme "conservation of Rhinos in Assam" was introduced in 1987 and is continued for effective and intensive management of Rhino habitats.

5. Snow-leopard project : This is being taken to create 12 snow-leopard Reserves throughout the Himalayas.

6. Project Elephant : This was launched in 1992 with the aim at ensuring long term survival of identified viable populations of elephants causing serious degradation. There have been drawn lines to restore the lost and degraded habitats of elephants including creation of corridors for their migration, intignation of man-elephants conflict and establishment of data base on the migration and population dynamics of elephants.It also aims at improving quality of life of people living around elephant habitats through sustainable development

Biosphere Reserves

In India the first Biosphere reserve came into being in 1986 to protect the flora and fauna of a biological community interacting with a single life zone where climate is similar (biome). Till to date (June 1992) there are 7 Biosphere Reserves in the country. They are :

(*i*) Nilgiri (Karnataka, Kerala, Tamil Nadu).

(*ii*) Nanda (U.P.).

(*iii*) Nokrek (Meghalaya).

(*iv*) Great Nicobar (Andaman and Nicobar Islands).

(*v*) Gulf of Mannar (Tamil Nadu).

(*vi*) Manas (Assam).

(*vii*) Sundarbans (West Bengal).

II. Ex-Situ Conservation

Different methods of ex-situ conservation are :

1. Long Term Captive Breeding : This method involves captive, maintenance and breeding in captivity on long term basis of individuals of the endangered species. Captive breeding and propogation or long term basis in usually undertaken for species which have last their habitats permanently or there are present certain such factors in the habitat which shall force it to extinction again. In majority of cases where poaching, excessive hunting etc. come in direct conflict with existence of the species long term maintenance and breeding in captivity is resorted to. ***Eg.*** **:** Siberian tiger, non tailed macaque etc.

2. Short Term Propagation and Release : Short term maintenance, captive breeding followed by release of the animal in their natural habitat is a method which is usually resorted to when the population of a specific declares due to some temporary set-back in their living conditions. There is no ineversible change in the habitat and the animal concerned can survive in its natural home after the factors casuing the set back are eliminated. ***Eg.*** **:** Cheetah, wolf, owl, American bison etc.

3. Animal Translocations : Translocation involves release in a new locality of animals which come from anywhere also other than the place in which they are being released. In some cases translocation may also involve removal of the animals from a natural community. The capture, transfer and release of animals from one locality to another usually involves maintenance of the animal in captivity for sometime. However, care should be taken that this period of captivity should be as short a possible. ***Eg.*** **:** Golden lion Tamains, squirrel sized monkey of Reo de. Janerio etc. Translocation is usually resorted to under following circumstances :

(*a*) The wild population may be threatened with prospects of extinction due to habitat destruction etc.

(*b*) The population within a locality may have become surplus.

(*c*) Translocation may be resorted to as an alternative to cutting.

(*d*) If the animal population become a nuisance to humans, threatening life etc.

4. Animal Reintroduction : Animal reintroduction involves release of animals either borne in captivity or caught in infancy from the wild and grown in captivity, into an area from which they either declined or disappeared as a result of human pressures (such as hunting) or due to natural causes (like an epidemic). These reintroductions may also involve rehabititation of the species as well. When an animal is borne in captivity or is captured as an infant and raised in captivity are naturally deprived of the process of learning, which enables them to live in the wild, hence should be trained. The process of training native animals to have in their natural habitat is referred to as rehabitation which is a very important step in the reintroduction procedure. ***Eg.*** **:** Eagle owl, Tailed sea eagle, goshawk etc.

Ex-situ Conservation of Flora

This can be done in the following ways :

(*a*) Botamical Gardens : A botanical garden can be described as a place where flowers, fruits and vegetables are grown. The basic purpose for the maintenance of these gardens was beauty, aesthetic sense and the calm and quite environment which a scheded place full of greenary and colourful flowers provide. A number of botanical gardens become institutions of scientific research and undertook the job of cateloguing and classification of plants. Many of them have contributed significantly to our knowledge of taxanomy and systematics of plant life.

(*b*) Conservation in Seed banks, Gene banks or Germ Plasm Reserves : A large number of plant species form seed with variable periods of dormancy following which they can be germinated to yield daughter plants. Most of such plants, therefore, can be preserved in the form of the seeds in small packets for long duration. Places where the seeds are stored are known as seed-banks or gene banks or sometimes germ-plasm banks. The germ plasm of a plant is any of its living organ or a part of it from which new plants can be generated.

WILDLIFE CONSERVATION BY NGO'S AND GOVERNMENT ORGANISATIONS IN INDIA

I. Non Government Organisations

There are a number of non government, voluntary, national and international organisations actively dedicated to wildlife conservation. Major or principal organisations are :

(*i*) **Bombay Natural History Society :** It was found in 1883, engaged in collection of information and specimens of flora and fauna of India, Burma and Ceylon.

(*ii*) **Wildlife Preservation Society of India, Dehradun :** It was founded in 1958 with several objectives of wildlife management.

(*iii*) **World Wildlife Fund for Nature India :** The World Wildlife Fund, Indian National Appeal was launched in India in 1969 at the time of the XIIth General Assembly of the International Union of Conservation of Nature and Natural Resources, held at Delhi. WWF International was formed in 1961, with its headquarters at Glands, Switzerland, and controlled by a board of International Trustees. It has set up National Appeals in several countries. WWF in India was founded with a Board of Trustees and has its Headquarters in Bombay. It has supported the wellknown "Project Tiger" and other similar projects.

II. Conservation Organisations

A number of Wildlife Acts have been made from time to time, by state as well as union Government for wildlife conservation. Some of these are :

1. Madras Wild Elephant Presevation Act, 1873.
2. All-India Elephant Preservation Act, 1879.
3. The Wild Birds and Animal Protection Act, 1912.
4. Bengal Rhinoceros Preservation Act, 1932.
5. Assam Rhinoceros Preservation Act, 1954.
6. Indian Board for Wildlife (IBWL) 1952.
7. Wildlife (Protection) Act, 1972.
8. Establishment of National Parks, Sanctuaries and Zoological Gardens.
9. India becasue a party to CITES (conservation of Internatioal Trade in Endangered species of Wild Flora and Fauna in 1976.
10. Indian National Man and the Biosophere Committee, 1972 for Bisopehre Reserve.
11. Projects to conserve individual endangered species like crocodiles (1974), lion (1972) and tiger (1973).
12. National Wildlife Action Plan, 1982 endorsed by IBWL.

Indian Board of Wildlife (IBWL)

This is the main advisory body to Govt. of India. It was first constituted in 1952 as an advisory body under the name Central Board of Wildlife. Later it was renamed as IBWL. At its first meeting, the Board made a recommendation for unified legislation for wildlife conservation in India. The Wildlife (Protection) Act was enacted in 1972, which has been adopted by all states.

The Wildlife (Protection) Act, 1972 and the provisions of the conservation on International Trade in Endangered Species (CITES) and Export and Import Policy of India are continued to be enforced through the officer of the Regional Deputy Directors of Wildlife Preservation located at Delhi, Mumbai, Kolkata and Chennai with the help of state wildlife wings and the customs Departments. The Wildlife (Protection) Amendment Bill, 1991 was passed by the parliament and promulgated as Act no. 44 of 1991, after it had received the ascent of the President of India in 1991. The new provisions of the Act regarding setting up of the Zoo Authority, protection of rare and endangered species would be enforced under this Act.

Indian Board of Wildlife has been reconstituted during January, 1991, under the Chairmanship of the Prime Minister. The functions of the IBWL are as follows :

(*i*) To advise Central and State Governments for promotion of conservation and effective control of poaching of wildlife.

(*ii*) To advise on the setting up of national parks, sanctuaries and zoological gardens.

(*iii*) To advise the Government on policy regarding export of living animals, trophies, skins, furs, feathers and other wildlife products.

(*iv*) To review the progress in the field of wildlife conservation in the country and suggest measures for improvement.

(*v*) To promote public interest in wildlife and on need of its preservation in harmony with natural and human environment.

(*vi*) To assist and encourage the formation of Wildlife Societies and to act as control coordinating Agency for such bodies.

(*vii*) To advise Central Government or any matter that it may refer to the Board.

QUOTATION FROM THE FORMER PRIME MINISTER OF INDIA, SMT. INDIRA GANDHI

For Conservation of Natural Resources

"The Environmental Problems of Developing Countries are not the side effects of Execessive Industrialisation but reflect the inadequency of Development. The rich countries may look upon Development as the cause of Environmental destruction, but to us it is one of the primary means of improving the Environment for living or providing food, water, sanitation and shelter; of making the deserts Green and the mountains Habitable. The Research and preserverance of Dedicated people Have given us an insight which is likely to play an important part in the shaping of our future plans. We see that however much man hankers after material goods, they can never given him full satisfaction. Thus the higher standardof living must be achieved without alienating people from their heritage and without despoiling Nature of its Beauty, Freshness and purity so essential to our lives".

SMT. INDIRA GANDHI
Prime Minister, Republic of India
Un Conference on Human Environment,

Stockholm,
June 5, 1972.

(First World Environment Day)

Courtesy: Prof. M.V. Subba Rao, Ph.D.

CHAPTER

16

FOREST MANAGEMENT AND CONSERVATION

M.V. SUBBA RAO

INTRODUCTION

A Forest is a natural ecosystem having multi species and multi-aged trees as dominant community. Of the total geographical area of India, 22.74% is forest as against a minimum of 33% forest cover prescribed under National Forest Policy.

Importants of Forests

Forests, forming the abode of Wildlife (includes both: flora and fauna account for an important land use in India, forming a quarter of land use. Forests provide goods and services.

The goods obtained from forests are :

(*i*) Domestic needs of rural based and economically poor populations

(*ii*) provide for industrial raw materials to wood based industries

(*iii*) Being, employment generative, form a resource base for providing continuous, year round and gainful employment where it is needed most

Causes of Destructions

Diversion of Forest Land to Agriculture

One of the main reasons for the destruction of forests in the developing countries is the clearing of forest lands for agriculture. Almost all the developing countries rely on labour intensive agricultural techniques to meet their growing demands of food and other agricultural products. Forests are cleared and the land is used for agriculture. In developed countries, capital intensive techniques are used in agriculture and the emphasis is upon obtaining higher and higher yield from the same land with greater use of machinery, improved seeds, fertilisers and insecticides.

The system of shifting cultivation has also resulted in large scale deforestation. This has been particularly marked in African countries. Africa, which was ones a dense forest area is now the least forested among the three tropical regions of Asia, Latin-America and Africa. Only *6* per cent of its land is covered with closed forests. According to Peterson, shifting cultivation has destroyed about 40 million hectares of forest. Permanent agriculture also reduces areas under forest. It is estimated that by 2000, the closed Forest Area of Africa will be reduced from 180 to 146 million hectares, if deforestation continues at the present rate.

Commercial Exploitation

Commercial exploitation of the existing forest is another major cause of deforestation. It is pointed out in the Global 2000 Report that the deforestation rate is closely related to the rate of commercial logging. In most of the developing countries deforestation after logging is left to chance. In densely populated regions farmers often follow the loggers and take over the land for agriculture. In less densely populated areas, natural regenerate generally degraded and seldom have commercial value. In the Amazon basin, the deforestation rate is estimated at 4 per cent per year. Earlier the forests were cut only along the perimeters and along rivers. But new roadway infrastructures are rapidly increasing the accessible area. By the year 2000, the Amazon forest will cover less than half the area it now does.

Industrialisation in the developing countries will add to the demand for forest produce for industries. Demand for paper, plywood will rise rapidly with the process of developing countries. Worldwide production of forests products including fuelwood, wood for construction, for paper and for other purposes totalled atleast 2400 million cubic metres in 1975.

Fuel Wood

Wood is still the main source of fuel in almost all the developing countries. Firewood collection is also an important contributor to forest depletion. It is pointed out by Eckholm that about half of all the wood cut in the world each year is burned as fuel, mainly by one-third of humanity who still rely on firewood for cooking and heating. Atleast 1.5 million people burn anywhere from one fifth of a ton to well over a ton of wood a year, putting an awesome pressure on the World's vegetation.

Cattle Ranching

The growing number of cattle is also increasing the pressure of eixsting forests. Grazing of cattle beyond the carrying capacity of the forests results in their depletion and also checks the process of natural regeneration. Large tracts of forests in Amazon region are being cleared by multinational meat companies for cattle ranching.

Irrigation, Hydroelectrocity and Projects

Desertification

Deforestation results in desertification and drought and adds to human misery. Deforestation leads to decline of environmental support systems essential for sustainable agriculture. The impact of deforestation is most seriously felt in a number of countries in Africa. As mentioned earlier only 6 per cent of the land of Africa is covered with closed forest. In 1985, 30 million Africans were affected by drought. A Scholar describes the African situation as follows: "Africa is the continent most at risk. Some 6.9 million square kilometres in sub-Saharan African area more than twice as big as India are under direct threat of desertification. Half of the worlds people most managed by desertification live in Sahel".

Forest Conservation Through Law

The National Forest Policy, 1952 enunciated that one-third of the geographic area of the country should be under forests However, there had been continuous deforestation in the country for various reasons, and it is estimated that 4.238 M ha. of forest land was officially diverted to non-forest purposes between 1951-52 and 1979-80. With a view to conserve forests, Government of India could enact the Forest (Conservation) Act, 1980 strictly.

Forest (Conservation) Act, 1980

The Act was enacted with a view to check indiscriminate dereservation and diversion of forest land to non-forest purposes. Under this Act, prior approval of Central Government is required before any reserved forest is declared as dereserved, or forest land is diverted to non-forest purposes. If diversion is permitted, compensatory afforestation is insisted upon any other suitable conditions imposed. Where non-forest lands are available compensatory afforestation be raised over equivalent area of non-forest land. Where non-forest lands are not available compensatory plantations be raised over degraded forests twice in extent to the area being diverted.

The Forests (Conservation) Act, 1980 was amended in 1988 to incorporate stricter panel provisions against violators Important amendments are as follows :

1. No State Government or other authority may direct that any forest land may be assigned by way of lease or otherwise to any person, corporation or agency or organisation (not owned by the Government) without prior approval of the Central Government.
2. No forest land or any portion there of may be cleared of trees which have grown naturally in that land or portion, for the purpose of using it for reforestation without prior approval of the Central Government.
3. Scope of existing "non-forest purposes" has been extended to other areas of cultivation of tea, coffee, spices, rubber, palms, medicinal plants etc.
4. Admissible punishment to the offender of the provision of Section 2 of the Act.

The Forest Developement and Conservation Act, 1980

The Forest Act was passed without the consent of States. The Act regulates the misuse of forest land and prohibits illegal removal or sale and purchase of forest goods of highly commercial nature. It prevents states from designating land from reserved forest status without prior approval of the Central Government although the earlier ligislation Indian Forest Act, 1927 empowered states to disignate state owned forest land as reserved forest and to regulate the use of such forests. It also prohibits states from approving any breaking up or clearing of forest land for any purpose other than reforestation without the approval of Central Government (S.2 (ii) Forest Act).

India has identified 12 sites as potential biosphere reserves, and currently, states have constructed some national parks and sanctuaries with some assistance of the Central Government. And the Indian Government proposes to amend the wildlife Act to implement the Biosphere Reserves of effectively since the Act is now being administered through State agencies. Infact the proposed amendment is already on the anvil of the Parliament awaiting its seal for approval.

And with a view to plug the loopholes in these two enactments and other previous enactments dealing with the problem of Water Pollution and Air Pollution and to make up by the deficiencies in the earlier legislations, the Parliament has enacted the supposedly more comprehensive and efficacious law than the previous legislations in the shape of the Environmental Protection Act,1986 to which the provisions under the newly passed Environmental protection Act, 1986. Significantly the Environmental Protection does not deal with problems of Forest Conservation and Wildlife Protection the omission of which seems to be deliberate with a wiew to treat them separately within the frame work of earlier Wildlife Protection Act and the recent Forest Conservation and Development Act. This calls for critical apprisal of the Environmental Protection Act, 1986.

Conservation of Forestry

It is necessary to see that the available forest resources are used to meet the basic needs of the people for fuel and fodder. Fuel is a basic necessity as food and nearly 80 percent of the need for fuel in developing countries is met by using firewood, It will be necessary to encourage the growing of forces that would meet this basic need. Many Governments appear to rely on regulatory measures to check deforestation. This is not possible. A drastic redistribution of agricultural land will be able to meet the hunger for and among the poor whereas the growing of woodlots would be able to meet the demand for firewood in these countries. It will be necessary to have three broad types of forests to meet the above objectives :

1. Conservation forest will help the maintenance of natural forest with all its stocks of animal and plant species.
2. Social Forest will meet the basic need of the people living in and around the forest.
3. Production forests will take care of the needs of forestbased raw materialistic industry, some of which can also be met through agro-forest. Forests must also provide as much employment as possible to the members of the forest dwelling

communities.Efforts should also be made to find out substitutes to the use of wood in industries.

***(i)* Social Forestry :** This type of forestry, started with NCA(1976) could succeed on private land. There are two main objectives in social forestry, (*i*) use of public and common land to produce in a decentralised way of firewood, fodder and small timber for the local poor men and also to manage soil and u/ater conservation, and (*ii*) to relieve pressure on conservation forests. This programme is in fact for poor, which aims at intensification of nursery operation at villages level for multipurpose species for firewood, fodder, pole, fruit etc., by involving villagers and school children. The area under social forestry increased from 15 M ha in First Plan to 1524 M ha in Sixth Plan.

***(ii)* Ecological movement :** The mass movement to hug trees to prevent their felling was people's response to the cutting of ash trees by a sports goods factory in the hill town of Gopeshwar in 1973. Villagers who were refused permission to cut a single ash tree to make agricultural implements were shocked to learn that the Government had given permission to a Sports goods factory to cut 50 trees and successfully resisted the attempt to cut trees by hugging them. The movement, with its peculiar technique, rapidly spread to the entire region. Activists moved from village to village spreading the message through songs, religious discourses,street plays, etc. A Poet described the method in the short poem that soon became a popular theme :

"Embrace the tree and,
Save them from beinq felled,
The property of our hills,
save them from being looted"

This movement is known as "Chipko Movement" done by Sunderlal Bahuguna. In the early stages, the movement was mainly economic and centred around the demands of replacing the contract system of forest exploitation with forest labour co-operatives as was done in some other states and providing raw materials to local forest based industries at concessional rates. Later on, there was a demand to ban the felling of trees in certain ecologically sensitive areas and this was accepted by the Government, of course, after the usual use of repressive measures.

Still later, there was demand for ban on felling green trees for 10 years in the catchment areas of the rivers in the region. This was in direct conflict with the concept of forestry by the officials who regarded resin, timber and foreign exchange as the main benefits of the Himalaya forests as against soil, water and pure air by the people. In April, 1981, the Government banned felling of green trees in areas over an altitude of 1000 meters.

The Ecological movement was major mass movement for the preservation of natural forests. People in other States in India also followed it and Appiko Movement took place in the Karnataka State in the Mid-eighties.(Appiko also means hugging).

***(iii)* Agro Forestry :** Agroforestry is actually a modified version of social forestry. According to ICRAF Agroforestry is a system of land use where woody perennials are deliberately used on the same land management units as annual agricultural crops and/

or animals, either sequentially or simultaneously, with the aim of obtaining greater outputs on a sustained basis." Agroforestry is indeed a new name for an ancient land practice where land is used for agriculture forestry and animal husbandry. It is however , a recent scientific activity depending upon the situation we may also have a mix of three basic elements i.e., agriculture forestry and animal husbandry. Agroforestry has certainly many advantage over the Traditional forestry $\frac{\text{created}}{\text{pressure}}$ Population explosion requires surveillance to prevent illegal grazing, illegal cutting and illegal clearing. Agroforestry $\frac{\text{responds to}}{\text{population pressure}}$ needs no surveillance; population pressure needs no unfamiliar technology; conserves the environment; produces fodder, fuel, crops, timber.

There are agri-silvicultural, agripastoral, or agri-silvi-pastoral systems (FAO,1984). Depending upon the situations we could have these individually. Infact agroforestry, social forestry and community forestry have much in common. Trees has to be on multipurpose species of use as firewood, fodder, food (fruits etc.), non-edible or even edible oil, plantation crops, tasar, silk worm, lac etc. This type would generate much employment also.

There must be massive afforestation under social and agroforestry programmes. Every village/town/city must be able to meet firewood, fodder and small timber needs by growing trees/shurbs in the land available in a cooperative system.

CONCLUSION

Over exploitation of both forests and wildlife may result in spurt in goods and services, but they loose permanently their productivity and service capacity. Forests and wildlife destroyed amounts to destruction of prosperity, plentifulness and adverse effect on civilisation and national economy.

CHAPTER

17

WILDLIFE CONSERVATION AND MANAGEMENT

M.V. SUBBA RAO

INTRODUCTION

The term *'wildlife'* is generally understood as referring to wild animals in the public mind. The wildlife Protection Act, 1972 defines it as including "any animal, bees, butterflies, crustacea, fish and moths and aquatic or land vegetation which forms of any habitat."

In India, there has been a long tradition of conservation of wildlife. It has been part of its culture right from the "Ashrams" of "Sages", in Kautilya, Arthasastra of the 3rd century B.C., upto recent times. Yet the scenario changed from 1950s, so much so, that wildlife dwindled very fast in the face of rapid development in the country. A stage has come when some species like the cheetah (*Acinomyx junatus*), pin headed duck (*Rhodoness sp.*) etc., are believed to be extinct and many are endangered and face the threat of extinction, if no specific and timely steps are taken to save them.

Wildlife Management in India

Due to continuous increase in the number of endangered species of flora and fauna of wildlife, steps have been taken to protect and manage the wilflife of the country. Non-Governmental voluntary organisations as well as Governmental organisations at state and central levels have been set up to protect the wildlife.

Forestry and wildlife from an organisational view point have been primarily under control of state governments. However, quite recently the subject has been given top priority and a separate Union Ministry of Environment Union and Forests has been entrusted with the task of Environmental Protection. The Department of Environment, and Forests and Wildlife under this Ministry has been set up with the view to have co-ordination between states and the centre and speedy and faithful implementation of the steps to be taken in programme of wildlife management in the country.

The wildlife management aims at :

1. Protection of natural habitats through controlled, limited exploitation of species.
2. Maintenance of the viable number of species in protected areas (National park, Sanctuary, Biosphere reserve etc.).
3. Establishment of Biosphere Reserves for plants and animal species.
4. Protection through legislation.

Wildlife can also be preserved by :

1. Improving the existing protected areas as Sanctuaries, National parks, etc.
2. Imposing restrictions on export of rare plant and animal species and their products.
3. Educating public for environmental protection at all levels of educaiton.

Non Governmental Organisations

There are a number of non-government voluntary national and international organisations actively dedicated to wildlife conservation. The principal organisations are :

1. Bombay Natural History Society - Founded in 1883; engaged in collection of information and specimens of fauna and flora of India, Myanmar and Sri Lanka.
2. Wildlife Preservation Society of India, Dehradun. Founded in 1958 with several objectives of wildlife management.
3. World Wildlife Fund, India. The World Wildlife Fund, Indian National Appeal was launched in India in 1969 at the time of the XIIth General Assembly of the International Union of Conservation of Nature and Natural Resources, held at Delhi. WWF - International was formed in 1961, with its headquarters at Glands, Switzerland, and is controlled by a Board of International Trustees. It has set up a National Appeals in several countries. WWF in India was founded with a Board of B Trustees and has its Head quarters in Bombay. It has supported the wellknown "Project Tiger".

Government Organisations

A number of Wildlife Acts have been made from time to time, by State as well as Union Governments for wildlife conservation. Some of these are :

1. Madras Wild Elephant Preservation Act, 1873.
2. All-India Elephant Preservation Act, 1879.
3. The Wild Birds and Animals Protection Act, 1912.
4. Bengal Rhinoceros Preservation Act, 1932.
5. Assam Rhinoceros Preservation Act, 1954.
6. Indian Board for Wildlife (IBWL) 1952.
7. Wildlife (Protection) Act, 1972.

8. Establishment of National Parks, Sanctuaries and Zoological Gardens.
9. India became a party to CITES (Conaention of International Trade in Endangered Species) of Wild Flora and Fauna in 1976.
10. Indian National Man and the Biosphere Committee, 1972 for Biosphere Reserve.
11. Projects to conserve individual endangered species like Crocodiles (1974), lion (1972) and tiger (1973).
12. National Wildlife Action Plan, 1982 endorsed by IBWL.

Wildlife Legislation

A comprehensive Wildlife (Protection) Act has been enacted in 1972. All States of the Indian Union expect Jammu and Kashmir and Nagaland have passed resolutions accepting the Wildlife (Protection) Act, 1972 - While Jammu and Kashmir have formulated their own legislation on the lines of the Wildlife (Protection), Act, 1972, the State of Nagaland has been addressed to adopt the Act at the earliest.

A significant step in the organisation of Wildlife has come in the wake of 42nd Amendment to the Constitution in the year 1976. The forests and protection of Wild animals and birds have been included in the concurrent list.

To control the thriving global, legal and illegal trade of endangered species, India became a party to an International Convention of Trade in Endangered species of Wild Fauna and Flora since 1976.

The Central Government since then have promulgated on 25th October, 1980 the Forest (Conservation) Ordinance, 1980 which prevents any forest land from being denotified or diverted to any non-forestry purpose without the prior approval of the Central Government. The Forest (Conservation) Bill, converting the ordinance into an Act of Legislation has been passed by both Houses of Parliament during December, 1980.

A separate department of Environment has been created directly under the charge of the Prime Minister to take care of the environmental problems.

The Indian Board for Wildlife recommended for starting of a separate training course for wildlife management at the Forest Research Institute and Colleges, Dehra Dun. Accordingly a six months specialization course in Wildlife management was started at the Indian Forest College. A fullfledged Directorate of Wildlife, Environment Education and Research within the F.R.I, and colleges, Dehra Dun, was sanctioned during the Fifth Plan and came into existence in the year 1977.

CHAPTER

18

MANAGEMENT OF WATER RESOURCES : USE OF WATER FOR VARIOUS PURPOSES

V. VENKATESWARULU

With the help in preserving native flora and fauna, maintaining fish and wildlife habitat, maintaining suitable quality of water for human consumption, Water conservation and management schemes should involve :

1. Recycling and treatment of waste water.
2. Pollution prevention.
3. Carefully designed river regulation and storage schemes.
4. Protection of riparian and aquatic habitats biological integrity-means.

Maintaining a balanced, integrated community of organisms, having a diversity comparable to that of the natural habitats.

Domestic water supply requires most stringent standards and water quality use of water ways for navigation, industrial cooling can be met with waters of poorest quality.

Consequences of Water Regulation

Dams create water reservoirs for domestic irrigation, industry, generation of help and solve the problem of flooding of downstream settled flood plains by regulating the natural pattern of flow.

Ecological conditions change dramatically due to dam construction-flow reduction fine sediment deposition-finally.

Sources of Water Pollutants

Natural Effluents

Organic pollution

Nutrient pollution

Eutrophication

Thermal pollution

Toxic pollution

Heavy metals

Ammonia, cyanides, phenols

Pesticides

Suspended solids

Extreme pH and acidification

Detergents

Oil and Petroleum products

Water Pollution

More serious, longer-term and large-scale water quality problems arise as a result of human activities.

Pollutants and their Effects

P = point source d = diffuse

Toxic effects	Physical effects
Acids and Alkalis (d, p)	Degergents (p)
Sulfide, Sulfate, Cynide (p)	Domestic sewage and farm manure (p)
Metals (Hg, Pb, Al) (p)	Food processing wasted (p)
Pesticides PCBs (d, p) (organochlorines)	Heat (p)
Formal Dehydes, Phenols (p) (org. Toxic wastes)	Nutrients (d)
Radionuclides (p)	

The most serious pollutants are those which are highly persistent in the ecosystem can bioaccumulate and biomagnify with :

1. Heavy industrial base, but low level water management poor legal controls on discharges and water treatment facilities.

In developing countries-high population the rivers contaminated by excessive organic pollution.

In developed countries e^- all straingent rules the problem is with diffuse inputs of pollutants and extensive use made of rivers.

Flood plain : Relatively level part of a river valley, adjacent to the river channel, formed from sediments deposited by river during flood periods some large flood plain rivers.

Europe	:	Danube (now much reclaimed)
Asia	:	Amur, euphrates-tigris, Indus, Ganges, Brahamaputra.
North America	:	Mississippi
South America	:	Amazon
Africa	:	Senegal, Niger, Nile

Delta : An accumulation of sediment at a river mouth. It forms when the rate of sediment deposition into sea or lake exceeds. The rate at which it can be removed. It is composed largely of alluvial sediment as in the flood plain main water uses.

Abstraction domestic supply	In stream uses
Industry : Manufacturing	Transport/navigation
Industry : Cooling	Flood control and water storage
Irrigation	Waste transportation
Flushing of canals	Exploitation of biological resources
Diversion between catchements	Recreation and culture

Downstream morphology will be altered completely dry below the dam for a part of the three year.

The regulation of water decreases or eliminates regular inundation and deposition of nutrient rich sediments on the flood plain, breaking the lateral links between channels and land in the lower reaches of the river. This will have profoud effects on both aquatic and terrestrial ecosystems. The river regulation can lead to the extinction of species from water course community level changes occur in down stream.

Changes in flow regime will have consequences in temperature regime in downstream water and impact on biological growth.

Flow rate : Flow rates can be increased not only by channelization and dredging but also through *inter-basin transfer*. It increases in future, so clearly more work is needed to identify and amelorate any possible detrimental effects.

Tourism and Sport Fishing

Leisure, bankside activities, sucha nagling, bird watching, picknicking directly effect river biota. It will threaten natural fresh water resource intr. of exotic species.

In New Zealand 26 out of 46 fish species native mosquito fishes (Gambusia affinis) introducted, for control of mosquitoes. Introduction of Tilapia and carp for weed control protection of species and habitats. Serious threat to biodiversity in river ecosystem is human. related *habitat* degradation. In Asian rivers it is caused by deforestation and over grazing (Dudgeon, 1992). Silt destroys habitats prefered by many invertebrates.

River restoration is gradually developing its own methodology and theoritical frame work drawing from geomorphology, hydrology, engineering and ecology.

Man has no moral right to cause extinction of another species. As the time is *short* and the rate of extinction is *Fast* (special in tropical regions) the habitats have to be protected against destruction.

Protect rivers as "National Rivers" substratum.

(a) Size

(b) Surface Texture : Coarse Surface Quite favourable for algal colonization.

(c) Chemical composition : Decides the occurence of particular species.

ALGAE IN FLOWING WATERS

Algal Communities

(*a*) Epilithic (Lithophytic) (*b*) Epiphytic

(*c*) Epizoic (*d*) Epipelic (*e*) Planktonic

Algal Groups

(*a*) Bacillariophyceae (*b*) Chlorophyceae

(*c*) Cyanophyceae (*d*) Euglenophyceae

Structural Adaptations

(*a*) Richly branched filaments, firmly attached water passes freely between branches. *e.g. Stigeoclonium.*

(*b*) Long, flexible cylinders, unbranched with slippery coat, offer little resistance to water movement *e.g., Spirogyra fluviatilis, Adnata sp.*

(*c*) Spherical or cushion like colonies, have smooth external surface offer little resistance to water current *e.g., Chaetophora, Nostoc.*

(*d*) Reduced, simplified plate like forms, thallus like thin appressed sheet, grow around the substratum, expose little surface to water *e.g. Phormidium.*

Water Current

Slower current (90 mm s^{-1}) : Stigeoclonium, Oedogonium, Tribonema.

Faster Current (380 mm s^{-1}) : Algal community dominated by diatoms.

Biological signficance of rate of water current "inherent current demand".

Strategies for Reservation and Conservation of Water Bodies

1. To protect water all environmental media are to be protected in Table 18.1.
2. Scientific survey of different water bodies in a region and their utilization.
3. Prevention of the entry of wastes into stagnant water bodies.
4. Wastes may be dumped in flowing waters after subjecting to preliminary treatment.

5. Entry of wastes have to be regulated to maintain ecological balance. Water bodies should not be overloaded.
6. Washing clothes, using detergents near a pond or lake should be avoided.
7. Control of excess weed growth in lakes and ponds.
8. Control of toxic, nuisance causing algae/blooms.
9. Desilting of lakes and ponds which are used for drinking purposes.
10. Biological methods should be employed as far as possible because they are quite safe and economical.
11. An integrated approach should be planned for this purpose.

Table 18.1 Water Quality Monitoring Criteria

The Following Criteria may be Followed in Environmental Monitoring of Lakes and Rivers

Factors	Lakes	Rivers
Sampling frequency	Fortnightly	Monthly
Physical	Colour, odour, turbidity	Turbidity, water current
Chemical	Acidity, alkalinity, Total Hardness, Total Solids	Acidity, Alkalinity, Total Hardness Total Solids
Nutrients	Nitrates, Phosphates Silicates	Nitrates Phosphates Silicates
Pollution indicators	B.O.D. Organic matter D.O., Ammonia, Chlorides	B.O.D., C.O.D., D.O. Organic Matter, Ammonia, Chlorides
Heavy metals	All	All
Biological	Phytoplakton, Macrophytes, Zooplankton Fishes	Phytobenthos (Benthic algae) Macrophytes (Rare) Zoobenthos Fishes
Bacteriological	Coliform count	Coliform count
Biochemical	Pigments organic acids (Glycollic acid) Total sugars Total proteins	Pigments Organic acids (Glycollic acid)

CHAPTER

19

MARINE POLLUTION : IMPACT ASSESSMENT, STRATEGIES AND POLLUTION CONTROL

V.V. SARMA

The oceans have supported a variety of activities of man since ancient times and are considered to be an inexhaustible source of many vital resources for meeting human needs. As land areas are gradually getting used up in endless process of human settlements and industrialisation practically throughout the world, the oceans have literally became the last frontier for man. The oceans are viewed as a reservoir of various kinds of living and non-living resources. Much attention should be paid to the new era of exploration and exploitation of its vast marine resources for economic and social development.

Not only the deep oceans, but also coastal zones can be evaluated in the economic terms *e.g.*, transportation, resources of water and minerals, industries and fisheries. These coastal zones are esthetically pleasing as used for various forms of recreation. But these coastal environments are being altered at an increasing rate, often without looking ahead to future consequences due to multitude of human activities. Coastal zone receives wide variety of substances brought to it primarily by sewage outfalls, dredge spoils, Industrial effluents and river runoff. These activities markedly affect the composition and quality of this particular coastal environment, causing concern for marine pollution.

The coast line of India's main land is about 7500 km long. The country being riverine, has 14 major, 44 medium and 55 minor rivers which discharge annually about 1566 thousand million cubic meters of water through land drainage into the seas transporting a wide range of pollutants generated by land based activities. Besides land drainage, there are large number of marine coastal outfalls discharging directly or indirectly industrial and municipal effluents into the sea. Uncontrolled disposal of land based waste into the seas, through rivers and effluent outfalls, is a major cause of pollution of coastal waters under tidal conditions, specially in semi-enclosed sea with shallow depths causing the pollutants to accumulate with longer residual time than in the open seas.

Andhra Pradesh has a coast line of about 980 km, and the state is endowed with a rich variety of minerals like barytes, copper ore, manganese, limestone, etc., Industrial development in Andhra Pradesh significantly contributing towards economic growth. Major industries include pharmaceuticals, fertilisers, leather, synthetics, cement and machine tools. Not less than 118 industries are located in the districts of Srikakulam, Godavari, Krishna, Prakasam, Visakhapatnam and Nellore districts in A.P. of which aqua culture farms and marine food process are dominating. The major coastal activities are ports and harbours, industrial cooling, industrial and municipal waste disposal, fishing, aquaculture, salt production, recreation and contact water sports.

Thus, in order to protect our coastal marine environment, proper environment strategies should be evolved and implemented. A probabilistic assessment of the environmental capacity to assimilate defined pollutants, is a vital component of any environmental management plan. However, development of a predictive capability for a given coastal area requires multidisciplinary expertise and intensive field data collection programme designed to accommodate temporal, spatial and seasonal variations. In this context, marine pollution monitoring programme in Andhra coast has been taken up by our institution since 1988. The main objectives of this pollution monitoring programme are : (*i*) To establish a baseline data in the coastal environment and estuarine regions, (*ii*) To predict environmental impact due to future developments in marine sucton. (*iii*) To know the dispersion potential and waste assimilation capacity of designated areas, (*iv*) To provide advisory and technical services to Government, Industry and Public institutions aimed at evolving pollution measures.

The results of our observations under this programme showed the impact of pollution mainly in the inland and near shore waters. The synoptic data along the Andhra coast shows that the coastal and inshore waters are clean, productive and biologically active.

In view of future developments in marine sector and establishment of coastal based industries in Andhra Pradesh, there is an essential need for Environmental Impact Assessment (EIA) in this region. EIA is an useful aid for decision making based on the understanding of environmental implications including social, cultural and aesthetic concerns which could be integrated with the analysis of the project costs and benefits. Preparation of Environmental Management (EM) plan is required for formulation, in Implementation and monitoring of environmental protection measures during and after commissioning of projects. Further improvement is necessary in present treatment and disposal systems through systematc monitoring in order to reduce the pollution load derived from land based industrial sources into the coastal waters.

Increasing stress on coastal areas form sea transport, Industrial growth as well as infrastructure underlines the need for both technical resources and environmentally related prevention planning. An understanding of the ecological systems, contingency planning, control and regular monitoring forms a solid basis in meeting these requirements.

CHAPTER

A NOTE ON ISO 14001, EMS

P.J. RAO

INTRODUCTION

Caring for the environment has become an intrinsic part of our lives. From neighborhood recycling efforts to global environmental protection regulations, heightened environmental awareness and activity are changing our attitudes and habits at home, in the market and in the place of work.

As focus on the environment intensifies, managing the environmental impact of any company's operations, products and services is becoming more closely linked to your market image and your ability to meet your business obligations and goals.

ISO 14001 is a new international standard that can help to build and enhance any company's environmental management system according to a widely recognized set of requirements, establishing and maintaining an ISO 14001 complaint system can help to improve any operational efficiency and meet today's environmental expectations.

About the Standard

ISO 14001 is a standard developed by the international organization for standardization *to provide organizations worldwide with a consistent and globally recognized structure for creating, implementing, monitoring and improving environmental management systems.* The ISO 14000 series includes both guidance and specification documents to help organizations of all types and sizes develop and maintain environmental management systems supportive of their stated environmental policy and goals.

ISO 14001 is the only specification standard in the series. It contains only those requirements that can be objectively audited. It addresses the fundamental elements of a company's operations, including system requirements and objectives, documentation, training, communication, operational control, emergency preparedness, monitoring and measuring, corrective and preventive action, records, and auditing. ISO 14001 can be used by companies wishing to benchmark their systems against internationally recognized standards and provide objective evidence of conformation through third-party registration.

Significance of ISO 14001

ISO 14001 provides a common language to define the elements of effective environmental management systems from company to company, industry to industry, country to country. It contains a series of requirements to help companies consistently identify and address environmental concerns. While ISO 14001 compliance does not indicate compliance to government performance standards, it can help to achieve any company's own environmental objectives and strengthen and ability to meet applicable customer and regulatory requirements.

Because *ISO 14001 can be used to integrate the environmental system with overall management structure, it can use the requirements in the standard as a framework to efficiently and thoroughly examine, manage and control the systems to achieve performance targets and continuous improvement.*

And, because of the international and comprehensive nature of the standard, an ISO 14001 environmental management system that meets the requirements will be recognized and accepted in the global community.

The Relationship between ISO 14001 & ISO 9000

ISO 14001 shares common management system principles with ISO 9000. Both contain requirements for policy, documentation, document control, auditing, training, corrective action and management reviews.

However, the standards are substantially different in that each addresses, the issues unique to its purpose. For example, ISO 14001 addresses environmental management system elements such as emergency preparedness and legal considerations. *Where compliance to ISO 9000 demonstrates an organization's ability to consistently meet the requirements of its customers, compliance to ISO 14001 demonstrates an organization's ability to meet the environmental policies, objectives and targets set by the company's own management.*

In addition, the ISO 9000 series includes three models for quality systems. ISO 14001 is the only specification standard for environmental management systems and can be used by companies to audit their environmental management system implementation.

Integration of Standards

ISO 14001 does not require a separate management system. Because ISO 14001 and ISO 9000 share common management principles, may choose to use the existing ISO 9000 system as a basis for environmental management system. Integrating the management systems will save duplication of functions and improve overall efficiency.

However, if should keep in mind that while the clauses in each standard are similar, the quality system and environmental system requirements are not identical. Adapting ISO 9000 management system to comply with the ISO 14001 requirements in most cases is possible, but will require modifying current management system to incorporate the environmental processes.

Third-party Registration

Third-party Registrars can provide an independent, unbiased assessment of entire environmental management system. When the registrar finds that company has fully implemented an ISO 14001 system, company is then "registered." The registrar's auditing team will continue to make periodic visits and to verify facility ongoing compliance.

It is not the function of a registration assessment to determine regulatory compliance. The registration assessment is a determination that company's system meets the ISO 14001 requirements, including the procedures to define as a part of system.

As a registered firm, to receive a certificate confirming system's compliance to the ISO 14001 requirements, and registration is recorded publicly in a directory. Because registration is considered a distinctive achievement, companies often generate their own public announcements through advertisements or press releases. Often, registered firms use the registration mark in their promotional materials.

The ability to publicly demonstrate ISO 14001 compliance is one of the main reasons companies choose to pursue registration. ISO 14001 registration is authoritative evidence of system's compliance for government regulatory agencies, customers, stakeholders, insurance companies, the public and other interested parties.

Value of ISO 14001

Because ISO 14001 registration provides others with an addition level of confidence that the company has fully implemented an environmental management system according to recognized international requirements, it becomes a valuable global credential.

ISO 14001 registration can help to:

- Work toward continuous improvement.
- Realize improvements in productivity, waste reduction, pollution prevention.
- Enhance image among work force and public.
- Comply with emerging trade regulations.
- Meet government purchasing or other customer or industry requirements.
- Gain a competitive advantage in the green market place.

In addition to the significance of registration outside the company, ISO 14001 registration offers many internal benefits. In particular, registration and associated follow-up assessments provide for an ongoing examination of system and objective feedback on its strengths and weakness, allowing opportunity for continuous improvement. In addition, registered firms often report time and cost savings resulting from more efficient operations.

Preparing for Registration

While the Company have a lot to gain from registration, it will require an investment of time and resources. Therefore, plan for registration carefully.

1. Identify the registration goals. Is it to gain a market edge and customer requirements and to improve operational efficiencies and pollution prevention?
2. Talk to customers and others in the environmental arena to identify their requirements and find out what registrations they will accept.
3. Get a sense for the registration process by talking to other companies who have achieved registration.
4. Consider taking advantage of training seminars or other pre-registration services, such as an accredited body's Preliminary Evaluation, which stimulates an audit situation and gauges the system's readiness for registration.
5. Gain company's commitment to registration and dedicate the time and resources necessary.

There are some key areas to consider when looking for the registrar that is right for company :

- Reputation and credentials in the market place.
- Experience and technical capabilities in the industry.
- Auditing resources and where they are located.
- Character, integrity and attitude.

  The relationship with registrar is important, because certification is ongoing. While auditors must always maintain their objectivity, they should also be approachable, helpful and responsive.

  It is a conflict of interest for a registrar to also provide consulting services, so you shouldn't expect your registrar to design your system or make recommendations for implementation. (In fact own people are really the only ones who can develop systems and processes that will work for them.) The auditors should, however, be able to provide with observations and constructive feedback that will help to keep the system in compliance with the standard.
- Finally, consider the value of registration.

  Don't compare registrars by cost alone. You owe it to yourself to examine exactly what you'll get for your money. For example, consider a program of continuous assessments vs. a complete re-assessment after few years. Continuous assessments can save you the time and expense of a complete re-assessment and can also help you to enhance your operations through periodic evaluations of your system.

Also, the range of services offered by a registrar could in the long run save you time and money. Identifying a single source for all your global assessment and information needs will give you the most for your investment.

Registration is not an end in itself, it is a means to help you attain your business goals. Therefore, it is critical to find a registrar with the service features that match your corporate goals and culture to get the most from your registration.

CHAPTER

21

HEALTH IMPACTS OF WATER POLLUTION

MANTRI SHYAM PRASAD

It is a well-known fact that clean water is absolutely essential for healthy living. Adequate supply of fresh and clean drinking water is a basic need for all human beings on the earth, yet it has been observed that millions of people worldwide are deprived of this.

Fresh water resources all over the world are threatened not only by over exploitation and poor management but also by ecological degradation. The main source of fresh water pollution can be attributed to discharge of untreated waste, dumping of industrial effluent, and run-off from agricultural fields. Industrial growth, urbanization and the increasing use of synthetic organic substances have serious and adverse impacts on fresh water bodies. It is a generally accepted fact that the developed countries suffer from problems of chemical discharge into the water sources mainly ground water, while developing countries face problems of agricultural run-off in water sources. Polluted water like chemicals in drinking water causes problem to health and leads to water-borne diseases which can be prevented by taking mear-ures can be taken even at the household level.

Groundwater and its Contamination

Many areas of ground water and surface water are now contaminated with heavy raetals, POPs (persistent organic pollutants), and nutrients that have an adverse affect on health. Water-borne diseases and water-caused health problems are mostly due to inadequate and incompetent management of water resources. Safe water for all can only be assured when access, sustainability, and equity can be guaranteed. Access can be defined as the number of people who are guaranteed safe drinking water and sufficient quantities of it. There has to be an effort to sustain it, and there has to be a fair and equal distribution of water to all segments of the society. Urban areas generally have a higher coverage of safe water than the rural areas. Even within an area there is variation; areas that can pay for the services have access to safe water whereas areas that cannot pay for the services have to make do with water from hand pumps and other sources.

In the urban areas water gets contaminated in many different ways, some of the most common reasons being leaky water pipe joints in areas where the water pipe and sewage line pass close together. Sometimes the water gets polluted at source due to various reasons and mainly due to inflow of sewage into the source.

Ground water can be contaminated through various sources and some of these are mentioned below.

Pesticides : Run-off from farms, backyards, and golf courses contain pesticides such as DOT that in turn contaminate the water. Leechate from landfill sites is another major contaminating source. Its effects on the ecosystems and health are endocrine and reproductive damage in wildlife. Groundwater is susceptible to contamination, as pesticides are mobile in the soil. It is a matter of concern as these chemicals are persistent in the soil and water.

Sewage : Untreated or inadequately treated Municipal sewage is a major source of groundwater and surface water pollution in the developing countries. The organic material that is discharged and surface water pollution in the developing countries. The organic material that is discharged with municipal waste into the watercourses uses substantial oxygen for biological degradation thereby upsetting the ecological balance of rivers and lakes. Sewage also carries microbial pathogens that are the cause of the spread of disease.

Nutrients : Domestic waste water, agricultural run-off, and industrial effluents contain Phosphorus and Nitrogen, fertilizer run-off, manure from livestock operations, which increase the level of nutrients in water bodies and can cause eutrophication in the lakes and rivers and continue on to the coastal areas. The Nitrates come mainly from the fertilizer that is added to the fields. Excessive use of fertilizers cause nitrate contamination of groundwater, with the result that Nitrate levels in drinking water is far above the safety levels recommended. Good agricultural practices can help in reducing the amount of Nitrates in the soil arid thereby lower its content in the water.

Synthetic Organics : Many of the 100 000 synthetic compounds in use today are found in the aquatic environment and accumulate in the food chain. POPs or Persistent organic pollutants, represent the most harmful element for the ecosystem and for human health, for example, industrial chemicals and agricultural pesticides. These chemicals can accumulate in fish and cause serious damage to human health. Where pesticides are used on a large-scale, groundwater gets contaminated and this leads to the chemical contamination of drinking water.

Acidification : "Acidification of surface water, mainly lakes and reservoirs, is one of the major environmental impacts of transport over long distance of air pollutants such as Sulphur dioxide from power plants, other heavy industry such as steel plants, and motor vehicles. This problem is more severe in the US and in parts of Europe.

Chemicals In Drinking Water

Chemicals in water can be both naturally occurring or introduced by human interference and can have serious health effects.

Fluoride : Fluoride in the water is essential for protection against dental caries and weakening of the bones, but higher levels can have an adverse effect on health. In India, high Fluorid content is found naturally in the waters in Rajasthan.

Arsenic : Arsenic occurs naturally or is possibly aggravated by over powering aquifers and by Phosphorus from fertilizers. High concentrations of Arsenic in water can have an adverse effect on health. A few years back, high concentrations of this element was found in drinking water in six districts in West Bengal. A majority of people in the area was found suffering from Arsenic skin lesions. It was felt that Arsenic contamination in the groundwater was due to natural causes. The Government is trying to provide an alternative drinking water source and a method through which the Arsenic content from water can be removed.

Lead : Pipes, fittings, solder, and the service connections of some household plumbing systems contain Lead that contaminates the drinking water source.

Recreational use of water : Untreated sewage, industrial effluents, and agricultural waste are often discharged into the water bodies such as the.lakes, coastal areas and rivers endangering their use for recreational purposes such as swimming and canoeing.

Petrochemicals : Petrochemicals contaminate the groundwater from underground petroleum storage tanks.

Other heavy metals : These contaminants come from mining waste and tailings, landfills, or hazardous waste dumps.

Chlorinated solvents : Metal and plastic effluents, fabric cleaning, electronic and aircraft manufacturing are often discharged and contaminate groundwater.

Disease

Water-borne diseases are infectious diseases spread primarily through contaminated water. Though these diseases are spread either directly or through files or filth, water is the chief medium for spread of these diseases and hence they are terminated as water-borne diseases. Most intestinal (enteric) diseases are infectious and are transmitted through faecal waste. Pathogens - which include virus, bacteria, Protozoa, and parasitic worms - are disease - producing agents found in the faeces of infected persons. These diseases are most prevalent in areas with poor sanitary conditions. These pathogens travel through water sources and interfuses directly through persons handling food and water. Since these diseases are highly infectious, extreme care are hygiene should be maintained by people looking after an infected patient. Hepatitis, cholera, dysentery, and typhoid are the more common water-borne diseases that affect large populations in the tropical regions.

A large number of chemicals that either exist naturally in the land or are added due to human activity dissolve in the water, thereby contaminating it and leading to various diseases.

Pesticides : The Organophosphates and the Carbonates present in pesticides affect and damage the nervous system and can cause cancer. Some of the pesticides contain carcinogens that exceed recommended levels. They contain Chlorides that cause reproductive and endocrinal damage.

Lead : Lead is hazardous to health at it accumulates in the body and affects the central nervous system. Children and pregnant women are most at risk.

Fluoride : Excess Fluorides can cause yellowing of the teeth and damage to the spinal cord and other crippling diseases.

Nitrates : Drinking water that gets contaminated with Nitrates can prove fatal especially to infants that drink formula milk as it restricts the amount of oxygen that reaches the brain causing the 'Blue baby syndrome. It is also linked to digestive tract cancers. It causes algae to bloom resulting in eutrophication in surface water.

Petrochemicals : Benzene and other petrochemicals can cause cancer even at low exposure levels.

Chlorinated solvents : These are linked to reproduction disorders and to some cancers.

Arsenic : Arsenic poisoning through water can cause liver and nervous system damage, vascular diseases and also skin cancer.

Other Heavy metals : Heavy metals cause damage to the nervous system and the kidney, and other metabolic disruptions.

Salts : It makes the fresh water unusable for drinking and irrigation purposes. Exposure to polluted water can cause diarrhoea, skin irritation, respiratory problems, and other diseases, depending on the pollutant that is in the water body. Stagnant water and other untreated water provide a habitat for the mosquito and a host of other parasites and insects that cause a large number of diseases especially in the tropical regions. Among these, malaria is undoubtedly the most widely distributed and causes most damage to human health.

Preventive Measures

Water-borne epidemics and health hazards in the aquatic environment are mainly due to improper management of water resources. Proper management of water resources has become the need of the hour as this would ultimately lead to a cleaner and healthier environment. In order to prevent the spread of water-borne infectious diseases, people should take adequate precautions. The city water supply should be properly checked and necessary steps taken to disinfect it. Water pipes should be regularly checked for leaks and cracks. At home, the water should be boiled, filtered, or other methods and necessary steps taken to ensure that it is free from infection.

The Water Borne and Other Diseases

I. Those caused by the presence of an Infected agent.

A. Bacterial Infections

1. Salmonellens group of bacteria Salmonelliosis.
2. Toxin producting bacteria, acute food poisoning.
   (*a*) Staphylo cocci.
   (*b*) Cloatridium welchii.
   (*c*) Cloatridium botalinum.
3. Toxin producing bacteria with prolonged incubation period.
   (*a*) Salmonella typhi (causes typhiod fever).
   (*b*) S. paratypin (causes para-typhiod fever).
   (*c*) Shigella bacillary (causes dysentery).
   (*d*) Streptococci abscesses (causes sore throat).
   (*e*) Mastitis endocridis (causes Rhematic fever).
   (*f*) Vibrio cholera (causes Cholera).
   (*g*) Brucciilosis bovine (causes Tuberculosis).

B. Viral Infections

(*a*) Infective hepatitis (causes jaundice).
(*b*) Polio myletis (causes Polio).
(*c*) Gastro enteritis (causes dysentery).

C. Ricketisial Infection

Cloxiella burneth (causes fever).

D. Protozoan Infections

(*a*) Entamoeba histolytica (causes Amoebiasis).
(*b*) Giardia lambella (causes Giardiasis).

E. Helminthic Infection

(*a*) Taenia saginata (causes stomach ache).
(*b*) Taeriia solium (causes stomach ache).
(*c*) Ascarisilumbrieoides .(causes stomach ache).
(*d*) Tridiinella spiralis (pork) (causes weils disease).
(*e*) Dibothric cephalus latus (fish tape worm).

F. Lepto Spiral Infection

Trichenella spiralis (due to pork causes Weils disease).

II. Those caused by the presence of an Aquatic host.

(*a*) Crustaceans like Cyclops (Guinea worm and Fish tape worm).
(*b*) Molluscans like Snails (causes Schistesomiasis through Blood fluke).

CHAPTER

ENVIRONMENTAL HEALTH : SANITATION MEASURES TO PREVENT CONTROL AND SPREAD OF INFECTIOUS DISEASES

S. RAMAKRISHNA RAO

The diseases that are spread through various sources like water, mosquitoes, soil etc., are to be tackled differently in different situations. The physiography of a town ship, climatic conditions and population are natural factors one should take into consideration before attempting to control. The area's contour levels, the types of soils and plantation and Industries in that area contribute to spread of the diseases and hence tackle the problem in more specific methods. The diseases spread through living and non-living agents such as towels, bed sheets, (fomites) and insects, dogs, rodents etc, and through water, soil and air. In such cases the prevention of spread of the disease to possible if enough precautions are taken to avoid such contaminated agents Personal hygiene also helps in prenttng diseases. The control is possible when sources of spread of diseases are known.

In this chapter the sanitation measures of water, food, milk, personal hygiene will be discussed to explain the prevention and control of common diseases.

Prevention of Water Borne Diseases

1. Water Treatment

Water is a very important medium in which number of organisms grow since it will have all the favourable conditions and nutrients to grow. Most of the life-cycles *i.e.*, from egg to adult occur in water. If water is not protected properly there is every possibility of contamination either direct or indirectly. Since water is used for different purposes like washing, bathing, drinking and ablution, the area close to the proximity of water is not devoid of contamination. The persons having disease, if defecate close to the area or upstream of the water fetching area the pathogems are carried to spread tne disease. The water source if contaminated with sewage continuously it is very difficult to prevent spread of the diseases unless adequate care is taken to preteat waters. Certain bacteriological standards are also stipulated for the raw water. The raw water source containing less than

10 Eschereschia coli bacteria per 100 ml should be regarded as clean and not likely to spread infections. A water source containing 10-100 E. coli per 100 ml is of poor quality and should be supplied only after treatment or the source should be abandoned. Water containing more than 1000 E. coli per 100 ml is regarded as grossly polluted hence one has to look for alternative sources if treatment is not possible.

The following criteria are considered to tap the source of raw water.

1. **Water requiring no treatment :** Underground water without any possibility of contamination.
2. **Water requiring disinfection only :** Ground and surface waters subjected for low contamination having 50-100 coliforms (entric bacteria) per 100 ml in a month.
3. **Water Requiring treatment including chlorination :** The water to be subjected to remove turbidity and chlorination is necessary.
4. **Water required to additional treatment to filtration and chlorination :** Raw water from rivers. Water requires sedimentation and long time storage before subjecting to treatment. Heavy chlorination is required.
5. **Water requiring unusual treatment measures :** When recycling of waste water is taken up, water requiring multiple chlorinations to remove heavy bacterial count. It can be used only when other sources are not available.

A. Disinfection

The chlorination is a disinfection process after treatment of water for physicochemical parameters such as coagulation, sedimentation and filtration. The waters are treated vvith chlorine gas or chlorine compounds such as bleaching powder The quantity and period of contact varies with varying water qualities. This requires special attention as to retain 0.2 and 0.3 mg/1 of residual chlorine at the consumer's end. The efficiency and intermittant pollution in the water supplies should be monitored from time to time by bacteriological examination of samples of treated water. The common methods for disinfection are :

1. By Boiling Water

The water can be disinfected by boiling water for 20 minutes. This is limite to house-hold and recontamination is possible if the boiled cooled water is handled unhygienically. Thus by this process only existing germs are killed and not protected by future contamination. During epidemic breaks, individual house-holds should adopt this process to ensure safe drinking water.

2. By Ultraviolet Radiation

Ultraviolet rays are of invisible spectrum with wave length of 1000 to 4000 mu, which Sun rays do have. In the modern gadgets for purification of water, the water is passed through this to ensure disinfection. It consists of mercury vapours enclosed in a quartz bulb and passing current through it. The water is passed through 10 cm column before the UV. rays. This process is very costly and not economical for treatment plants. It is used generally in swimming pools to ensure disinfection without affecting the quality of water.

3. Disinfection with Ozone

Ozone gas is also used as a disinfectant as it has a capacity to oxidize the organic matter. The ozone usage is costly and excessive usage results in nausea to operators as well as to the consumers.

4. Chlorination

It is a cheap process by which the water is treated before filtration and post-filtered water to ensure complete oxidation of organic matter. The minimum residual chlorine at consumer end ensures the protection against any intermittent contamination during repairs or plumbing installation. Chlorination is also affected by the change in temperature and pH. The disinfection power depends on the compound's inherent chlorine content.

The chlorine compounds generally used are chlorinated lime or Bleaching powder having about 40% of chlorine and liquid chlorine in cylinders. In the water treatment plants the automatic chlorinators will be used for chlorination. The residual chlorine should be checked from time to time by using comparator and comparing with standard discs of chloroscope.

B. Water Supply

The treated water supply is also prone for contaminations at the cross connections. Same times the regular water supplies are connected to some emergency water source which is used when regular water supply fails. This connection between public water supply aad emergency water supply is called the cross connection. The unsafe emergency water supply may enter through defective values thus leading the contaminated water supply of poor becterial quality.

In addition, faulty plumbing can also provide cross connections between sewer system and water system. This results in possible back siplionage of water used in toilets, wash basins, Kitchen wastes etc. into water supply pipes when a vaccum or negative pressure in the water system. The Amoebic dysentery out-break in Chicago was due to the entry of sewage into supply pipes due to defective plumbing.

C. Personal Hygiene

The diseases are mostly spread through water by contamination by a carrier. Certain people possess the diseases like amoebiasis but never exhibit it but spread the disease in the rest population. The improper hygienic conditions in many restaurants and hostels where groups occur are prone to spread the disease in large numbers by single "carrier". The Amoebic cysts get attached or lie in nails when a person doesn't clean properly after defecation. The servers carry these oysts in their hands and carry the water or contaminate the food they supply. Thus the spread is invitable. Another common way is 'infection' is in the persons habits of chewing and nail biting leads to entry of new cysts making the person sick.

D. Protected Water In Public Places

The public places such as schools, swimming pools, hotels etc., where large number of people visit daily are also to be protected from contamination. The children especially in schools after play in soil will drink water. Often taps get contaminated making water a source to transmit the water borne disease. The swimming pools should be maintained hygenically since body of the infected persons get in touch with water; further leads to spread the disease in other healthy population who take a swim.

II. Milk and Food Sanitation

(a) Milk Sanitation

The Milk and food are two important commodities that are used daily. Hence it is very important to protect them from infectious agents, since they provide nutrients and promote growth once contaminated. The prevention of milk infections increases the rate of consumption of milk in addition to projection to public life. The unclean vessels for the entry of dust, storage in high temperatures help the growth of bacteria. The diseases like the tuberculosis, dengue feaver, undulant fever etc. are transmitted which originate from cows or buffallows or the workers in the plant. The following steps should be regulated in all the milk processing plants.

1. **Healthy Cows :** The infection carrying cows should be discarded. A thorough examination should be done to know whether they are suffering from T.B. or Mastitis.
2. **Healthy and Hygenic Workers :** The worker in a dairy should have sound health and should not have any respiratory diseases. The handling of milk requires a constant touch with milk or other products. The workers suffering with diseases should be refrained.
3. **Clean Surroundings :** The plants should be clean, dust proof and floor should be periodically cleaned as it will attract all types of insects. The dairy plants should be erected awaj from the cow-sheds etc.
4. **Vessel and Equipment :** The handling utencils and machines should be so simple that they can be easily washed and cleaned. The retention of fat or milk sediments will promote bacteria growth.
5. **Cooling and Storage :** The handing of milk is importan including milking storage and transport. Any laxity in the maintainance of temperature during transport or storage promote the growth of bacteria.

Pasteurisation

It is a process in which milk is subjected to heat destroying the pathogerms in the raw milk. It provide: safe milk. The different bacteria are killed at different temperatures : the diptheria bacteria are killed at 130° F after an exposure of 30 minutes which streptococi dies at 133° F. The typhoid bacilli live upto 136° F. and T.B. bacilli upto 139° F So the desired effect is obtained after exposure of 15 minutes at 160° F. The reduction of bacteria would be 99% hence the souring of milk is not prevented but delayed. The subjection of milk to 194° F for 0-75 sec. is also tried which provides protection from the surviving bacteria.

6. Food Sanitation

Food is a very important source of infection spread since it affects the infectious carrying agents. The food affects health in many ways since the unbalanced nutrition toxic materials in food and different parasitic stages in them promote the spread of infection. The following are the possible hazards through food.

1. Food harbours various parasitic worms such as Trichina worm, tapeworm and also dysentery-causing organisms. They enter the healthy beings through consumption of meat or meat products which are improperly cooked or pickled.
2. The micro organisms such as cholera, typhoid, salmonellosis etc. enter the food through different agents or natural polluted environments cause the spread of the diseases.
3. The release of toxins by some bacteria that come in contact with food causes poisoning of food. The effects are known only after consumption.
4. The different colouring agents used to attract consumers such as colours used in ice-creams, sweets etc. are hazardous.
5. Eating the foods containing certain inherent, natural poisonous substances without proper knowledge.

1. Parasites

Among the food borne infection, the common tapeworms and nematodes occur more frequently in human beings. The 'parasite' is an organism that lives at the expense of another organism called 'host'. So they will depend on food shelter and their exitenence solely depends upon the existence of other organisms. The life-cycles are complicated and needs intermediate hosts. The common pork tapeworm, Teania, solium and beef worm Teania saginata are very common in Western World. The infective beef of pork when eaten in improperly cooked condition, they will develop in human beings causing deficiency in 'B' vitamin in the hosts. The fish tapeworms cause anaemia and they are very common in East Asian countries (China, Philippines etc.) where fish is eaten in raw or pickled forms.

The nematodes such as Trichinella spiralis is common in Western World since they eat the sausages made of pork. This may lead to fatality whose autopsy revealed millions of larvae choked in muscles. The infection spreads when the garbage having infected portion parasite and fed to healthy pigs, the larva erupt in muscles and further consumption spreads the disease in population. The worms are killed when subjected to 137°F.

2. Food Poisoning

Food poisoning generally is due to activity of already existing bacteria such as clostridium sp. and salmonella grow and release toxic material during break down of nutreints. The food poisoning is followed by vomiting, abdominal pain, diarohoea, chills, prostration and gasteroenteritis. These symptoms occur after 4-12 hrs of consumption.

The entry of bacteria like Typphococci to food is through the hands of food handlers with skin infections such as boils, pus wounds and nasal drops. They develops and grow in food in favourable temperatures. Generally in the restaurants have food poisoning.

The foods which are processed and tinned cans also be subjected to food poisoning by Clostridium botulinum which causes head-ache, weakness, constipation, paralysis symptoms are exhibited after 15 hrs. Generally this occurs in home processed uncooked foods, meat etc.

3. Chemicals in Food

Food poisoning with chemical usually occurs due to negligence with the pesticides, rat poisons' or to mistaken identity of packets having hazardous chemicals. The insecticide residues on fruits and vegitables are also responsible for trouble. The chemicaks used to colour different foods to attract a consumer are mostly not cleared by the Food inspector. The cheap ice-creams are given different flavours using organic compounds, such chemicals can cause concern among people who constantly get exposed.

4. Shell Fisheries

The use of shell fishes specially clams (Bivalves) for different groups and other preparations is very common in Western World. The shell fish produced in sanitary conditions such as contaminated water or handled by handlers with infection will lead to typhoid, dysentery gastro-intestinal problems and jaundice. The constant monitoring of quality of water in the areas cultured and thorough cleaning in fresh water will prevent spread of such diseases.

At certain times of the season the mussels, arid clams may be toxic causing paralysis. This is due to shell fish feeding on a plankton called dino flagellates close to the coastal areas. Hence fishing for shell fish is totally controlled in such areas and seasons.

CHAPTER

23

ELECTRONIC HEALTH RECORDS

DR. MADHAVI, MADI REDDY, M.S. (USA), FEnRA

With the growing emphasis on providing the right information to the right person anywhere ai any time across the globally interconnected world, the healthcare industry across the world has been moving toward an electronic health record (EHR) system. It has become apparent that the paper record system is incapable of providing caregivers the patient information they need in a way they can utilize it.

The DIGHT (Distributed Information store for Global Healthcare Technology) project is addressing the challenges of building a scalable and highly reliable information store for EHRs for the citizens of India. The project partners are SICS and the Indian Centre for Development of Advanced Computing (C-DAC), where SICS is responsible for the distributed storage aspects of the project, while C-DAC will work towards evolving an EHR standard for India. The project will embrace both open-source technology and open standards to ensure that information is managed run information and secured in an accountable and transparent manner.

Issue

Factors or driving forces for implementing EHR systems were the need to

- Improve clinical The motivating processes or workflow efficiency
- Improve quality of care
- Share patient record information with healthcare practitioners and professionals, and
- Reduce medical errors

Physician satisfaction is an important component of the success of an electronic implementation. User satisfaction is described as essential to the survival of a system. Implementations that have failed or have been plagued with difficulty have often been those with which physician-users are dissatisfied.

Satisfaction with electronic health record systems is multifactorial. A number of studies have identified factors contributing to or predicting user satisfaction with new electronic implementations. Among factors that may affect user satisfaction with computer systems are gender, age, and computer satisfaction or familiarity with technology. For each of these factors, controversies exist about the degree and direction of its influence on satisfaction.

CHAPTER

CHILD HEALTH CARE : A PERSPECTIVE

DR. AVR BRAHMANANDAM, M.S.

In last few decades the world has changed drastically in terms of Family structure, Economy, Scientific progress, State sponsored programs and life style changes of present generation. The traditional family support system we proudly associated with India is fast disappearing. With the increasing Nuclear family culture, the demands and organization of Health have also changed to ensure complete Health of a Child. This change has a direct bearing on how we as a society take care of our children... Today and in Future!

Child health care refers to care of children from Conception to Birth and after Birth till the age of five years and it implies that Health care of Child starts even before the child is born i.e.) Antenatal care and Maternal Health care.

Health care of Neonates from birth to 28 days, Infants from 1 month to 12 months of age, Toddlers from 1 year to 2 years and Preschool children from 2 years on wards is taken care with different parameters specific to the age of the Child.

The Objectives are to ensure:

(a) Proper Antenatal care.

(b) Every child to get adequate Health care and proper nourishment.

(c) Monitoring of Growth & Development and identification & treatment of any deviations from normal.

(d) Prompt detection and treatment of Childhood ailments.

(e) Availability of trained persons and facilities.

(f) Education and training of mothers and family members.

Antenatal care:

Antenatal care is monitoring the progress of Fetus with an objective to ensure birth of a live, mature, and healthy Baby. The state of health of pregnant mother and fetus are assessed periodically from conception up to birth. The basic parameters are recording of Weight, Haemoglobin levels, Urine analysis and clinical Examination of the mother in Antenatal Clinics. The Antenatal Ultrasonographic Examinations from time to time forms main stay of antenatal care to record progress of Pregnancy and health & growth of fetus. Presently we have many technical tools like Amniocentesis, Chorionic Biopsy, Fetoscopy, CT Scans and MMR for detecting any Congenital Abnormalities in fetus and ensure timely interventions or resort to Medical Termination of Pregnancy in case of nonviable situations. Proper maternal Nutrition and care can prevent Low Birth Weight babies and ensure normal growth of Fetus.

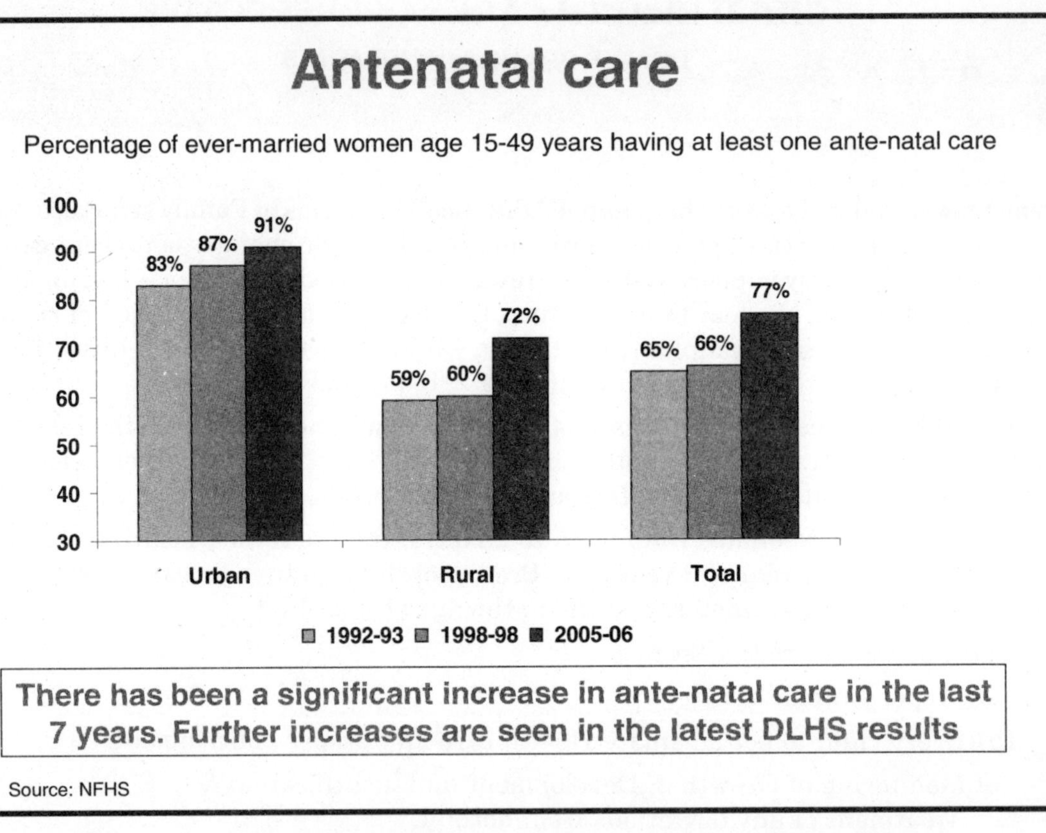

Fig. 24.1. Percentage of women having at least one Antenatal Care in India.

In India maternal deaths are also high due to inaccessibility of skilled birth attendants and quality of Emergency Obstetric Care. Only 15% of mothers receive complete Antenatal Care and only 58% receive Haematinics during pregnancy. The State vide incidence of Maternal Mortality is depicted in Figure 2, highest being in UP and lowest in Kerala.

There are many preventable causes for maternal deaths in India many of which occur due to lack of awareness and inaccessibility to ideal maternity facilities and skilled technical personnel.

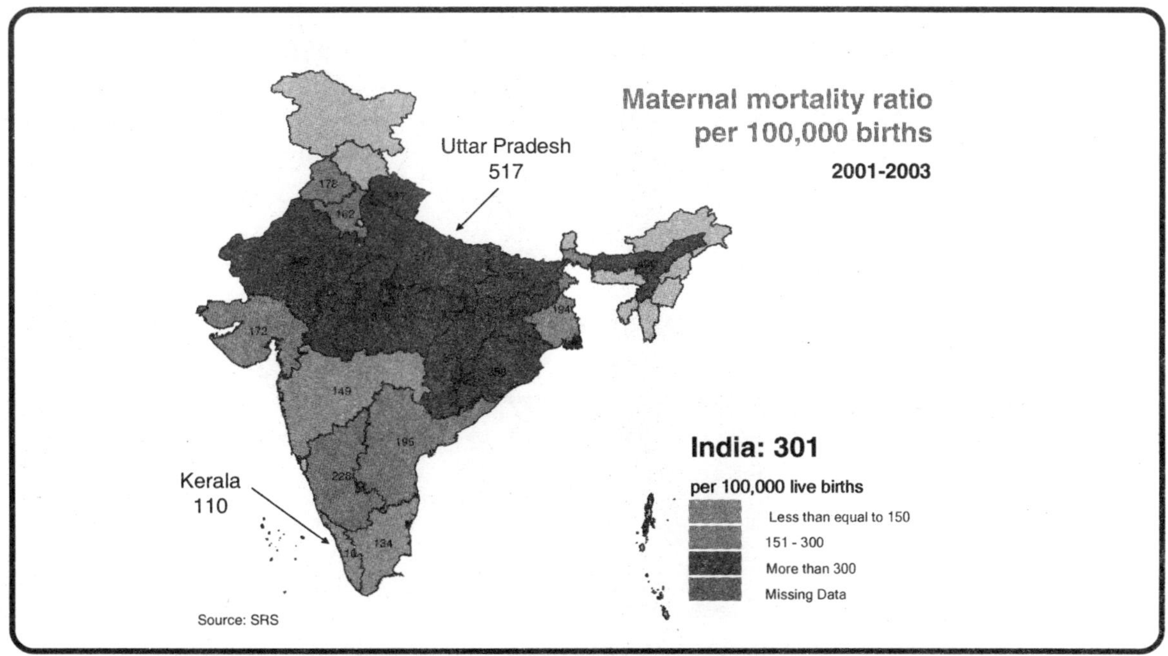

Fig 24.2. Incidence of Maternal Mortality in India.

Care of Neonates:

Health care of new born from birth to 28 days is rendered by combined services of Obstetrician, Paediatrician & allied Specialists and Nursing Personnel. Care during 24-48 Hours to 1st week is crucial in preventing Neonatal Mortality. Statistical figures show that the infant mortality in India is as high as 63 per 1000 live births, majority of the deaths occurring in the 1st month and up to 47% in 1stweek it self.

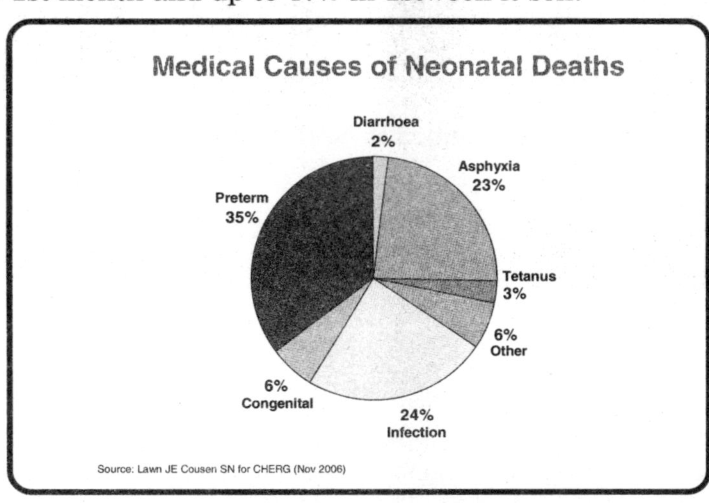

Fig 24.3. Medical causes of Neonatal Deaths.

Tetanus in New Born period is the major cause of death, in the States of Uttar Pradesh, Uttaranchal, Madhya Pradesh, Chatteesgarh, Rajasthan, West Bengal and Assam. Vaccine preventable diseases such as Measles are also responsible for deaths of a number of children in India. The proportion of children in India who received Measles vaccine dropped from 72% in 1995 to 50% in 1999 and is at 61% in 2009.There is a decline in number of cases of Polio from 1934 in the year 1998 to 225 in 2004 and India is on a path to eradicate this disease.

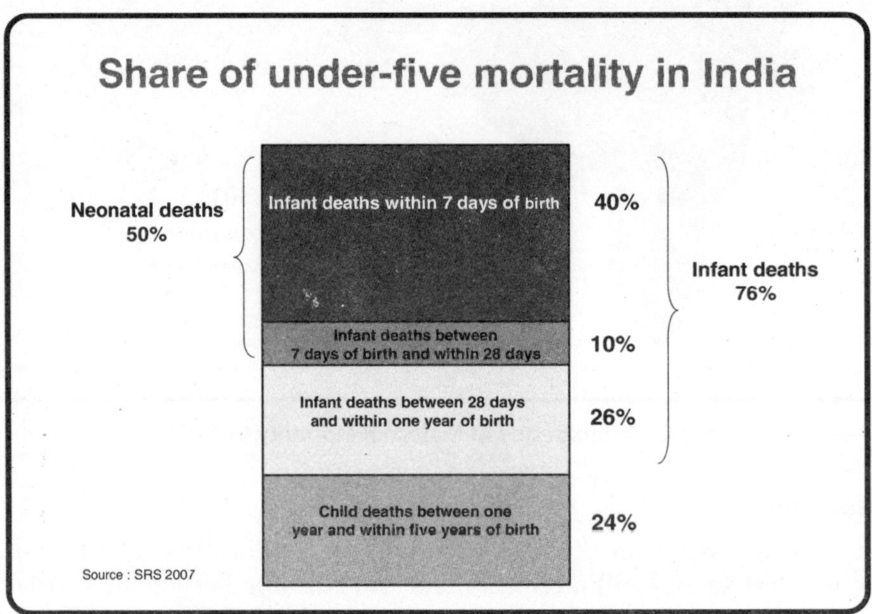

Fig. 24.4. Share of under- five mortality in India.

Governments action to prevent Neonatal deaths involves a) Strengthening existing Health System by increasing the number of Health Workers b) Prevent New Born deaths through home based medical visits and c) Increase children's access to immunization.

Common Health Problems in Newborns and Infants:

(A) Low Birth Weight (LBW Babies):

The birth weight of Babies born to well nourished mothers is usually about 3.5 Kgs.The birth weight is measured within 60 Mts. of birth and the average for an Indian baby is 2.7 to 2.9 Kgs.

There are two types of LBW babies :

(1) Preterm Babies- are babies born prematurely or before time ie) 37 weeks of gestation. Their Intrauterine Growth is normal, that is, their Weight, Length and Development are within normal limits to the gestational age. In developed countries most of the LBW babies are Preterm babies. The preterm Deliveries are often due to multiple

pregnancies, severe infections, toxemia, teenage Pregnancy, hard physical work etc and in some the cause may be unknown.

(2) Small for date Babies(SFD Babies). They can be either Preterm or Full Term born babies but their weight is less than 10th Percentile of the Gestational age and majority of SFD babies are in developing countries.

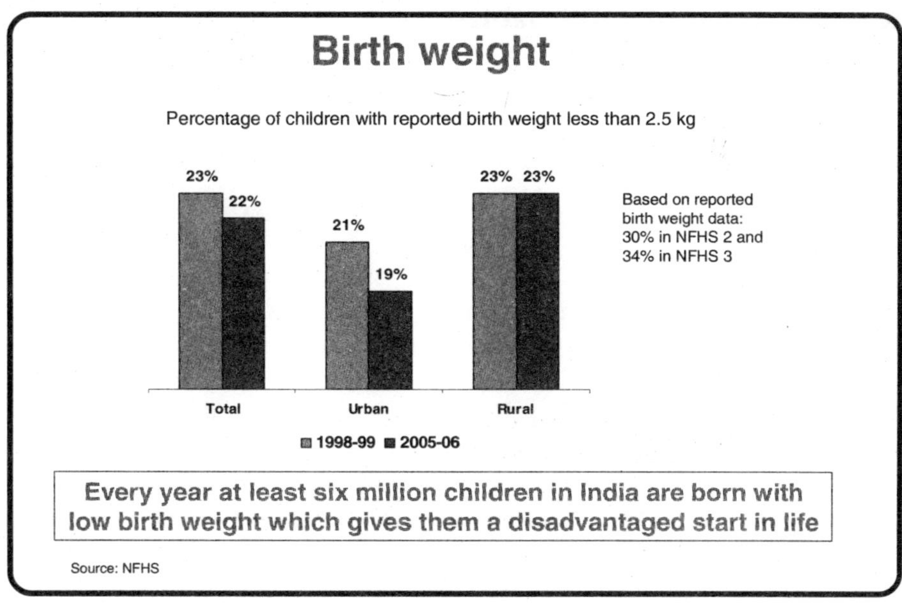

Fig 24.5. Percentage of LBW babies in India

The factors associated with this category of LBW babies are related to Mother, Fetus and Placenta. *The Maternal factors* are malnutrition, severe anaemia, young age and short stature, multiparity, close birth spacing, hypertension, toxiemia, and malaria etc during pregnancy. They are also attributable to family's low Socio economical& educational status at large. *The Fetal factors* are Twins or Triplets, Intrauterine infections, Fetal & chromosomal abnormalities etc. *The Placental Factors* such as structural, positional or placental vascular abnormalities and placental circulatory deficiencies can cause birth of SFD babies.

Around 1/3rd of all adult women in India are under weight resulting in LBW babies. Nearly 30% of all newborns are LBW and their socioeconomic status making them vulnerable to Malnutrition and disease as they grow. This is a global problem with the incidence varying from 4% in developed countries to 30% in under developed countries.

Prevention:

National and State level policies enforcing and enacting: (a) Good antenatal care and planned interventions. (b) Early registration of all pregnant women and identification of women at risk. (c) Improving maternal nutrition by balanced and supplementation diet and distribution of Iron, Folic Acid tablets. (d) Early detection and treatment of Non infectious diseases like Diabetes, Hypertension etc. (e) Discouraging smoking, self medication and intervention by Quacks. (f) Encouraging small family norms, proper spacing and timing of conception. (g) Improving Socio economical status of women. (h) Promoting gender sensitivity.

Treatment/management of LBW babies:

LBW babies less than 2 Kg of weight are nursed under intensive care in N.I.C.U s in Hospitals at Institutional level. Babies between 2 to 2.5 Kgs can be managed at Home under the supervision of Health Workers taking care to provide warmth, adequate feeds, taking steps to prevent Infections and insisting early breast feeding and regular weight checks.

(B) Malnutrition:

Malnutrition like LBW is a global problem-even though it is more common in India. About 50% of all childhood deaths are due to Malnutrition in India. As per a study by National Institute of Nutrition and National Family Health Survey (NFHS) the most vulnerable age group concerning malnutrition is between 6 months and two years. In India 46% children below 3 years are small for their age, 47% are underweight and at least 16% are wasted. This is not only due to intake of food but also due to inaccessibility to Health Services for care of child & mother, hygiene and socioeconomical status. In India the highest prevalence rate at 55% is in Madhya Pradesh and lowest at 27% is in Kerala State with girls at more risk than boys.

Nutritional facts of Infants and Children in India	
• % of LBW infants, in India (2003-2008)	28
• % of children who are exclusively Breastfed (2003-2008)	46
• % of children Breastfed plus complimentary food(6-9 months)	57
• % of under 5s with **moderate** under weight (NCHS/WHO-2003-2008)	48
• % of under 5s suffering from **severe** under weight (WHO-2003-2008)	16
• % of under 5s with moderate to severe wasting(WHO 2003-08)	20
• % of under 5s with moderate to severe stunting (WHO 2003-2008)	48
Source: UNICEF	

Anemia, Vitamin and Mineral deficiencies affect 74% of children under 3 years, over 90% of Adolescent girls and 50% of women. Iodine deficiency which affects learning abilities is wide spread because fewer than 50% of house holds use Iodized salt. Blindness and eye afflictions are also remarkably high in Pre school children due to Vitamin A deficiency.

Preventive Measures:

(a) Implementation of National and State level policies for prevention of Malnutrition and Low Birth Weight, and providing Vit A, Iodine and Iron supplements to population at large.

(b) Exclusive Breast Feeding up to 6 months of age.

(c) Supplementation of Breast Feeds by suitable food rich in nutrients after 6 months of age.

(d) Providing complete diet rich in Protiens, Vitamins and Minerals to toddlers and pre school children.

(e) Providing adequate and nutritious diet to especially GIRL CHILD and pregnant mothers.

(f) Early recognition and treatment of any nutritional deficiencies in pregnant mothers and children.

(C) Infectious Diseases:

Several millions of children in the world suffer from Respiratory Infections, Diarrhea, Hepatitis, Enteric Fever, Malaria, Intestinal worm infestations, Eye and skin infections, Polio and Tuberculosis. A study in 1997 shows that 19% of Neonatal deaths are due to Diarrhea and 13% due to Polio in developing world. Most of these ailments are caused by Poor Hygiene and unsafe drinking water. In some parts of India and world excessive Arsenic and Fluorides in drinking water has posed serious health hazards. Apart from these infective conditions, environmental hazards like accidents and poisoning at home, school or on road are other causes of death amongst above 3 years old children.

Prevention:

(a) Implementation of State and National Schemes to provide clean drinking water, sanitation and achieve full coverage of Rural Population especially at Schools.

(b) Educating the Population through schools for cultivating Hygienic practices at Home and School.

(c) Providing disinfectants to sterilize the areas identified for Mosquito breeding & water born diseases.

(d) Prevention and treatment of worm infestations, skin infections and blindness amongst school going children.

(D) HIV and AIDS :

Though 1st case of AIDS was reported in 1998 in Tamil Nadu the virus has spread very fast from high risk group to general population. Today there are 5.7 million people living with AIDS in India. Women and children are increasingly becoming vulnerable to HIV/ AIDS with about 38% of patients being women. The mothers unknowingly pass the virus to their children.

India has an estimated 220,000 children infected with HIV/AIDS and that about 55,000 to 60,000 children are born every year to mothers who are HIV positive. Without treatment about 30% of these Newborns are likely to be infected during mother's pregnancy, labour or through Breast feeding up 6months of age. *There is effective treatment to prevent this, but this information is not reaching the vulnerable women and children.*

Measures to be taken:

A simple Anti- Retrovirus drug administered to mother during labour and a spoonful of syrup to the Baby soon after birth can prevent transmission of virus to the newborn.

Government of India under National Aids Control programme phase 3 works in 4 key areas to contain the HIV/AIDS menace, which they call '4Ps'.

(1) Primary prevention.

(2) Prevention of parent to child transmission.

(3) Pediatric HIV/AIDS.

(4) Protection, care and support of affected children.

(E) Neonatal Jaundice :

Also referred as Neonatal Hyperbilirubinemia or Physiological Jaundice of the newborn. It is usually harmless and caused by the inability of immature liver to get rid of Bilirubin (a yellow pigment).It is often seen on 2nd day of birth and may last up to 8 days in normal births and up to14 days in premature births.

Treatment – mild jaundice clears on its own in 8 to 10 days, however high levels of Bilirubin in blood need some measures to prevent complications. The steps to be taken are: A) Breast feeding the Baby more often. B) Exposure to morning sunlight or indirect Sun light. C) Phototherapy- exposing the baby to special blue lights under medical supervision. D) Exchange blood transfusion in extreme cases.

Health care of Infants, Toddlers and Pre school children:

This is discussed as Health care of children under five years of age. The basic health care of this group is based on regular monitoring of growth and development (both physical and mental) of children. This care is given by various Health personnel at Health Centers and clinics in the Hospitals. The patterns of normal growth is governed by the Standards set by both National and International organizations. ICMR (Indian Council of Medical Research) has set up standards of growth for Indian Children and similar reference standards are set up by World Health Organization for under five children any where in the world.

The health of children is monitored in terms of these standards of growth by regularly measuring the Weight, Length/Height, Head and Chest circumference, Mid arm circumference and Body Mass Index (BMI). Apart from these parameters the Child Growth Standards also include 'Windows of Achievement' to describe the Range and Time Line for key Motor Developmental Milestones such as Sitting, Standing, Walking etc. Growth of a child is also refers to Development of skills and functions related to Intellectual, Emotional and Social aspects.

Normal Patterns of Growth: Growth and development of children is influenced by various factors like genetic Inheritance, Age and Nutrition of Mother and child after birth, Socioeconomic conditions, Environment, Prevention and Control of Infections, Birth spacing, Number of Siblings etc.

Below is a chart showing the height, weight and head circumference- the green marking shows the range of head circumference in centimeters (cm) likely in a normal child with the dividing line showing the average growth. The orange-red marking shows the range of weight measurements in Kilogram (kg) and the dividing line shows the average increase in weight. The light blue-dark blue markings show the range of height measurements likely in a normal child with the dividing line showing the average increase in height.

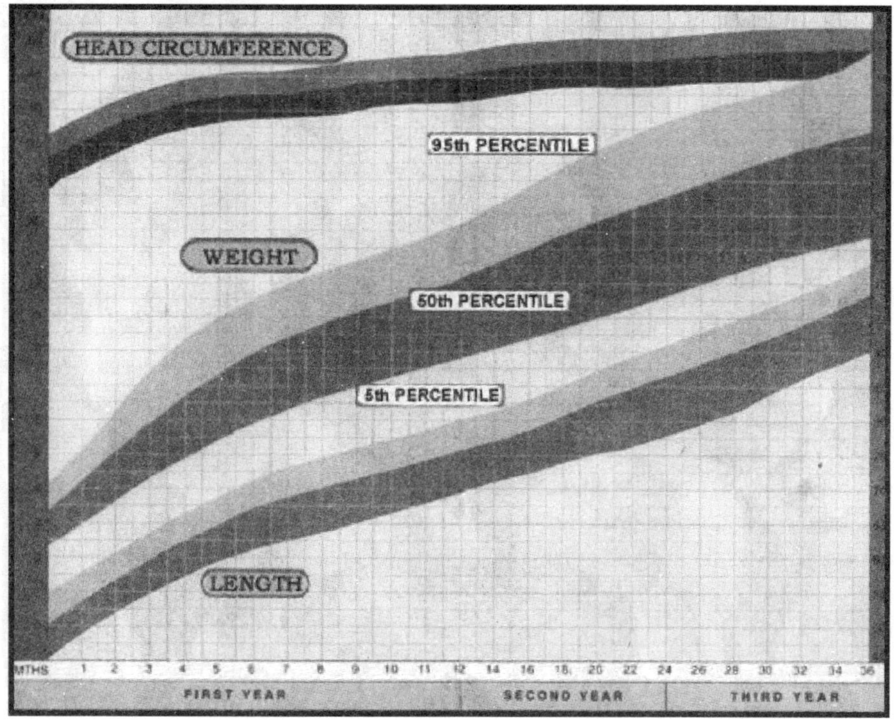

Source: National Center for Health Statistics (NCHS)

Fig 24.6. Growth chart for assessing growth of child in terms of 'Percentile'.

Weight: At birth weight of a normal newborn is between 2.7 to 3 kgs. All most all babies lose weight in first 2-3 days and regain it by 7 to 10 days. The body weight increases by 25 to30 Gms. per day for 1st 3 months there after, it is less rapid. Normally the baby doubles its weight by 5 months and triples it at 1 year. After 1 year the weight gain is gradual and steady.

Height: The height of a newborn baby is 50 Cms (20").The height increase in 1st year is 25 Cms, in the 2nd year 12 Cms, in 3rd 4th and 5th year the increase is 9 Cms, 7Cms and 6Cms.

Head and Chest circumference: Normal head circumference at birth is 34Cms (14"). It is about 2 centimeters more than chest circumference. As the baby grows the chest circumference over takes the head circumference.Mid arm measurement shows rapid increase in 1st year at 12 Cms and at 5years it reaches about 18 to17 Cms.

YOUR BABY-a mother's guide:

Here is a brief guide to track the progress of your Baby from 1st month onwards. What to expect and what to do with unexpected!

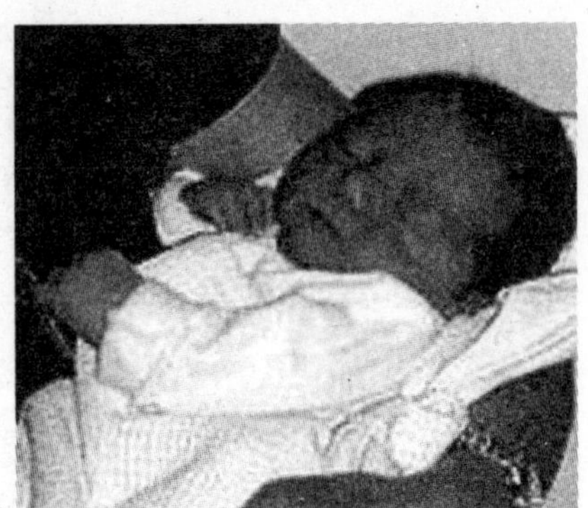

(1) 1st steps:

Month 1: Baby slowly responds to sounds and movements. Sleep, cry, feed pattern is set up. Brings out some 'noises'. Starts focusing on objects. By end of 1st month attempts to smile.

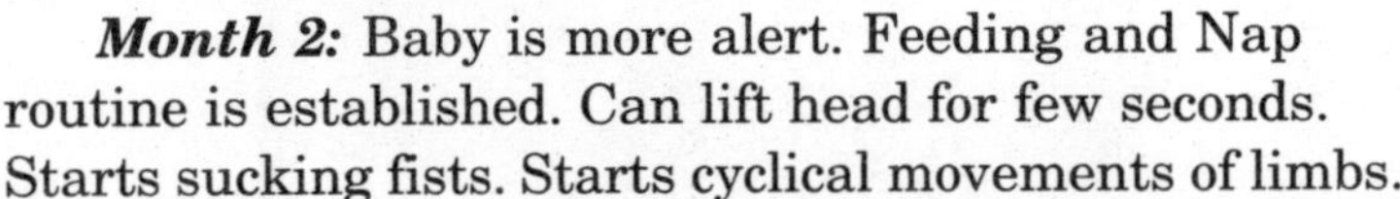

Month 2: Baby is more alert. Feeding and Nap routine is established. Can lift head for few seconds. Starts sucking fists. Starts cyclical movements of limbs.

Month 3: Sleeps through the night. Neck is firm and can hold the head. Tries to get her hands and feet in to mouth. Shows signs of memory and know time of feeds. Distinguishes speech sounds from other sounds. Recognizes close family members and smiles a lot. Gets on her stomach and leans on her elbows. Can hold a toy and wave. Facial expressions appear.

Month 4: Can roll over from tummy on to back and vice versa. Starts 'swimming' moments in the crib. Can focus her eyes at different distances. Slowly becomes 'Social Animal' responding with smiles when happy and cries when angry. Invents new sounds and tones.

Month 5: Utters vowel sounds. Squeals, grunts and shouts. Dislikes strangers and cries in their presence. Rocking, rolling and twisting movements. Aims well to reach and grasp objects/ feeding bottle with one or both hands.

Month 6: Can creep along on tummy and can sit for a while. Displays mood changes, protests loudly, laughs loudly. Learns to compare two objects. Acts shy with strangers but don't cry. Recognizes her name and turns when called. Develops taste preferences. Likes to hold as many objects as she can.

Month 7: Shows concentrated attention and able to say "ma", "da","du","Do".etc.Attempts to recognize pictures and shows signs of sense of Humour. Balances head well. Starts crawling. Pushes herself on hands and knees. Increasingly uses fingers.

Month 8: Crawls rapidly, stands, leaning against things and able to put one foot in front of other. Pushes away things she doesn't want. Picks up objects, Attached to parents and shows fear of strangers. Shouts for attention. Doesn't like confinement. Claps and waves hands.

Month 9: Stands up holding to objects. Able to turn around while crawling. Able to hide and find toys. Can remember some thing she saw previous day. Able to follow simple instructions. Begins to recognize moods of people. Performs for audience and is delighted by applause!

Month 10: Can sit and stand easily. Imitates others actions. Picks up words and repeat it constantly. Understands and obeys commands. Able to open drawers. Enjoys playing in water. Actively seeks approval from adults. Shows signs of moods. Responds to Music. Learns to play hide and seek.

Month 11: Baby is able to lean over while standing and can stand on her toes. Squats and stoops. Enjoys games. Shows guilt and responds to verbal chastisement. Able to turn pages in a book, some times in a clump. Can pick up minute articles and can lift lids of boxes. Can connect meanings to words. Speaks gibberish with some intelligible sounds.

Month 12: Baby can walk, stand and cruise. Can climb out of crib. Attempts to climb up and down steps. Learns to play with Blocks. Preference of use of one hand over the other comes. Starts to throw tantrums. She 'mothers' her Doll or Teddy Bear. Starts saying few words. Identifies animals and objects in a book.

Months 13 to 24: Baby can walk pulling along a toy. She will be extremely possessive about her Mother. Imitates adults and mimic their actions. Able to ride a Baby bike or toy car. Starts precise speech and starts to use crayons on paper. She starts to identify and name body parts.

Months 25 to 36: At this stage she will be asking questions on every thing around. She can solve small puzzles and jigsaws. Learns to color in the given squares in a book. Shows eagerness to learn new things every day. Jumps and runs. Starts to learn dressing up. Likes to be independent. Begins to show signs of imagination. Likes to play with other children and share toys. Shows interest in books and starts to identify alphabets.

2) Breast is best (Breast versus Bottle):

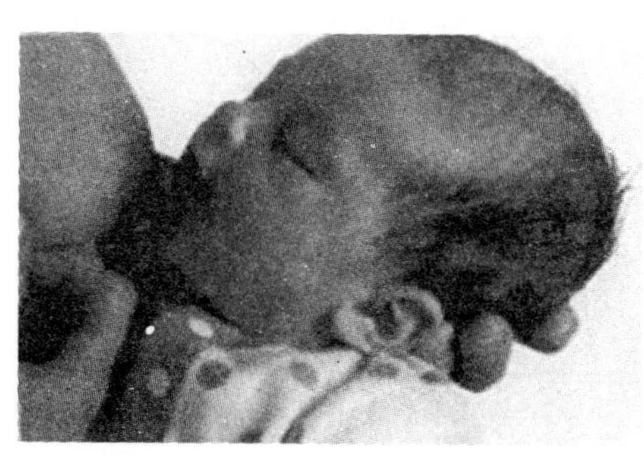

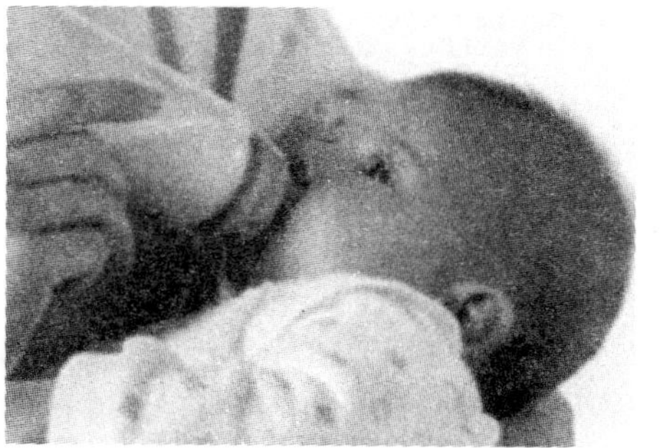

A quick review why Breast feeding is better for the Baby suggests **1)** Breast milk is **nutritionally most suitable form of milk** available. The iron from mother's milk is completely and effectively absorbed. **2) Colostrum** produced by the breasts in 1st 48 hrs after delivery contains Antibodies that give baby protection against post natal diseases thus reducing neonatal infections. **3)** Breast feeding avoids allergic reactions to Cow's or other forms of milk in families with history of allergy as Breast milk is nature's hypoallergenic food. **4)** Breast feeding is convenient, always available and does not require any equipment. **5)** The stools of breast fed baby are soft and acidic in nature helping to prevent Nappy Rash. **6)** Breast feeding has great psychological and emotional benefits to both mother and baby. **7)** Some studies show that breast fed babies grow to be smarter, with up to an 8 point IQ difference, than Bottle fed. It may be due to certain fatty acids and amino acids present in mothers milk.

3) The 10 health worries: (Listed here are top 10 health worries, which are meant to be for guidance only.....you should have a Pediatrician available – in person or over Phone when needed).

1. Cold: It is 'COMMON' in first 2 years with most babies having between 8 to 10 episodes accompanied by sneezing, coughing, sore throat, runny noses, and fever. It needs to be treated at Pediatric clinic to avoid serious complications like viral infections or Pneumonia.

2. Ear Infection: Two thirds of all babies have at least one bout of Ear Infection (Medically known as Acute Otitis Media) before they are two years old. In a number of cases body immune system takes care of it and rest will have to be treated at a Pediatric clinic.

3. Vomiting: Most vomiting cease on it own but make sure that Baby is not dehydrated, by giving extra fluids. In few cases it can be symptom of a serious illness like Pneumonia, Meningitis, or abdominal infection. Hence consult a Pediatrician if the vomiting persists for more than 24Hrs.

4. Dehydration: This is a serious condition because it can lead to kidney failure, shock and even death in few cases. Symptoms include Parched tongue, sunken eyes, dry skin, scanty urine, irritability and listlessness. Give the baby constantly small amounts of Electrolyte solutions containing Suger, salt and Minerals. Severe cases may require IV fluids in a Hospital.

5. Wheezing: Wheezing is not always Asthma but it is a symptom of Upper or Lower Respiratory Tract Infection. Saline nasal drops for keeping nasal passages clear and keeping the home free of Cigarette or any other form of smoke is essential. If symptoms worsen or baby becomes blue Hospitalization will be necessary.

6. Fevers: In many cases fever is body's natural defence against infection but all fevers need to be monitored closely. Any fever above 100 degrees F or any fever lasting for more than two days needs Pediatric attention.

7. Rashes: Common skin rashes include nappy rash and impetigo which are common in 2 and 3 year olds. Rashes accompanied by fever indicate more serious Bacterial infection. These require Medical attention.

8. Diarrhoea: Passing loose motions some times is a common condition in babies. Most will subside with correcting dehydration by fluids. Intractable diarrhoea is a serious condition and needs to be treated at a Pediatric center.

9. Accidents: These mainly include falls from bed level or higher. All cases need to be evaluated for excluding any serious injury to internal organs. Minor injuries can be treated at home with mild pain killers and antiseptic ointments.

10. delay in Milestones of development: Consult your Pediatrician in case of gross delay in the development of the baby with reference to the normal growth as described in previous section'1St Steps".

(5) The Food facts:

Babies can not, and will not, stay happy on just a liquid diet. However, not all solids suit their delicate systems. **(A)** GRADATIONS: The ideal time to start semisolids is when the baby is four months old. Rice is best starting diet, slowly going on to wheat and cereals. Initially they all should be topped with milk. Starting from miniscule amounts the cereal servings are increased gradually and the milk intake is reduced slowly. Offer alternative to cereals in the form of mashed fruits. Fruits ideal for mashing/ stewing/ straining are Bananas, Peaches, Pears, and Prunes etc. If any fruit intake results in loose motions omit that fruit and try others. By eight months of age the baby can start on raw but softened fruits like apples, berries and different kinds of fruit juices. Another addition at this age is egg yolk for its Iron content. It can be boiled and given finely mashed. **(B)** THE RIGHT FOOD: By one year the baby can be started on strained, cooked vegetables like Peas, Beans and Carrots. Potatoes, Cabbage etc can also be tried at this age. Non vegetarian food may be started when the baby is well in to second year…latter the better. Some foods will cause vomiting, diarrhoea, Rashes, Breathing problems, and even skin reactions. The usual culprits are Dairy Products, Nuts, Egg white, Corn, wheat and Soya products. Consult a Doctor to avoid allergy causing foods. **C)** AMBIENCE: Baby needs about 800 calories a day. See that it gets them in one form or other. The babies don't follow adult time table of three square meals a day till they are above two years, so a meal time routine should be set up as early as possible. Make meal times fun with much talk and laughter. New foods may be presented in a novel fashion to attract the baby to try it out. A study shows that Breast fed babies are more open to new foods. **D)** EATING HABITS : Get the baby used to good, healthy, nutritious food from the start.. These are learned early in life hence it is very important, in present day pollution-ridden environment that the baby learns to avoid unhealthy foods which in later life can lead to High Blood pressure, Heart ailments, Diabetes or over weight problems. By the time the baby is three years it should be eating a **Break fast** of Cereal, egg yolk, toast and milk; **lunch** of vegetables, potato, rice, fruit and milk; and **dinner** comprising of Cereal, fruit, rice and milk

(6) **Shots for the Tots**:

Every baby is born with a natural immunity which is further strengthened by Colostrum in mother's milk. But that protection quickly wears of leaving the baby vulnerable to any infection. Germs enter the body through **inhalation** (Tuberculosis, Measles, Chicken pox etc), by **ingestion** (Typhoid, Cholera etc).Vaccination (introducing small, non lethal amounts of the disease toxins in to the body) prepares the body to produce Antibodies to fight these organisms. The vaccines are given over a period of time as Primary or Secondary immunizations.

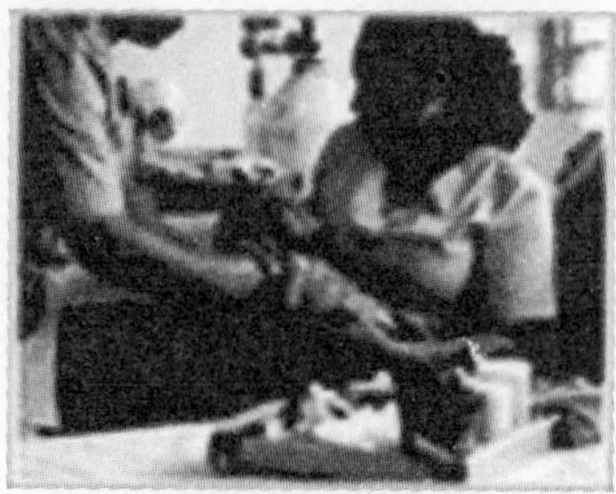

Indian National Immunization Schedule

(as approved by Ministry of Health &FW and Indian Academy of Pediatrics)

Beneficiary	Age	Vaccine
Infants	Birth	BCG* and OPV**
	6 weeks	DPT&OPV
	10weeks	DPT&OPV
	14 weeks	DPT&OPV
	9 months	Measles vaccine
	18 months	DPT&OPV (Booster dose)
Children	5 years	DT vaccine
	10years	Tetanus toxoid
	16years	Tetanus toxoid

*At birth or at the time of DPT/OPV;

** dose called as Zero dose and can be given till 14 days of age, if missed early.

ABBREVIATIONS: BCG=Bacillus calmitte Guerin;
DPT=Diphtheria, Pertussis & Tetanus; OPV =Oral Polio Vaccine;
DT=Diphtheria & Tetanus vaccine.

Watch out your baby for

Disease: Measles
Vulnerable age: 16 to 24 months.
Symptoms: Rashes, Fever, Dry cough & cold.
Form of Vaccination: Injection.

Disease: Chicken pox.
Vulnerable age: one year onwards.
Symptoms: Fluid filled rashes on body & chest, Abdomen and Back.
Form of vaccination: Injection.

Disease: Poliomyelitis.
Vulnerable age: 4 months onwards.
Symptoms: Fever, Headache, Vomiting Constipation.
Form of vaccination: Oral Drops.

Disease: German measles.
Vulnerable age: 12 to 36 months.
Symptoms: Sore throat, Mild cold, swollen neck glands, Pink Rashes.
Form of vaccination: Injection.

Disease: Mumps.
Vulnerable age: 16 to 24 months.
Symptoms: Swollen Glands in front of ears, Fever, pain on swallowing.
Form of vaccination: Injection.

Disease: Whooping cough.
Vulnerable age: 10 to 14 months.
Symptoms: Severe persisting cough with vomiting.
Form of vaccination: Injection.

The Indian Academy of Pediatrics (IAP) supplements the above schedule further ,with 2 additional vaccines namely Hepatitis B vaccine to be given in three doses (at birth, one month and six months of age.). The IAP also recommends MMR (Measles, Mumps & Rubella vaccine) at about 15 to 18 months of age. The decision to use the newer vaccines such as Hepatitis A vaccine (Water borne jaundice), Hem.B vaccine and Varicella (chicken pox) vaccine can vary amongst pediatricians. The parents and the doctor can discuss their usage for their child, as presently; these vaccines are not included in the routine immunization program of our country. Their rational use should be based upon the cost, child's age, parent's concern, exposure risks to the child and the doctor - parent decision.

CHAPTER

FAQS ABOUT HEART FAILURE

DR. A.V. SUBBA RAO, MD

What is meant by "Heart failure"?

A. Heart failure (HF) is a condition in which a problem with the structure or function of the heart impairs its ability to supply sufficient blood flow to meet the body's needs. It should not be confused with cardiac arrest, which means sudden stopping of heart.

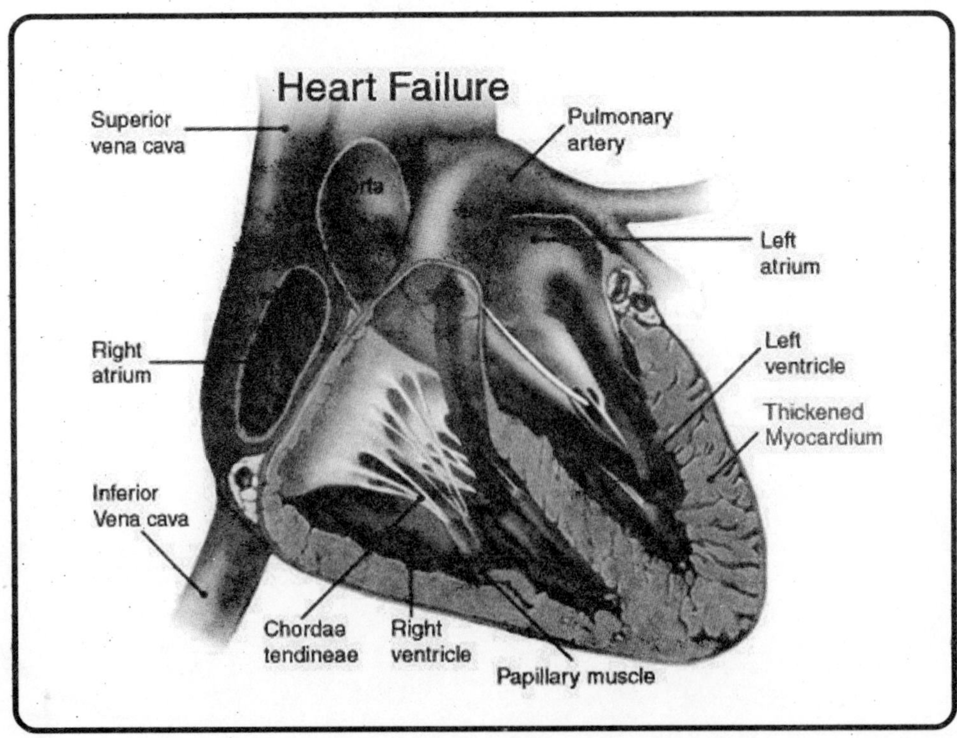

What are the differences between Heart attack, Heart failure, Heart stoppage and "Heart enlargement"?

- Heart stoppage or Cardiac arrest, and asystole both refer to situations in which there is *no* cardiac output at all. Without urgent treatment, these result in sudden death.
- Heart attack refers to a blockage in a coronary (heart) artery resulting in heart muscle damage.
- Heart enlargement is often due to Cardiomyopathy. This refers specifically to problems within the heart muscle, and these problems usually result in heart failure

FAQS ABOUT SCD AND CARDIAC ARREST

Q. We often come across news that a young or middle aged person dies suddenly without any apparent cause? Is there any medical cause? Can we prevent such deaths?

A. Sudden death is a catastrophic event, whether due to accident, suicide, homicide or even natural causes. As the means to prevent accidents and to prevent suicides and homicides are outside the purview of this present discussion, we will confine to only those deaths which occur due to natural causes. Certainly every death has an explanation and the old adage that "The coming of rain and the going of life cant be predicted" is no longer scientifically true. With prompt medical help and following simple procedures many of these deaths can be prevented or aborted!

Q. Then what are the causes of natural Sudden death?

A. 90% of them are due to Cardiovascular causes. Other forms of sudden death may be noncardiac in origin. Examples include respiratory arrest (such as due to airway obstruction, which may be seen in cases of choking or asphyxiation), toxicity or poisoning, anaphylaxis. Most of the Natural sudden deaths can be prevented.

Q. What is the definition of Sudden cardiac death?

A. The term **sudden cardiac death** refers to natural death from cardiac causes, heralded by abrupt loss of consciousness within one hour of the onset of acute symptoms. The most common cause is **cardiac arrest**, which refers to cessation of cardiac pump function which may be reversible. The phrase *sudden cardiac death* is a public health concept incorporating the features of *natural*, *rapid*, and *unexpected*. It does not specifically refer to the mechanism or cause of death.

Q. What is meant by Cardiac arrest?

A. cardiac arrest, also known as **cardiopulmonary arrest** or **circulatory arrest**, is the abrupt cessation of normal circulation of the blood due to failure of the heart to contract effectively during systole. A cardiac arrest is different from (but may be caused by) a *heart attack* or myocardial infarction, where blood flow to the still-beating heart is interrupted (as in cardiogenic shock).

Q. Can we treat Cardiac arrest and prevent Sudden death?

A. Cardiac arrest is a medical emergency that, in certain groups of patients, is potentially reversible if treated early enough The primary first-aid treatment for cardiac arrest is *cardiopulmonary resuscitation* (commonly known as CPR) which provides circulatory support until availability of definitive medical treatment, which will vary dependent on the rhythm the heart is exhibiting, but often requires defibrillation.

Q. How do you diagnose Cardiac arrest in a pt lying unconscious?

A. In many cases, lack of carotid pulse is the gold standard for diagnosing cardiac arrest, but lack of a pulse (particularly in the peripheral pulses) may be a result of other conditions (e.g. shock), or simply an error on the part of the rescuer. Studies have shown that rescuers often make a mistake when checking the carotid pulse in an emergency, whether they are healthcare professionals or lay persons. In face of evidence, the current recommendation is that cardiac arrest should be diagnosed in all casualties who are unconscious and not breathing normally.

Q. Does Cardiac arrest mean the person is dead?

A. Cardiac arrest is synonymous with clinical death. All disease processes leading to death have a period of (potentially) reversible cardiac arrest: the causes of arrest are, therefore, numerous. However, many of these conditions, rather than causing an arrest themselves, promote one of the "reversible causes" (see below), which then triggers the arrest (e.g. choking leads to hypoxia which in turn leads to an arrest). In other words, CPR or Cardiopulmonary Resuscitation is like bringing back the dead to life.

Q. If I see a person having an apparent Cardiac arrest, what should I do?

- **Early recognition** - If possible, recognition of illness before the patient develops a cardiac arrest will allow the rescuer to prevent its occurrence. Early recognition that a cardiac arrest has occurred is key to survival - for every minute a patient is in cardiac arrest, their chances of survival drop by roughly 10%
- **Early CPR** - This buys time by keeping vital organs perfused with oxygen whilst waiting for equipment and trained personnel to reverse the arrest. In particular, by keeping the brain supplied with oxygenated blood, chances of neurological damage are decreased.
- **Early defibrillation** - This is the only effective treatment for ventricular fibrillation, and also has benefit in ventricular tachycardia[and should be employed in such cases if the patient has signs of hemodynamic compromise, or if the patient has pulseless ventricular tachycardia. If defibrillation is delayed, then the rhythm is likely to degenerate into asystole, for which outcomes are markedly worse.

- **Early advanced care** - Early Advanced Cardiac Life Support is the final link in the chain of survival.

FAQS ABOUT CPR (CARDIO-PULMONARY RESUSCITATION)

Q. What is meant by CPR?

Cardiopulmonary resuscitation (**CPR**) is an emergency medical procedure for a victim of cardiac arrest or, in some circumstances, respiratory arrest CPR can be performed in hospitals, or in the community by laypersons or by emergency response professionals. CPR involves physical interventions to create artificial circulation through rhythmic pressing on the patient's chest to manually pump blood through the heart, called chest compressions, and usually also involves the rescuer exhaling into the patient (or using a device to simulate this) to inflate the lungs and pass oxygen in to the blood, called artificial respiration. Some recent protocols now downplay the importance of the artificial respirations, and focus on the chest compressions only.

Q. What is the purpose of CPR?

CPR is unlikely to restart the heart; its main purpose is to maintain a flow of oxygenated blood to the brain and the heart, thereby delaying tissue death and extending the brief window of opportunity for a successful resuscitation without permanent brain damage. CPR can help the patient come into a "shockable" rhythm

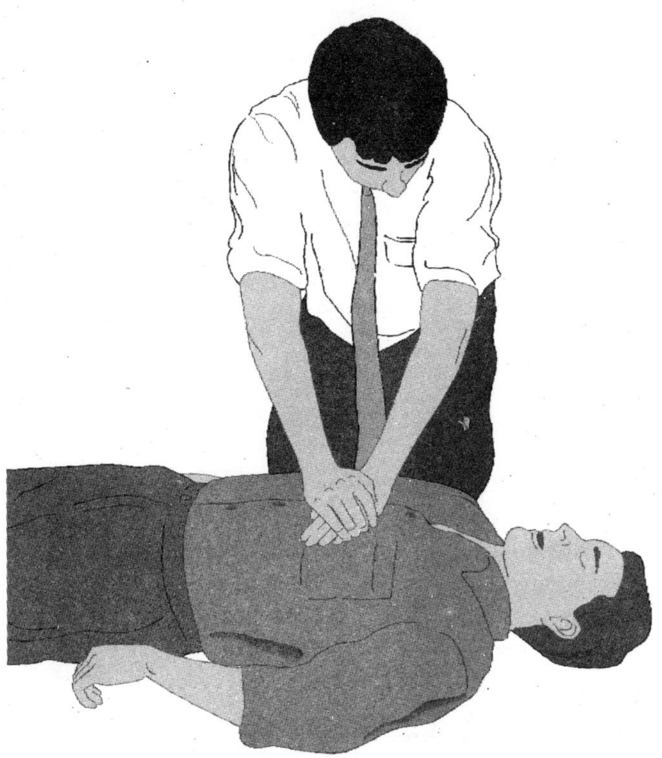

Q. How long should I continue CPR?

CPR is generally continued, usually in the presence of advanced life support (such as from a medical team or paramedics), until the patient regains a heart beat (called "return of spontaneous circulation" or "ROSC") or is declared dead.

Q. What are the consequences of cardiac arrest if CPR is not given immediately?

A. Blood circulation and oxygenation are absolute requirements in transporting oxygen to the tissues. The brain may sustain damage after blood flow has been stopped for about four minutes and irreversible damage after about seven minutes. CPR is generally only effective if performed within seven minutes of the stoppage of blood flow. The heart also rapidly loses the ability to maintain a normal rhythm.

Q. Can a pt be in Cardiac arrest and survive even after 15 min?

Low body temperatures as sometimes seen in near-drownings prolong the time the brain survives. Following cardiac arrest, effective CPR enables enough oxygen to reach the brain to delay brain death, and allows the heart to remain responsive to defibrillation attempts.

Q. What if the pt has a pulse but still does not breathe?

A. If the patient still has a pulse, but is not breathing, this is called respiratory arrest and artificial respiration is more appropriate. However, since people often have difficulty detecting a pulse, CPR may be used in both cases, especially when taught as first aid.

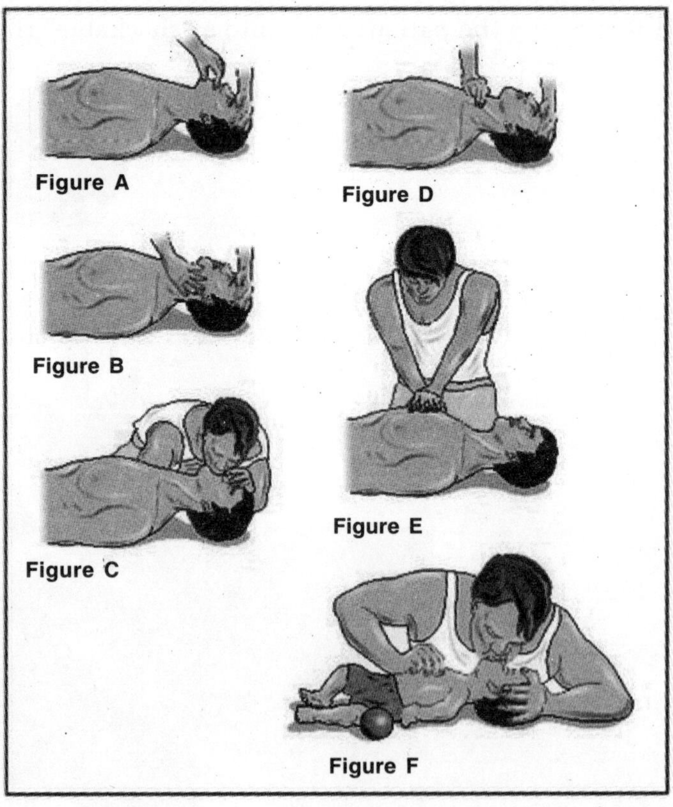
Figure A
Figure D
Figure B
Figure E
Figure C
Figure F

Q. How do I perform CPR?

In 2005, new CPR guidelines were published by the International Liaison Committee on Resuscitation (ILCOR), agreed at the 2005 International Consensus Conference on Cardiopulmonary Resuscitation and Emergency Cardiovascular Care Science. The primary goal of these changes was to simplify CPR for lay rescuers and healthcare providers alike, to maximize the potential for early resuscitation.

Q. How many times should I press the chest and how many times should I give artificial breathing?

A universal compression-ventilation ratio (30:2) recommended for all single rescuers of infant (less than one year old), child (1 year old to puberty), and adult (puberty and above) victims (excluding newborns).

- Now it is the absence of *normal* breathing as the key indicator for commencing CPR.

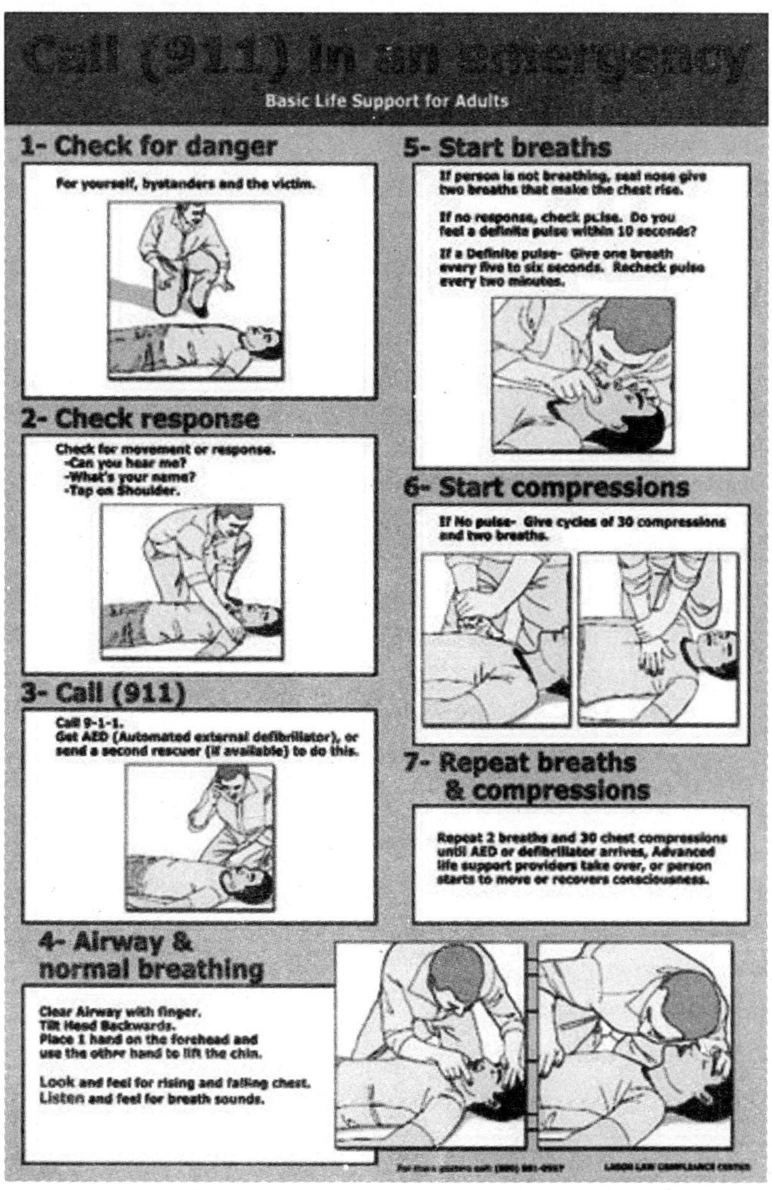

- All pts should undergo CPR irrespective of whether the pulse or the breathing is absent

Q. How can I be certain the pulse is absent?

A. It has been shown that lay personnel cannot accurately detect a pulse in about 40% of cases and cannot accurately discern the absence of pulse in about 10%. The pulse check step has been removed from the CPR procedure completely for lay persons and de-emphasized for healthcare professionals.

Q. What is the latest recommendation for a pt with Cardiac arrest?

A. The traditional International Liaison Committee on Resuscitation approach described above has been challenged in recent years by advocates for compression-only CPR, also known as cardiocerebral resuscitation (CCR). This technique is simply chest compressions without artificial respiration.

The CCR method has a three times success rate compared to traditional CPR. Except in Drowning and with Drug overdose.

Q. If I suspect that I have a cardiac arrest but I am still conscious, how can I rescue myself?

A. A form of "self-CPR" is termed "Cough CPR" Rapid coughing has been used in hospitals for brief periods of cardiac arrhythmia on monitored patients. One researcher has recommended that it be taught broadly to the public. However overuse of Cough CPR may aggravate the condition of a pt with heart attack. The American Heart Association (AHA) and other resuscitation bodies do not endorse "Cough CPR", which it terms a misnomer as it is not a form of *resuscitation*. The AHA does recognize a limited legitimate use of the coughing technique:

The AHA protocol for CPR. In AP, we can replace 911 with 108 (Emergency services)

CHAPTER

CHILDHOOD BLINDNESS

DR. N.K. CHANDRASEKHAR, M.S.

Definition

Childhood blindness refers to a group of diseases and conditions occurring in childhood or early adolescence, which, if left untreated, result in blindness or severe visual impairment that are likely to be untreatable later in life.

How common is childhood blindness?

According to the World Health Organization, an estimated 1.4 million children are needlessly blind. Three quarters of those children live in the poorest regions of Africa and Asia. Each year almost half a million children go blind — approximately one child every minute.

The vast majority of childhood blindness happens before the age of five - a period when 75 per cent of learning is through sight. Also, as many as 60 percent of blind children die within a year of losing their sight, mainly as a result of the condition causing their blindness.

According to Gilbert and Foster, the prevalence of blindness in children varies according to socioeconomic development and under-5 mortality rates. In low-income countries with high under-5 mortality rates, the prevalence may be as high as 1.5 per 1000 children, while in high-income countries with low under-5 mortality rates, the prevalence is around 0.3 per 1000 children. Using this correlation to estimate the prevalence of blindness in children, the number of blind children in the world is approximately 1.4 million.

India shoulders the world's largest burden of blindness. Of a total population exceeding 1 billion, as many as 15 million people are blind, with an additional 52 million visually impaired. Among those are 320,000 children under the age of 16, constituting one fifth of the world's blind children.

Combating childhood blindness has been identified by the World Bank as the most cost-effective of health interventions. It is considered a priority area in global blindness prevention due to the number of years of blindness that will ensue — devastating families and keeping children from contributing to their communities.

Causes

The major causes of blindness in children vary widely from region to region, being largely determined by socioeconomic development, and the availability of primary health care and eye care services. In high-income countries, lesions of the optic nerve and higher visual pathways predominate as the cause of blindness, while corneal scarring from measles, vitamin A deficiency, the use of harmful traditional eye remedies, ophthalmia neonatorum, and rubella cataract are the major causes in low-income countries. Retinopathy of prematurity is an important cause in middle-income countries. Other significant causes in all countries are congenital abnormalities, such as cataract, glaucoma, and hereditary retinal dystrophies

Many of the causes of childhood blindness are avoidable, being either preventable or treatable. Only three per cent of the world's blind population are children. However, because children have a lifetime of blindness ahead of them, the number of 'blind person years' resulting from blindness starting in childhood is second only to cataract. As the causes of childhood blindness differ from that of blindness in adults, different strategies, personnel, infrastructure, and equipment are required to combat it. There is also a greater urgency when managing children, as delays in treatment can lead to amblyopia (lazy eye).

Classifying the causes of blindness in children

The World Health Organization's (WHO) system for classifying blindness and low vision in children uses two methods. The first method, a descriptive classification, refers to the anatomical site most affected. The following categories are used:

- whole globe (e.g. anophthalmos, microphthalmos)
- cornea (e.g. corneal scarring, keratoconus)
- lens (e.g. cataract, aphakia)
- uvea (e.g. aniridia)
- retina (e.g. retinal dystrophies)
- optic nerve (e.g. atrophy)
- glaucoma
- conditions where the eye appears normal (e.g. refractive errors, cortical blindness, amblyopia).

The information necessary for this descriptive classification can be collected on every child following examination and clinical assessment.

The second method, an aetiological classification, classifies blindness according to underlying cause. This method uses categories based on the time of onset of the condition:

- hereditary (at conception, e.g. genetic diseases, chromosomal abnormalities)
- intrauterine (during pregnancy, e.g. due to rubella or thalidomide)
- perinatal (e.g. retinopathy of prematurity, birth injury, neonatal conjunctivitis/ophthalmia neonatorum)
- childhood (e.g. vitamin A deficiency disorders, measles, trauma)
- unknown/cannot be determined (e.g. congenital abnormalities).

Information about underlying causes of blindness, although often more difficult to collect, is more useful for planning.

The data suggest that the causes of blindness in children vary widely from region to region. Corneal scarring due to childhood factors (measles, vitamin A deficiency disorders, traditional eye medicines) and neonatal conjunctivitis/ophthalmia neonatorum are more important in poorer developing countries. In affluent regions, lesions of the central nervous system (often associated with prematurity) predominate, whereas hereditary diseases are more important in industrialised countries and the Middle East. Perinatal factors, such as retinopathy of prematurity, are important in middle-income regions, i.e. Latin America and the former socialist economies of Eastern Europe. In all regions, the underlying causes could not be determined in a high proportion of children.

The anatomical site most commonly affected is the retina (353,000 children), followed by corneal scarring (265,000), and lesions of the whole globe (258,900). Hereditary factors (381,300) are the commonest underlying causes, followed by acquired conditions of childhood (241,200).

Prevention and treatment

Prevention and treatment of childhood blindness is disease specific. For Vitamin A deficiency, at a cost of only 5 US cents a dose, vitamin A supplements reduce child mortality by up to 34% in areas where Vitamin A deficiency is a public health problem. As vitamin A deficiency manifests often during an outbreak of measles, properly planned and implemented national vaccination programmes against measles has reduced the prevalence of eye complications. In middle income countries, retinopathy of prematurity (ROP) is among the leading causes of blindness, the incidence of which can be reduced through availability and affordability of screening and curative services. Early treatment of cataract and glaucoma can be beneficial, while low vision devices are helpful in children with residual vision.

Reducing childhood blindness depends on the availability of primary health care. This includes a proper diet replete with vitamin A, rubella immunization for young women and infants, and a clean, hygienic environment. Also important are increasing public awareness of the harm that can arise from eye trauma, traditional medicine or home remedies for eye injuries, and marriages between blood relatives.

Because a child's eye is very different from an adult's — it is especially susceptible to nutritional deficiencies and infections — the diagnosis and surgical treatment of children requires specialized equipment and training in paediatric ophthalmology. Resources for paediatric ophthalmology, however, are extremely limited in developing countries, and public awareness and government initiatives are also lacking.

APPENDICES

(COURTESY : PROF. M.V. SUBBA RAO, Ph.D.)

APPENDIX 1 : 12TH MEGA BIODIVERSITY IN INDIA

India extending over a 329 million hectares has one of richest Biological diversity due to its diverse physical and climatic factors. India is one of the 12 identified Megabiodiversity Centres.

•Plant Species		• Animal Species		
45,000	Plant Species (7.0% of World's flora)	81,000	Animal Species (6.4% of World's fauna)	
15,000	Flowering plants (About 4,900 Endemic and 1,500 Species Threatened or Extinct)	5,000	Molluscs	
64	Gymnosperms	57,000	Insects	
2,843	Bryophytes	2,546	Fishes	
1,012	Pteridophytes	204	Amphibians	110 Endemic
1,940	Lichens	428	Reptiles	156 Endemic
25,000	Fungi	1,228	Birds	69 Endemic
12,480	Algae	372	Mammals	38 Endemic

India is also considered as one of the *World's 12 centres of cultivated plants.* This *includes 51 species of cereals and millets.*

104 Species of Fruits

27 Species of Spcies

55 Species of Vegetables and Pulses

24 Species of Fibre crops

2 Species of oil seeds

India is also very rich in *domesticated animals.*

8 Breeds of Buffalo

26 Breeds of Cattle

8 Breeds of Camel

2 Breeds of Horses

40 Breeds of Sheep

20 Breeds of Goats

18 Breeds of Poultry

2 Breeds of Donkeys

APPENDIX 2 : MORE SPECIES IN THE RED

The 2007 Red List of endangered plants, animals, birds, and sea life released by the World Conservation Union (IUCN) offers a gloomy forecast for many species that make the earth unique. If unrelenting pressure from human activity continues, these evolutionary marvels, like others before them, will become extinct sooner rather than later at least in the wild. Global populations of several species have declined so dramatically that the IUCN has added 188 species to last year's tally of 16,118 that may be wiped out in the wild. The animals facing serious threat include the Western lowland gorilla in Africa, the Sumatran and Bornean Orangutans, and India's gharial, a reptile belonging to the crocodile order. The gharial population has come down as a result of net fishing and irreversible loss of habitat. Their numbers have plunged by about 60 per cent in the last decade and their habitat has shrunk in the Ganges, Brahmaputra, and Mahanadi rivers in India and Nepal. The gharial is now critically endangered — just a step away from extinction in the wild; The rescue of the gharial now depends on whether the damagingly huge impact of human activity — the construction of dams, barrages, and irrigation canals — on habitats is recognised. The absence of far-sighted action is resulting in species that evolved over millions of years vanishing owing to pressure from a single species, our own. This tragedy has been described by naturalist, E.O.Wilson as the silent haemorrhaging of the world's biodiversity.

Governments, international organisations, and scientists view the IUCN Red List — statured by well-defined criteria and now comprising a total of 41,415 species — as a vitally important index of the state of nature. The IUCN methodology also helps to estimate the health of species at national and regional levels. But it is important to remember that many more species that may be similarly endangered do not make it to such lists on account of data deficiencies and therefore get low priority in conservation measures. Researchers reported in *Current Science* in 2005 that some Western Ghats plants listed in various Red Lists, including that of the IUCN, were abundant in forest sites in comparison with other endemic plants. Such findings do not detract from the tremendous value of the IUCN list, On the contrary, they draw attention to the need for even more intensive research into the state of India's natural heritage. The wider message from the IUCN Red List should be read as the need to have a land use plan for a fast-growing India and above all the political and social will to enforce it. (Courtesy: The Hindu, Sept. 29, 2007).

APPENDIX 3 : HEALTH CARE : DO YOU KNOW?

- 90% of World Population is without safe water and those water borne diseases kill nearly 30,000 people every day.
- 7% of Human body contains water as a result of which only mans density is more or less is equal to that of water.
- Man can survive for 5 weeks without food but for less than 5 days without water.
- Deficiency of water causes Acidosis, Dehydration, Edema, Fever, Shocks, Urinary tract infections, Indigestion and Constipation.
- Water acts as a buffer that neutralizes the acids produced within our body.
- For Good Health, an adult man should take 2 to 3 liters of water every day. Meals before half an hour and after half an hour don't take water.
- Water in contact with natural deposits of Fluoride caused Fluorosis (common in Nalgonda of AP).
- In India, about 30 million people are suffering from Flourosis (dental and bone problems).
- Today, Hussein Sagar of Hyderabad is not an ocean of Sweet water but an Oxidation pond.
- Nearly 80% of the Worlds diseases espeically in developing countries are linked with water.
- Preventive Measures (Solutions) for Pure Water are :

  1. Filtering and Boiling.
  2. Cooling and Treating with $KMNO_4$.
  3. Dissolving a piece of Alum.
  4. Using Commercial Filters and Electronic UV Filters.
  5. Water contains less than 10 *E.coli* bacteria per 100 ml is safe to drink.

INDEX